Towards a better use
of the ocean

SIPRI

Stockholm International Peace Research Institute

SIPRI is an independent institute for research into problems of peace and conflict, with particular attention to the problems of disarmament and arms regulation. It was established in 1966 to celebrate Sweden's 150 years of unbroken peace. The financing is provided by the Swedish Government. The staff, the Governing Board and the Scientific Council are international.

The Board and Scientific Council are not responsible for the views expressed in the publications of the Institute.

Sveavägen 166, 113 46 Stockholm, Sweden

Telephone 08–34 96 00

Towards a Better Use of the Ocean

Contemporary Legal Problems in Ocean Development
by
Professor W. T. Burke

Comments and Recommendations
by an International Symposium

A SIPRI MONOGRAPH
Stockholm International Peace
Research Institute

Almqvist & Wiksell
Stockholm

Humanities Press
New York

Gerald Duckworth & Co. Ltd.
London

First published by Almqvist & Wiksell,
26 Gamla Brogatan, Stockholm 1

in collaboration with

Humanities Press, Inc.
303 Park Avenue South
New York, N.Y. 10010

and

Gerald Duckworth & Co. Ltd.
3 Henrietta Street
London. W.C. 2.

SBN 7156 0509 7

Printed in Sweden by
Almqvist & Wiksells Boktryckeri, Uppsala 1969

PREFACE

The Royal Committee which recommended the creation of SIPRI to the Swedish Parliament suggested that amongst its research work it might examine some of those instances where technological progress is creating new international problems. One of these is the problem of the oceans. Technological progress is rapidly increasing the possibilities of exploiting the oceans for military and economic purposes. This is straining the present framework of international law and is creating new risks of conflict—and new opportunities for co-operation.

Since it appeared that the framing of international policies was already getting underway, it was decided that the Institute should study the problem, adopting an approach that would yield quick results. Professor William T. Burke, then of the Ohio State University, was therefore commissioned to prepare in a matter of months a report on contemporary legal problems of ocean development, including a full description of the technological and policy background to the problems. Seven scholars from different countries were invited to submit their comments in writing on Professor Burke's paper and then to attend a symposium held in Stockholm from June 10th to June 14th, 1968.

Professor Burke's paper and the written comments form the main body of this report. Also included are a paper which I prepared on alternative regimes for the ocean, approaching the problem as an economist, and a summary of the conclusions reached at the meeting.

Since the problem of the oceans was being debated in an *ad hoc* committee established by the United Nations General Assembly at the suggestion of the Maltese delegation, and since a growing volume of work was being carried out in various international organizations and institutes in different parts of the world, this report was issued immediately after the meeting of the symposium in a preliminary form. This printed edition is the same, apart from the addition in the Annex of the General Assembly Resolutions concerning the oceans adopted in December 1968.

I hope that the report will make a contribution to the achievement of a fair and peaceful regime for the oceans in the future. If it does so, it will be the result of the hard work of the participants in the symposium. I am particularly indebted to Professor Burke, who prepared the main paper for the symposium, and to Jan Mårtenson, the rapporteur.

Robert Neild
Director, SIPRI

CONTENTS

The Symposium

List of participants 9
Summary of the discussions, with recommendations 9

Contemporary Legal Problems in Ocean Development   13

Professor W. T. Burke

Introduction 15
Aquisition of mineral resources 20
    Claims by coastal states to an area of special rights 20
    Delimitation of the area of special rights 22
    The nature of the regime to govern mineral exploration and development
    beyond the area of presently recognized special rights 30
Aquisition and control of marine fishery resources 62
Military uses of the continental shelf and the seabed beyond 83
Scientific research in the oceans 114

Comments on Professor Burke's Report, and General Remarks   133

Professor R. Bierzanek 135
    General remarks—Delimitation of the area of special rights of adjacent
    coastal States—Aquisition of mineral resources—Aquisition and control of
    marine fishery resources—Military uses of the continental shelf and the
    seabed beyond—Scientific research in the oceans

Dr. I. Brownlie 148
    Aquisition of mineral resources—Aquisition and control of marine fishery
    resources—Military uses of the continental shelf and the seabed beyond—
    Scientific research in the oceans—General observations

Dr. W. M. Chapman 155
    Concerning fishery jurisdiction and the regime of the deep sea bed

Captain C. Girard 175
    Military uses of the continental shelf and the seabed beyond

Professor E. J. Manner 183

Mr. R. R. Neild 187
    Alternative forms of international regime for the oceans

Professor S. Oda 197

Outer limit of the continental shelf—Scientific investigation of the continental shelf—Twelve mile fishery zone—Special or preferential right of the coastal state relating to the fisheries—Treatment of sedentary fisheries—Fithery management on the high seas—Pollution of sea water by radioactive waste—Military use of the high seas

Annex: United Nations Documents   207

General Assembly, A/6695, 18 August 1967;
REQUEST FOR THE INCLUSION OF A SUPPLEMENTARY ITEM IN THE AGENDA OF THE TWENTY-SECOND SESSION: Declaration and treaty concerning the reservation exclusively for peaceful purposes of the sea-bed and of the ocean floor, underlying the seas beyond the limits of present national jurisdiction, and the use of their resources in the interests of mankind. *Note verbale dated 17 August 1967 from the Permanent Mission of Malta to the United Nations addressed to the Secretary-General* 209

General Assembly, A/RES/2340 (XXII), 28 Dcember 1967;
RESOLUTION ADOPTED BY THE GENERAL ASSEMBLY: 2340 (XXII). *Examination of the question of the reservation exclusively for peaceful purpose of the sea-bed and the ocean floor, and the subsoil thereof, underlying the high seas beyond the limits of present national jurisdiction, and the use of their resources in the interests of mankind* 211

Economic and Social Council, E/4487, 24 April 1968;
MARINE SCIENCE AND TECHNOLOGY: SURVEY AND PROPOSALS, *Report of the Secretary-General:* III. The need to maximize international co-operation efforts and related proposals 214

General Assembly, A/RES/2467 (XXIII), 14 January 1969;
RESOLUTION ADOPTED BY THE GENERAL ASSEMBLY: 2467 A–D (XXIII). *Examination of the question of the sea-bed and the ocean floor, and the subsoil thereof, underlying the high seas beyond the limits of present national jurisdiction, and the use of their resources in the interests of mankind* 225

PARTICIPANTS

in the SIPRI Symposium, Stockholm, June 10–14, 1968

Professor H. Eek	Stockholm	Chairman
Professor R. Bierzanek	Warsaw	
Dr. I. Brownlie	Oxford	
Professor W. T. Burke	Columbus, Ohio	
Dr. W. M. Chapman	San Diego, California	
Captain C. Girard	Paris	
Professor E. J. Manner	Helsinki	
Professor S. Oda	Sendai	
Mr. J. Mårtenson	SIPRI	Rapporteur

SUMMARY

of the Discussions, with the Recommendations Adopted by the Symposium

The agenda for the symposium followed the order of subjects in Professor Burke's paper, namely: Acquisition of Mineral Resources, Acquisition and Control of Marine Fishery Resources, Military Uses of the Continental Shelf and the Seabed Beyond, and Scientific Research in the Oceans.

The proceedings can be summarized briefly, as the discussions are reflected in the recommendations. They were focused on three questions: the *problems resulting from the elastic definition of the continental shelf* made in the Geneva Convention of 1958; the *need for a moratorium* or freeze on present claims of national sovereignty and exclusive rights; and the *possibility of an international structure* to manage the use of the ocean and its resources in the future.

It was felt that the definition of the continental shelf provided in the Convention does not give a sufficiently clear indication of the extension of the shelf area. This is the very core of the problem of the future use of the seabed, for the wording in the Convention could lead to the establishment of a "national lake" system, a division of the oceans between the coastal states. The symposium advocated a clarification.

The participants were also of the opinion that a moratorium, or freeze, on the present claims of national sovereignty and exclusive rights should be established. This would ensure that the coastal states did not take advantage of the existing situation by claiming a further extension of their sovereign rights and thus placing themselves in a more favourable position for future negotiations.

The question of an international regime over the areas beyond national jurisdiction was discussed at length. Some participants were of the opinion that an internationalization of the seabed and the ocean floor was not justified or necessary as of today, the knowledge of mineral and other resources being too small to allow for the establishing of clear and firm guidelines at present. Others advocated an international regime. It was, however, agreed that a form of international structure for managing the use of the ocean and its resources was needed for the future. This structure would include a mechanism for achieving a more equitable division of the benefits of such uses. It was also agreed that it was necessary to make better provision for the maintenance of the public order of the oceans, and, by creating an international regime for the seabed outside the limits of the continental shelf, to provide a definitive solution to the problem of preventing the process of extension of exclusive claims by coastal states. Such a regime would prevent the making of claims to exclusive and sovereign rights by states, but would not prejudice the content of the freedom of the seas.

The symposium made the following recommendations:

I. 1. A clarification of the definition of the continental shelf should be undertaken. The present situation is not satisfactory, its vagueness allowing a variety of interpretation. Different methods of delimitation might be contemplated, as well as different means of arriving at the delimitation: the use of a mileage or depth criterion or the geological concept; a revision of the Geneva Convention, a resolution adopted by the United Nations.

2. Without prejudice to the present rules of general international law, no government should claim a territorial sea beyond 12 miles from the baseline. A moratorium or "freeze" on claims of exclusive rights regarding the ocean floor, as well as on extension of the shelf limits, should be established. Future negotiations would be of little value if in the meantime the states concerned rushed to establish sovereign rights so as to hold a more favourable position when such negotiations begin.

3. A better international structure for managing the use of the ocean and its resources, including a more equitable sharing of the benefits of such uses, should be established.

4. The governments of the member states of the United Nations and the various United Nations agencies should give early and thorough consideration to the advisability and feasibility of establishing an intergovernmental ocean organization to deal with all aspects of ocean investigation and the uses of the seas.

5. Pending the establishment of such an intergovernmental ocean organization, such member governments should:

(a) Support the recommendations of the Secretary-General of the United Nations for increasing the effectiveness of the existing international structure for managing the use of the ocean and its resources, as set out in UN/ECOSOC E/4487, 24 April 1968 (see Annex, pp. 214–224);

(b) Notify the World Data Centers, through the Intergovernmental Oceanographic Commission (IOC), of the location, nature and estimated permanence of any structure or apparatus moored to, erected upon, or laid on the seabed outside internal waters, together with pertinent recognition signs, the whole of which will be promulgated at appropriate intervals by IOC in Notices to Mariners;

(c) Notify the World Data Centers at regular intervals of the amount and nature of the resources removed by the governments concerned from the ocean or the seabed, together with the location of such removal;

(d) Settle disputes arising from the use of the ocean in accordance with the appropriate measures provided in the United Nations Charter;

(e) Avoid introducing foreign materials in the ocean except in accordance with norms established by the appropriate specialized agencies of the United Nations, as promulgated by the Intergovernmental Oceanographic Commission;

(f) Provide for freedom of research on their continental shelves by vessels engaged in declared national programs within the meaning of that term in the IOC usage, i.e. the list of research cruises and plans operation have been submitted to IOC for publication in the quarterly "International Marine Science" prepared and promulgated jointly by UNESCO and FAO and the data from which will be exchanged in accordance with the procedures of IOC.

A maximum of freedom should be given to scientific research projects, including logistics. Permission for research in inner and territorial waters should be given in a very liberal spirit, with provision for control measures if that should be required by the coastal states.

6. The problems of smaller seas must be taken into consideration. All the rules established for the oceans cannot be automatically applied to these areas without disadvantage.

7. The rules regarding international straits should be re-examined.

8. The problems concerning the military use of the ocean and the seabed should be dealt with by the United Nations.

The symposium discussed what should be done to permit economic activity to continue to expand pending the introduction of a new structure. For this purpose the following recommendations were agreed upon:

II. 1. Without prejudice to the application of the rules of general international law governing the exploitation and exploration of the seabed of the high seas beyond the limits of the continental shelf, there should be introduced a system of registration of claims to quiet possession *ad interim* for purposes of exploitation and exploration of the resources of the seabed.

2. The object of the system of registration would be to eliminate uncertainty as to the priority of use of a particular area and consequently to reduce the possibility of breaches of public order. Subsidiary objects would include the reduction of tension caused by unpublicized activity, especially in the vicinity of coastal states, and the reduction and elimination of hazards to other users of the oceans.

3. The existence of a registration would not be a condition of the legality of seabed activity: the legal status of unregistered activity would still depend on existing rules. The only legal significance of a registration would lie in the creation of a presumption that parties to the registration system had knowledge of the existence and priority of quiet possession *ad interim* and of the limits of the claim. In case of an issue of international responsibility arising or a complaint of a threat to the peace or breach of the peace in a United Nations organ, the registration would have a significant evidential role.

4. Registration would be required only if exploitation or exploration necessitated the creation of fixed installations or the temporary reservation of a certain area of the seabed for the undertaking of an economic extractive process or the making of scientific investigation in reasonable conditions.

5. An application for registration would comply with conditions laid down by the international registration authority. Such conditions would deal *inter alia* with the creation, where appropriate, of safety zones, the establishment, where necessary, of warnings to shipping, including submarines, and to other seabed vehicles, and the observance of a reasonable standard of precision in delimiting the area to which the claim to quiet possession *ad interim* applied.

6. Applications for registration of claims would be made on behalf of persons of private law and public corporations with distinct legal personality by their governments.

While the rapporteur assumes full responsibility for the summary of the discussions, the two sets of recommendations, as listed above, were approved by the participants during the symposium.

Stockholm, 18 June 1968

Jan Mårtenson
Rapporteur

Contemporary legal problems in ocean development

William T. Burke

Professor of Law, Ohio State University
on leave with
Mershon Center for Education
in National Security

Introduction

Recent activities by the governments of influential nation-states, on the international level as well as within internal policy-making processes, provide convincing evidence of a growing concern over the legal and political problems arising from intensified use of the ocean for many purposes.[1] Decisions made by public international organizations, partly in response to initiatives by individual member states, are additional indications of the relatively sudden emergence of the ocean as a major focus of national and international political consideration.[2] Private agencies, too, primarily national in orientation, are now organizing for examination of the problems expected to emerge as various groups seek to realize greater benefits from the oceanic part of the planet.[3] Although there are some indications of con-

[1] Both the United States and the Soviet Union have taken the initiative on the international level to ask for investigation or, even, resolution of certain problems. United States government officials claim major responsibility for General Assembly resolution 2172 (Resources of the Sea) adopted in December, 1966. The First Report of the President to the Congress on Marine Resources and Engineering Development, Marine Science Affairs—A Year of Transition 35 (1967); Bellman, Deputy Legal Adviser, U.S. Department of State, Address before American Bar Association National Institute on Marine Resources, p. 2, June 8, 1967.

As is well known, the Soviet Union took the lead in pressing for the study of legal problems of scientific research and ocean resources within the Intergovernmental Oceanographic Commission of UNESCO.

Influence is a relative term, of course. Events within the United Nations over the past year, including the 22d and 23d General Assembly sessions, indicate that neither the United States nor the Soviet Union, perhaps even the two combined, exercise decisive influence in shaping affairs within the United Nations affecting potential decisions about the oceans. The large number of developing states obviously played a highly important role in establishing the Committee on the Peaceful Uses of the Sea-bed and the Ocean Floor Beyond the Limits of National Jurisdiction at the 23d Session of the General Assembly.

[2] Reference is made to the Economic and Social Council resolution 1112 (XL), March 7, 1966; General Assembly Resolution 2172 (XXI), December 8, 1966; General Assembly Resolution 2340 (XXII); and, Resolution V-6 adopted at the Fifth Session, Intergovernmental Oceanographic Commission, Oct. 19–28, 1967, entitled "The Establishment of an IOC Working Group on Legal Questions Related to Scientific Investigations of the Ocean."

[3] Without attempting exhaustive enumeration, the following groups and activities may be listed within the United States: The American Bar Association has three committees at work in the Section on Natural Resources and the Section on International and Comparative Law; the Law of the Sea Institute has held annual week-long meetings since 1966 at the University of Rhode Island; the Mershon Center for Education in National Security of The Ohio State University and the Carnegie Endowment for International Peace jointly sponsored two conferences in 1967 on Law, Organization and Security in the Use of the Ocean; the American Assembly of Columbia University

cern by international private organizations, the extent of this has been slight to the present time.[4] A part of the purpose of this paper, and the meeting which is to convene to examine the problems discussed herein, is to enlarge and to encourage the international dialogue by private scholars and observers in order to contribute to the process of protecting the common interests of all peoples in development of ocean resources.

The problems to be confronted by states in attempting to maintain a viable public order for the oceans, to the extent such problems can now be identified with useful certainty, are compounded both of novel legal conflicts and of recurring controversies that have acquired new connotations or urgency. The occasion for the emergence of this mixture of problems consists of several elements, including the rapid progress now being made in scientific and technological developments affecting man's relation to the oceanic environment, the perception that the enlarged capacities in ocean use made possible by science and technology permit mankind to turn to the ocean to relieve certain social and economic problems created by a rapidly increasing population, and the awareness that the nature of the ocean environment requires international consideration and disposition of controversies over its use.[5] Summary mention of these factors, and others, is made below in connection with the discussion of background information relevant to particular problems that can be expected to emerge.

The problems to be discussed could be identified, or formulated, in a variety of ways, as by location of the events in the ocean,[6] by the specific

sponsored an Assembly on The Uses of the Sea in May, 1968; the American Branch of the International Law Association has recently established a Committee on Deep Sea Mineral Resources.

[4] The principal activity is that of a newly-formed Deep Sea Mining Committee of the International Law Association. See American Branch Committee on Deep Sea Mineral Resources, Interim Report, July 19, 1968. The subject of deep-sea mineral resources was ventilated at the 1968 meeting of the International Law Association in Buenos Aires.

The text statement does not accurately describe the work of scientists. The Scientific Committee on Oceanic Research (SCOR) of the International Council of Scientific Unions has been especially active and influential, including efforts in the international organization of scientific endeavors in the ocean.

[5] The text statement is not intended to affirm that the ocean is the source of enormous riches merely waiting to be plucked, as one picks fruit from a tree. However it is to be expected that marine resources and the environment can be used in ways that, with ingenuity and effort, will provide measurable assistance of various kinds to what may be hoped is a widening circle of beneficiaries.

Perhaps the best concise treatment of the factors mentioned in the text is in the Report of the Secretary-General, Marine Science and Technology Survey and Proposals, U.N. Doc. E/4487 (24 April 1968).

[6] The following are illustrative: Jessup, The Law of Territorial Waters and Maritime Jurisdiction (1927); Strohl, The International Law of Bays (1963); Bouchez, The Regime of Bays in International Law (1964).

legal technicalities invoked,[7] or by functional description of the demands being contraposed.[8] The more traditional approaches utilize the former two methods. These studies are organized about areas of authority in the ocean and the inquiry centers on all disputes arising out of events in the area under scrutiny. Still other studies center upon certain doctrinal concepts, seeking, for example, to analyze such terms as "freedom of the seas" or "innocent passage". The course to be followed here is that of identifying certain conflicts over particular uses of the oceans and to examine the congery of issues of legal policy raised by each such conflict. The remainder of this paper, therefore, is concerned with claims to acquisition of mineral resources, similar claims relating to fishery resources, potential problems in military use of the ocean and, finally, some problems connected with scientific research in the ocean. As will be indicated, each of these problem areas involves a number of issues, some of which are presented in terms of such familiar disputes as over the permissible width of the territorial sea, whether the ocean bottom may lawfully be appropriated by a state, whether contiguous zones for fishing are lawful, and so forth.

It is perhaps useful, and important, to account for this selection of problems for consideration. The principal criteria have been that of potential for important political controversy over the next decade, beginning in the relatively near future, and potential for resolving certain economic, social, and political difficulties. All of these problems have already, in fact, been under consideration in international arenas in one form or another and have inspired varying degrees of dispute. International concern over the extractive resources of the seabed and subsoil outside national territory began almost immediately after World War II and in important measure the community of nations has identified certain common interests which merit protection by international agreement. Yet, because of progress in science and technology, new vistas in mineral exploitation of the ocean bottom, only dimly perceived a decade ago, now appear to be opening which pose new difficulties in recognition of common interests. It is, thus, not overly important for present purposes whether it is realistic to expect that states will soon recover enormous mineral wealth from the sea. The search for international mechanisms to control or regulate exploitation is already underway and

[7] Reppy, The Grotian Doctrine of The Freedom of the Seas Reappraised, 19 Fordham L. Rev. 243 (1950); Margolis, The Hydrogen Bomb Experiments and International Law, 64 Yale L.J. 629 (1955); Slonim, The Right of Innocent Passage and the 1958 Geneva Conference on the Law of the Sea, 5 Columbia J. of Transnat'l 6. 96 (1966).
[8] Johnston, The International Law of Fisheries (1965); Christy and Scott, The Common Wealth in Ocean Fisheries (1965); Hydeman and Berman, International Control of Nuclear Maritime Activities (1960); Oda, International Control of Sea Resources (1963).

gives signs of considerable potential for political conflict. The latter is not necessarily bad, of course, since out of such conflict may emerge highly desirable solutions. But the present task is that of identifying and establishing conditions which will be considered as desirable enough to achieve general acceptance in the community of states so that the benefits of the resources are realized while minimum order is maintained.

Access to ocean fisheries is a source of conflict that may be traced back for centuries, yet here too recent developments pose the problem in new forms or in intensified versions of old difficulties. Although on some occasions disputes over fisheries cause serious political difficulties between states, the impact is generally rather minor and, hence, the reason for considering this problem area stems not from its potential for consequential disruption in relations between states, but from its potential for alleviating the world-wide problem of protein deficiency. The objective is to promote the use of marine food sources and to avoid unreasonable interference with the most effective employment of such sources. The yield from the ocean has been increasing faster than population for the past several years and there is reason to believe that under certain conditions it can be increased several times more over the next decade or so. Access to the sea for realizing such increases in ways consistent with sustainable production, and division of the yield or the benefits of it on the most equitable possible basis, call for continued scrutiny and research on an international basis.

Military uses of the ocean are, again, nothing new under the sea, but contemporary recommendations about this use and new technological possibilities combine to focus attention on such activities. Among several special reasons for concern is that consequential military operations, both offensive and defensive, are spreading from or penetrating beyond, the upper layers of ocean waters to regions of the deep sea. At the same time, on the civilian side, man is beginning to look to the deeper ocean bed as a locale for the production of wealth. It seems realistic to anticipate a necessity for seeking to accommodate what may be conflicting uses or, in some views, to forbid certain kinds or all kinds of military uses of the deep sea environment. However the issue might ultimately be resolved, it is now timely to devote disinterested attention to the various alternatives and the strategies for realizing desired options.

Inclusion of the problem of free entry into ocean areas for scientific research is justified primarily to assure that our concern for gaining wealth and other values from the sea does not lead to undue restriction upon research activities aimed at producing basic knowledge of the environment. It is already apparent that expansions of national boundaries (either of national territory as such or of special purpose boundaries) are working against freedom of scientific inquiry. Since the latter is basic to achievement of all goals in the ocean, efforts should be exerted to protect against unthinking or unwise restraints. It is possible that certain institutional innovations may be required, or at least could be helpful, to establish an adequate framework for carrying on this highly important ocean activity.

The organization of discussion of the four problems follows a scheme employed by numerous contemporary international law scholars.[9] In each instance the initial section seeks to describe the legal problems involved in terms of potential conflicting claims. Normal problem-solving procedures are then employed, including clarification of the goals at stake in the resolution of conflicting claims, description of trends in decision relevant (or purported to be relevant) to the problem, and, finally, an appraisal of the congruence of decisions and policy with appropriate recommendations.

[9] McDougal and Burke, The Public Order of the Oceans (1962); Murty, Propaganda and World Public Order (1967); Johnston, *op. cit.* supra note 8; Chen and Lasswell, Formosa, China and the United Nations (1967); Higgins, The Development of International Law through the Political Organs of the United Nations (1963).

I. Acquisition of Mineral Resources

The legal and political problems arising from ocean mineral exploitation appear likely to focus upon three principal issues, or, in some cases, sets of issues. It is useful to consider these issues in terms of claims states advance, or may advance, that certain authority is (or should be) accepted as lawful and the counterclaims by other states opposing such assertions. The claims may consist of interpretations of previously (allegedly) accepted principles of international law, proposals for new principles, or even exercises of authority over the ocean which, it may be said, are novel but should be accepted by other states either by explicit agreement or tacitly as evidenced by similar behavior on their part.

The three issues to be considered here are:

A) Claims to an area over which coastal states may exercise certain special rights pertaining to the resources or activities within the area;

B) Delimitation of the area of special rights;

C) The nature of the regime to govern mineral exploration and development beyond the area of special rights.

A. *Claims by coastal states to an area of special rights*

Claims and Counterclaims

In the past two decades numerous states have made claim, principally through unilateral pronouncement, to the natural resources of the "continental shelf" contiguous to their coasts.[10] Although definitions of the shelf observably vary somewhat in these various declarations, the basic claim to exclusive control over the resources of an adjacent submarine area has been repeatedly advanced by a large number of states. Counterclaims in opposition are notable mostly for their absence, except in connection with efforts by some states to include the waters above the shelf within the ambit of coastal control.[11]

[10] Schedule of National Claims to Continental Shelf and Submarine Area (1967), listing the claims of 58 states. This Schedule, and a Schedule of Selected Concessions Granted in Continental Shelf Areas, were furnished to the writer by Mr. Robert B. Krueger of the Los Angeles, California, bar, and are used with the permission of Mr. Coleman Morton, President of International Geomarine Corporation. The cooperation of Mr. Krueger and Mr. Morton is gratefully acknowledged.

Another recent compilation and analysis of state claims is in Battelle Memorial Institute, Legal Aspects of the Continental Shelf and Seabed 4–18 (1967) (Report No. 8 prepared for the U.S. Arms Control and Disarmament Agency).

[11] Id. at 19–21.

Clarification of Policy

In light of previous decisions, outlined briefly below, there is no substantial policy problem regarding recognition that resources in an area of adjacent ocean bottom should be considered as subject to the special rights of the coastal state. In accordance either with international agreement, or substantial international practice in the form of reciprocal claims, it is now well accepted that coastal states have "sovereign rights" over an adjacent "continental shelf" for the purpose of exploration and exploitation of its natural resources. Very substantial activity in both exploration and exploitation is now occurring in reliance on the national laws enacted pursuant to the general consensus that such an area is subject to national controls.[12] In the interest of stability in the expectations of states and private groups, this allocation of competence over an adjacent area should not be disturbed. Furthermore, despite advances in technology over the past decade the policies originally served by such an allocation are relevant to preserving that allocation. For reasons of efficiency in exploitation, ease of administration, and national security, it continues to be desirable policy that coastal states exercise limited control over a defined area of adjacent ocean floor. Plausible projections of future conditions do not indicate any need for change in this community policy.

Trend in Decision

Even prior to 1945 it was widely accepted that all coastal states had some measure of authority over the resources of ocean floor, but the area concerned was of minimal size. In general understanding the floor beneath the areas of internal waters and territorial sea was wholly within the disposition of the coastal state; and no other state, or a national thereof, could lawfully engage in exploitation of resources thereon without the consent of that state. As is well known, the notion of an additional area of ocean bottom under exclusive coastal control emerged during the Second World War and within a dozen years thereafter this notion too became widely accepted. Finally in 1958 the states of the world meeting together for this purpose determined that the area of the continental shelf, as defined in international agreement, adjacent to a state was to be considered subject to its sovereign right for the purpose of the exploration and exploitation of the natural resources of the shelf.[13] Although the Continental Shelf Con-

[12] Approximately 75 states are now involved in some form of offshore oil exploration or exploitation. Weeks, Offshore Operations Around the World, 27 Offshore No. 7, p. 41 (June 20, 1967) (Annual Drilling and Production Report).
[13] Convention on the Continental Shelf, Article 2(1).

21

vention of 1958 is now in effect as a treaty between only a minority of states,[14] it is widely regarded as reflecting the state of customary international law. There is, then, presently no doubt that states accept that some area of the ocean floor, whose area is imperfectly defined, is to be allocated to the control of one state for limited purposes relating to exploration and exploitation of resources.

Appraisal and Recommendation

Nothing that has been observed, or that appears likely to develop, in the (as yet) limited debate regarding allocation of ocean mineral resources even remotely suggests a tendency to withdraw the decision to allocate the "continental shelf" to coastal states. Insofar as can be determined, then, the strong expectation still prevails that some area of "shelf" will continue to be subject to certain "sovereign rights" of the adjacent coastal state.

B. *Delimitation of the area of special rights*

Claims and Counterclaims

The expansible definition of the continental shelf contained in the Convention of 1958 is the crux of the problem of state claims to delimit the area of coastal control over exploration and exploitation of the natural resources of the seabed and subsoil. The question is: what claims have states made to ocean areas beyond 200 meters, either through national legislation or, perhaps more importantly, through the issuance of exploration and exploitation permits. It is, apparently, widely believed that issuance of either type of permit (or grant of concession for either activity) constitutes a claim that the area concerned falls within the Convention definition or is otherwise subject to coastal control.[15]

[14] The number changes and at this writing is thirty-seven.
[15] Presumably unless the area covered by an exploratory permit is within the "continental shelf", there would be no need to secure authorization for exploration from a coastal state. *But see* Remarks of Frank J. Barry, Solicitor, Department of the Interior, on Administration of Laws for the Exploitation of Offshore Minerals in the United States and Abroad, delivered at American Bar Association National Institute on Marine Resources, June 9, 1967, wherein it is stated (p. 7):
"Whether the granting of these permits might be taken as a precedent in interpreting the Convention's definition of the Shelf is an open question. Until it is resolved I see no reason why companies voluntarily seeking permits for exploration in that zone [i.e., the zone beyond depths admitting of exploitation] should not receive them, if they otherwise should be issued."
The purport of the final qualifying phrase is unclear, but it might be interpreted as vitiating the notion that the question is still open. The various papers delivered at the American Bar Association National Institute on Marine Resources are now available in volume 1 Natural Resources Lawyer, No. 2 and No. 3, June and July 1968.

At the present writing about fifteen states have issued permits for activity beyond the 200 meter isobar, but the deepest producing oil well is located in only 340 feet of water off the coast of Louisiana.[16] None of the present non-fuel mineral exploitation efforts, except those conducted by means of tunnels from adjacent land, are located in deep water. Currently, surface operated mining machinery is largely limited to the depths of 50 to 100 meters.[17] Hence the critical technology for the present problem is that employed for petroleum development.

Developments in the United States and elsewhere illustrate the range of state claims. An authoritative source, Under-Secretary of the Interior Charles F. Luce, summarizes the U.S. position as seen by the Department of the Interior:

... the United States has taken action consistent with a claim of sovereign rights to the seabed and subfloor some distance from its coasts, by the granting of a phosphate lease some 40 miles from the California coast in the Forty Mile Bank area in 240 to 4000 feet of water; by the granting of oil and gas leases some 30 miles off the Oregon coast in about 1500 feet of water; and in the threatened litigation against creation of a new island by private parties on Cortez Bank, about 50 miles from San Clemente Island off the coast of California, or about 100 miles from the mainland. Each of the California areas is separated from the coast by troughs as much as 4000 to 5000 feet deep. The Department of the Interior has published OCS Leasing Maps indicating an intent to assume jurisdiction over the ocean bottom as far as 100 miles off the Southern California coast in water depths as great as 6000 feet.[18]

In addition, permits for exploratory drilling have been issued off the Atlantic coast, apparently in the continental slope region, to depths of 4000–5000 feet.[19] In the Gulf of Mexico an exploration permit was granted for drilling in over 3000 feet of water more than 100 miles from the coast.[20]

Other states have made comparable or even more extensive claims. Australia, for example, has issued an exploration permit for an area as far as 200 miles from its coast and Honduras and Nicaragua have licensed

[16] Schempf, Crude Lines Off Louisiana, 28 Offshore, No. 1, p. 19 (January, 1968); Wilson, Oil Hunters Will Hasten Quest for Marine Reserves, 27 id., No. 13, p. 42 (December, 1967).

[17] Bascom, Mining the Ocean Depths, in Subcommittee on International Organizations and Movements of the House Committee on Foreign Affairs, Interim Report on The United Nations and the Issue of Deep Ocean Resources, H.R. Rep. No. 999, 90th Cong., 1st Sess. 120, 139 (1967) (Hereinafter this report is cited as H.R. Rep. No. 999.); Remarks of Michael Cruickshank in Panel Presentation on Ocean Mining, in Supplement to Proceedings of OECON (Offshore Exploration Conference) p. 61 (1967).

[18] Luce, The Development of Ocean Minerals and the Law of the Sea, Address before American Bar Association National Institute on Marine Resources, p. 4, June 8, 1967.

[19] 9 Ocean Science News, No. 22, p. 3 (June 2, 1967).

[20] Schedule of Selected Concessions Granted in Continental Shelf Areas 11 (1967).

exploration in an offshore area out to 225 miles.[21] By legislation, or even constitutional provision, other states have sought to claim the continental shelf out to a distance of at least 200 miles.

Clarification of Policy

On the assumption that desirable community policy continues to justify limited exclusive rights to coastal states, the major policy problem is whether a precise limit on such rights should be established and, if so, how it shall be defined.

Initially it seems reasonable to posit that at some point, in relative proximity to the coast, there should be an end to the authority of a particular coastal state. The alternatives to this postulate are unacceptable. On the one hand, as already indicated, it is neither realistic nor equitable to expect that present areas of control can be wholly and completely abolished, so that coastal control would recede to the limit of national territory, i.e., the boundary of the territorial sea. The effect of this in spurring even greater expansion of the already extensive claims to the territorial sea needs hardly to be emphasized. On the other hand, for reasons explained more fully below, neither is it acceptable to allow coastal states continually to expand "their shelf" out further and further into the sea, eventually to meet each other at some alleged median line as technology and economic feasibility permit exploitation in deeper and deeper regions. The disadvantages of confusion and conflict ensuing from this latter approach are likely to far outweigh the supposed advantages of certainty and predictability that allegedly would accrue.[22] This projection, coupled with the near certainty of rapid technological progress in deep ocean operations and the eventual emergence of their economic feasibility, provides every reason for discarding exploitability as a criterion for determining the limit of coastal rights.

The reasons just cited for rejecting continued use of the exploitability criterion, or any variant thereof, apply also to suggestions for dividing up the entire ocean bed among coastal states by somehow determining the segments attributable to each. In the end this solution and use of an exploitability concept would achieve about the same result and would have similarly undersirable consequences.

In terms of balancing the interests of coastal states and those of the

[21] Id. at 7.
[22] Partial indication of the results of this method may be seen in the map showing a division of the Atlantic Ocean in H.R. Rep. No. 999, p. 88. Dr. Francis Taggart Christy, Jr., and Henry Herfindahl prepared this map and also one for practically all of the world ocean. The latter will appear in the 1967 proceedings of the Law of the Sea Institute held at the University of Rhode Island, June, 1967.

general community, the remaining problem is to define the point at which coastal states can claim no greater interest than the rest of the community. A fundamental difficulty in such an exercise is that there are very few concrete indicia for giving guidance in making such a determination.

Perhaps the most easily identifiable consideration at the moment derives from the policy of maintaining stability of expectations on the part of states and private groups. In reliance, at least in part, on present treaty provisions and on general consensus, states have asserted certain "sovereign rights" over areas more than 200 miles from the coast and in waters as deep as 6000 feet and in exercise of that authority have held themselves out as competent to offer assurances to exploiters that the area concerned, and the exploitation thereof, is governed and protected by coastal laws. So long as these claims rest on reasonable interpretation of the Shelf Convention, and especially of the requirement that coastal rights extend only to "adjacent" submarine regions, it would be desirable to include them within a new formulation of coastal exclusive rights.

In arriving at this formulation, decisive weight should be attached to the concept of "adjacency" lest the area of special rights become completely detached from any rational nexus with relevant coastal interests. This implies, specifically, that the topography of the ocean bottom, i.e., depth of water, should be given little weight in fashioning a precise definition. Bottom topography varies enormously around the world, and also offshore particular states and, in itself, is wholly neutral in determining the reach of coastal interests. Moreover, if depth alone were used to define the exclusive area, the latter would sometimes be enormous indeed if the criterion of 6000 feet were employed for general use because it was necessary to preserve existing particular claims. The proposal of 600 meters, advanced by Senator Pell as embracing all conceivable regions of the geologic shelf in the world,[23] would also mean that very large areas would be included

---

[23] "I am more or less fixed on the idea that it (the limit) should be 600 meters, because if you use the depth of 600 meters, you then automatically exclude any areas that can conceivably be a continental shelf anywhere in the world." Remarks of Senator Claiborne Pell, in Hearings on S.J. Res. 111, S. Res. 172, and S. Res. 186 before the Senate Committee on Foreign Relations, 90th Cong., 1st Sess. 31 (1967).

The statements in the text to the effect that use of a depth criterion of 6000 feet would result in an enormous area within exclusive coastal control do not appear to be accurate. It appears that on the average the continental shelf, if it were defined in terms of 2500 meters, would extend 100 miles from the land–water interface. See, generally, the report of the Committee on Deep Sea Mineral Resources of the American Branch of the International Law Association, supra note 4. The American Branch Committee, on which the writer served as rapporteur, concluded that the limit of adjacency may be regarded as coinciding with the foot of the submerged portion of the continental land mass. In this sense the Committee placed heavy emphasis upon the geological characteristics of the adjacent ocean bottom, emphasizing the profound natural boundary which is formed by the interface between the continental land mass and the true ocean basin.

within the control of some states. A major difficulty with any limit based on depth alone, whether 200, 600, or 2000 meters, is that states would be alloted submarine regions of very different sizes, with some gaining huge areas and others relatively little. However unrealistic it may sometimes be in practical effect to speak of unequal treatment in this connection, it is not unrealistic to expect vigorous opposition to a formula which has differential application. If there are advantages even to an arbitrary limit for the shelf, they would appear to attach more to a limit expressed in miles than in depth of water.

Of course, using a distance criterion could also lead to extreme results in terms of measuring the interests of some states. If security were considered especially relevant, some states might be able to project their exclusive interests out to remote reaches of the ocean. Although, in general, it is very difficult to translate security interests into reasonable quantitative terms, there is no doubt whatsoever that states would feel little pleasure, and much apprehension, if other states could lawfully emplace installations for military or other purposes in relatively close proximity to the coast. Admittedly, such a reference to "close proximity" does not answer, but merely poses, the question of how close is too close for comfort. Since some value should be attached to security for this purpose, and since it cannot be confidently expressed in concrete terms, perhaps it is wise not to succumb to the temptation to place great weight upon it. Accordingly it is assumed that a narrow limit for the shelf, one well within the policy of protecting stability of expectations, is compatible with a reasonable regard for coastal security. Those who would, for security reasons, establish a wide limit for coastal control should bear the burden of establishing this need by reference to facts and not to surmises.

Such weight as may be accorded depth as a factor important for policy in this context arises from consideration of the multiple uses to which shallow areas are now being put and the need for a regulatory system to provide for accommodation of such uses. While it is true that technology promises to open deeper and deeper regions to effective use for some purposes, the major region for intensive multiple use is likely to continue for some time to be in waters of less than 1000 feet depth. But even here, due account of the need for administration and regulation of numerous, potentially conflicting, activities is possible by confining the exclusive area to a space adjacent to the coastal state.

In the end the question of what is "adjacent" cannot be determined with any exactitude in terms of coastal interests. But the common interest in confining exclusive state authority within reasonable limits would suggest, nonetheless, that even an arbitrary determination might gain wide acceptance. If there is to be any opportunity to reserve the vast reaches of the ocean floor to the common patrimony, whatever form such reservation might take, there appears to be little alternative than to specify some particular width in miles for the exclusive area.

Suggestion has been made that one means of encouraging the adoption of a relatively narrow exclusive area by states is to provide for an "escape valve" in the form of buffer zones beyond the area of exclusive or limited "sovereign rights". In such zones coastal regulation and administration would continue to provide the framework of operation, perhaps with greater leeway for operation by "foreign" enterprises. Additionally there might be provision that revenues produced in such a zone or zones would accrue in some agreed distribution to both the coastal states and the community generally. Considerable variation in such arrangements is easily imaginable. The virtue of this concept might also be enhanced by linking it with negotiations about an acceptable regime for regions beyond the exclusive area and buffer zone.

Trend in Decision

There is no need either to attempt any extensive survey of the decisions on this point or to attempt a summary of the debate at Geneva in 1958. It is well, however, to mention certain aspects of the definition of the shelf in the 1958 Convention in relation to contemporary developments, especially in relation to the issuance of exploitation and exploration permits.

First, it appears to have escaped notice that the definition in the Convention can be read so that the word "adjacent" qualifies both the alternative formulations that follow it defining the shelf. In this view the area out to a depth of 200 meters is subject to certain sovereign rights of the coastal state only so long as that region is "adjacent" to such state. If such an interpretation were accepted, and unless the term "adjacent" is to be deprived of any meaning, there are instances in which a part of the 200 meter region would be beyond coastal authority. Everyone accepts the idea that the exploitability criterion is subject to the limitation of adjacency.

Second, it does not seem very clear, from examination of the summary records of the Geneva discussions, what content was to be given the phrase "to where the depth of the superjacent water admits of the exploitation of the natural resources". Presumably the admissibility of exploitation was to be established by actual demonstration, i.e., a showing that an area of a particular depth was actually subjected to exploitation. Of course this would not necessarily mean that in fact resources in every area of that depth could actually be exploited, for making such a determination in every case would not appear to be feasible or even necessary. If it were technically possible to exploit at a particular depth in one area then such exploitation elsewhere at that depth would fall within coastal control, at least so long as the region were adjacent to the coastal state.

But what seems most noteworthy is that states, in asserting authority over the shelf, have paid little attention to the exploitability criterion if it is taken to mean that oil production actually takes place at a certain depth. Instead the assertion of coastal rights beyond 200 meters rests not on demonstrated production but on employment of the means for determining potential production, i.e., exploration. The issuance of permits for exploration has been taken as an indication of a claim to control, yet the areas involved are far deeper than the present capability for exploitation. Thus far this method appears not to have been challenged, but it is still perhaps too early to conclude that a sufficient pattern exists to call such activity lawful. Generally speaking, the areas concerned have been in reasonable proximity of the coastal state, not much more than 100 miles, but in some instances the distance from shore has exceeded 200 miles.[24] So long as the area concerned *is* reasonably proximate there probably is little ground for making objection, but the trend could become disquieting if the distances involved from shore become more extended than is now generally the case.

Nothing in present decisions appears to offer any reliable hope for limiting state claims in this regard. It is true that doctrinal bases for challenge exist in the "adjacency" criterion, and even in the exploitability standard itself, but there is reason to wonder whether coastal states feel inclined to put a stop to expansion. Perhaps the only reliable means for halting the continued extension of exclusive rights is by revision of the 1958 Convention to provide for a specific limit on the shelf. To the present time there has been no authoritative impartial interpretation of the 1958 Convention definition of the shelf which would establish what is meant by "adjacency" and prospects for obtaining one quickly do not appear bright.

Appraisal and Recommendation

If one accepts the policy of placing some specific limit on coastal rights over adjacent ocean floor resources, a major concern for the near future must be for the method of establishing such a limit. And if, at the same time, there is a preference for assuring stability in expectations based upon

[24] The authorization for exploratory drilling referred to in note 19 supra is reported to include areas as far as 300 miles from the coast. Krueger, The Convention on the Continental Shelf and the Need for Its Revision 8, Paper Delivered at American Bar Association National Institute on Marine Resources, June 9, 1967. Mr. Krueger believes that "the claims being made by our Department of Interior seem to be testing the outside limits of the open-end definitions adopted at the Geneva Conference, as those there present appear to have understood it." Id. at 10.

current claims to authority over the continental shelf, such concern is heightened and it then becomes rather critical to prevent continued expansion of coastal claims to regions further and further from the coast. Since the very notion of a specific limit suggests that different regimes for exploitation will apply within it and beyond it, there may well be a stimulus to coastal states, and to those groups which would benefit from the control of such states, to seek continued expansion of coastal authority during the period in which the new regime is being negotiated. As the process of establishing a regime for the region beyond the limit is quite likely to occupy an extended period of time, perhaps a decade at least, there will be ample opportunity for states unilaterally to expand their limits, at least unless, and until, a halt is somehow called.

These considerations suggest that there is both urgency and importance in the recommendations, advanced most notably during the First Committee discussion of the Maltese item at the 22d General Assembly, for a freeze upon the *"status quo"*.[25] While these suggestions were aimed specifically at potential claims beyond present national jurisdiction, the basic policy underlying them would appear also relevant for determining what the limit is on such jurisdiction at present. Expansion of the shelf by unilateral interpretation of the Shelf Convention will determine, just as will territorial claims to the floor in deep sea regions, what there is left to negotiate about when negotiations finally get underway. Indeed greater encroachment on deep sea regions could be achieved by expansion of shelf limits than by territorial claims formulated in some other way.

Accordingly, whatever else may or may not be done at the 23d General Assembly, states should take the opportunity of speaking collectively and authoritatively to the effect that all states should forthwith declare a moratorium on assertions of jurisdiction to areas alleged to be part of the shelf or to areas beyond, until either the 1958 Shelf Convention is revised to set a specific limit or another agreement is negotiated establishing a limit, whichever event occurs earlier. If action of this kind is not feasible at this session, there is at least the theoretical possibility of an early convening of a conference to revise the Shelf Convention. In view of the time elements involved, however, it would be unlikely that such a meeting would occur until 1970 at the earliest and perhaps not then if the General Assembly of the United Nations, which is authorized to decide what shall be done about requests for revision, were to convene a meeting at which a great many legal issues in addition to this one would be considered. In view of the ferment now attending ocean development of many kinds, it would

[25] 22 UN GAOR, Provisional Verbatim Record of the 1527th Meeting of the First Committee 56 (U.N. Doc. No. A/C.1/PV. 1527) (14 November 1967).

certainly not be surprising if another general conference on the law of the sea were convened within the next five years. Since there are many sound arguments for refraining from piecemeal revisions of the law of the sea, it is conceivable that a decision on a specific limit for the shelf would be delayed until the general conference. This underscores the desirability of an early recommendation of a moratorium by the General Assembly.

C. *The nature of the regime to govern mineral exploration and development beyond the area of presently recognized special rights*

Claims and Counterclaims

To place this problem in appropriate perspective, it should be made clear at the outset that there are at this writing no competing claims, whether by states or private groups, to deep ocean mineral deposits.[26] The only current problem, already examined above, concerns the extent of the area of limited sovereign right by coastal states. Reference to that issue is repeated here since one potential claim to disposition of deep ocean deposits beyond the present "shelf" area that has been urged by some is the extension of national boundaries so that the entire ocean bed is divided up among the coastal states of the world. Such extensions could be achieved in two different ways: by interpretation of the Shelf Convention or by a new agreement explicitly alloting the ocean bed to coastal states. The former route is already available, at least theoretically, since states are now authorized to extend their boundaries to the limit of technological exploitability, so long as such area is adjacent to the state. The proviso of "adjacency", of course, is the basis for grave doubt whether the Convention can be reasonably interpreted so as to divide up the entire ocean bed. The latter route would require both another general conference of states and an extremely high degree of consensus to achieve a successful and peaceful outcome. For reasons briefly mentioned below, neither of these approaches can be regarded as desirable policy.

[26] Insofar as is known, the claims thus far made, by way of exploration permits, to regions of such depths as 6000 feet affect the continental slope only and thus retain a connection with the land mass of the coastal state.

On October 1, 1968, the Saudi Arabian government promulgated a decree claiming ownership of ocean floor resources in the Red Sea beyond the area regarded as part of the continental shelf. The Saudi Arabian oil minister was quoted as stating "Although Saudi ownership of these resources appears both equitable and justified, we have found it necessarry to issue a law declaring this ownership. In the meantime the law does provide for the possibility of joint exploitation of these resources with our neighbor, Sudan, and we will contact them about this." 11 Middle East Economic Survey No. 50, p. 2 (11 October 1968).

Beyond the contemporary, but still only potential, difficulty arising from the Shelf Convention, the question of a regime for ocean minerals is uncomfortably hypothetical in nature. The fact is that there is no deep ocean mining industry and no one appears to have any reliable idea of when it will be feasible to undertake a deep sea mining operation. The reasons for this uncertainty are several. First, our knowledge of the magnitude, density of distribution, and composition of deep ocean mineral deposits is seriously deficient. Second, the technology for extracting and processing such deposits does not exist. Third, while technology for extraction could probably be developed if someone wished to make the required investment, and while difficulties in processing might be overcome, it does not now seem to be profitable to make the attempt. Fourth, if the assumption is correct that enormous quantities of mineral deposits are to be found on the deep sea floor, there could be great risk for the initial entrants into mining them. Additional entrants could make the whole enterprise nearly useless. Fifth, and last in order of importance, no one has any clear idea of what legal protection is available for such operations. But even if protection of exclusive rights were available, the other unanswered questions enumerated present a serious obstacle to those interested.

Although it is, plainly, difficult to speak with much assurance of the claims states will in fact make to establish control over mineral resources, three major types of potential claims can be identified. Initially it is conceivable that a state may advance a mixed kind of claim by asserting that certain resources of a particular area, or *all* resources therein, are subject to exclusive appropriation by a single state and that while other states may make similar claims elsewhere in the high seas no state or group may, without consent, have access to or even seek access to the resources of area already claimed. Such a claim would probably be limited both in terms of the locale involved and its duration. Support for this demand for exclusive access and control may be sought in previous policies and decisions allocating some ocean resources, such as those of the territorial sea, contiguous fishing zones, and continental shelf. The counterclaim most likely to be offered in opposition to this demand for unilaterally established exclusive appropriation is that the mineral resources of the sea are open to free access by all and that no single state or organization is authorized, or should be authorized, to acquire exclusive power and dominion over them unless in accordance with explicit international agreement. Justification for this position might be urged in terms of the ancient doctrine of freedom of the seas, according to which the animal resources of the high seas have been kept open to exploitation by all comers.

The second major type of claim, whose outlines, at least, have already attracted attention, is inclusive in nature but demands that mineral resources be developed under the aegis of an international institution which either engages in direct exploitation or provides a framework and supervision for exploitation by states and private groups. The structure and functions of such an institution could take a variety of forms but the major feature would be the subjection of mineral resources to organized community controls.

The third type of claim, alluded to above, is that these resources are already allocated among states by the Continental Shelf Convention of 1958 or that they should be divided among the coastal states of the world. The considerations underlying such a claim were discussed previously.

Clarification of Policy

The uncertainties referred to above underscore that the policy recommendations to be made at present must be dominated by the understanding that we know very little of the context in which ocean mining will occur. In general, therefore, clarification of policy must be highly tentative in nature. It seems more likely that we are presently able to advance negative recommendations with more firmness and assurance than can be found for positive statement.

Perhaps the most general policy statement, possibly because it is so general, is not controversial. In keeping with general community policy directed at realizing the greatest net gain from ocean resources, there is a clear common interest in all states in promoting the exploration and production of the mineral resources of the ocean floor. The more specific policy problem is that of achieving an allocation of competence over such resources that is most likely to facilitate both the orderly, peaceful development of such resources and their productive, rational exploitation. Several alternatives are most frequently mentioned:[27]

a) division of the ocean bed among "coastal" states;

b) provision for completely free access, leaving assurance of rights, the adjustment of conflicts, and accommodation with other uses to be resolved

[27] There is a growing body of literature examining this policy question. See, e.g., Chapman, Legal Problems in Harvesting Minerals of the Deep Sea Bed, Paper presented April 13, 1963 at "Symposium of Chemicals from the Sea", 144th National Meeting of the American Chemical Society, Chemical Marketing and Economic Division, at Los Angeles, California; Burke, Legal Aspects of Ocean Exploitation—Status and Outlook, 1966 Transactions of the Marine Technology Society 1, 10–14; Ely, The Laws Governing Exploitation of the Minerals Beneath the Sea, 1966 id. 373; Ely, American Policy Options in the Development of Undersea Mineral Resources, 2 The International Lawyer 215 (1968); Christy, A Social Scientist Writes on Econo-

as controversy arises and in accordance with available international law principles;

c) establishment of an international agency, either one already in existence or one to be created, to allocate rights among claimants and to regulate exploitation;

d) provision for an international recording system, leaving regulation to national systems of law;

e) provision for exploration and exploitation to be undertaken by a public international group on behalf of all states.

Of these policy choices for allocation of competence the most certainty can be displayed in rejecting some alternatives. Thus, an allocation of competence over ocean mineral resources by dividing them among "coastal" states has too many serious shortcomings, in terms of the general objectives stated above, to be regarded as desirable. Such a method would be completely arbitrary, being built upon a present structure of states which includes many that have little or no access to the sea. The bottom of the ocean, and perhaps even the waters above, would resemble a crazy quilt of artificial boundaries determined in substantial measure by the existence of remote islands and rocks. Similarly, identification of the states who would benefit by such a system would be determined in major degree by the possession, rooted in the accidents of history, of distant island groups. Some major maritime states would find themselves without any substantial control over or access to the floor of the sea. Finally, such an extension of national boundaries would, without more, pose the definite threat that the waters above the seabed would also become subject to some form of national, or exclusive, controls.[28] In sum, even casual concern for promoting effective and equitable development of ocean resources warrants rejection of this means of allocation.

At the other extreme, provision for exploitation of ocean minerals by

---

mic Criteria for Rules Governing Exploitation of Deep Sea Minerals, 2 id. 224; Brooks, Deep Sea Manganese Nodules: From Scientific Phenomenon to World Resource, Paper presented at the Law of the Sea Institute, University of Rhode Island, June 27, 1967; Goldie, Comments on the Geneva Convention and the Need for Future Modifications, in Alexander, ed., The Law of the Sea 273 (1967); Burke, A Negative View of a Proposal for United Nations Ownership of Ocean Mineral Resources, Paper presented at the American Bar Association National Institute on Marine Resources, June 8, 1967; Cheever, The Role of International Organization in Ocean Development, in Papers presented at the Second Conference on Law, Organizations and Security in the Use of the Ocean 37 (1967) (sponsored by Mershon Center for Education in National Security and the Carnegie Endowment for International Peace, October 5-7, 1967, Columbus, Ohio).

[28] Dr. John Craven has asserted that in his opinion the "trend of law" is toward "the careful extension of municipal jurisdiction seaward along the sea bed *and from thence to the vertical column* above and the subterrain below." 2 First Conference on Law, Organization and Security in the Use of the Ocean p. C35 (1967). Dr.

a public international agency composed only of states seems unrealistic and ill-designed to result in productive development. Lack of realism stems from the fact that this approach would probably place severe limits on exploitation by private groups and it could be expected with some confidence that some major states would be wholly unable to concur for this reason. In the United States, for example, there is already considerable concern over, and opposition to, potential federal government activity in development of mineral resources. Even without this spur, however, states would be extremely hesitant to vest complete control over the production of mineral supplies critical, at least potentially, for national purposes in the hands of an international agency. Assuming such obstacles could be overcome, however, it does not seem likely that an international agency could, without the investment of very substantial resources by states, undertake effective development of ocean minerals. The crucial elements of capital availability and technological skill are now in the hands of private groups and some states; and these would somehow have to be diverted to the international agency if it were to have any prospects for successful operation. The likelihood of such diversion seems minimal presently; hence the likely result of this approach would be to hinder rather than to promote development.

Whether or not one is optimistic about the creation of an international agency for exploitation, however, one possibility that should be investigated is that of an international consortium, composed of public and private groups representing interested states, to engage in ocean mineral (perhaps including fuel) development. Within the U.S., for example, thought has been given to the creation of a group comparable to Comsat which would be responsible for certain types of ocean enterprises. The structure, organization and operating procedures for such a consortium obviously present grave and complex questions, but further inquiry into them would seem to be extremely valuable if there were any conceivable prospect that this approach could provide a forum for peaceful resolution of the greatly complicated issues raised by ocean mineral development. The experience of Intelsat, although directed at a different type of resource, might prove extremely valuable as a guide to the rocks and shoals that attend the establishment of an international enterprisory group.[29]

Craven adds his conclusion that "the long-term, stable solution (which ought not be reached in this century or even in the early part of the next) is one in which every area of the ocean bottom and its resources are under the clearly recognized municipal jurisdiction of an appropriate 'coastal' state, and the international enjoyment thereof carefully delineated by agreement or treaty with the 'coastal' state." Id. at C35–36.

[29] A repeat of the problem of management and control faced by Intelsat would be especially undersirable. See Vlasic, the Growth of Space Law 1957–65: Achievements

The remaining policy choices are the employment of the laissez-faire system, sometimes called the "flag nation" approach, some form of international institution for regulation or supervision or lesser authority, or some combination of these either consecutively or simultaneously. It is with this set of choices in mind that it is proposed to survey the more significant factors that appear relevant to policy. The purpose of calling attention to these factors is, in part, to seek to identify difficulties which might be encountered in working out an acceptable international regime. Whether or not these factors do pose obstacles, they do suggest some of the reasons why policy clarification must be tentative at this stage.

Factors Relevant to Policy

1. *Characteristics of Resource*

The first, and perhaps the most important, category of data relevant to policy concerns the characteristics of the resource and the environment in which it is found. The deep ocean basins are almost completely unexplored and it is therefore not surprising that there is virtually no knowledge of the structure and composition of the ocean floor (beyond the continental slope) below the sediments. It is believed that the underlying rock of the ocean basins may be substantially or even completely different from the composition of the continents and of those undersea regions which are part of the continents. This leaves the possibility open that new types of minerals may be discovered there or that potentially valuable supplies of familiar metals could exist.[30] In any event there is ample testimony to the breadth of our ignorance regarding this part of the planet. The leading study of deep ocean minerals, that by Dr. John Mero, observes that very little is known of this region and focusses attention on the sediments above the floor of the sea.[31] So far as fuel minerals are concerned, the situation is similar except that there is some basis for believing that the oceanic ridges may contain valuable deposits of petroleum and gas.

The sediments of the deep sea, and especially the surficial deposits, have

and Issues, in 1965 Yearbook of Air and Space Law 365, 395–400 (1967); Doyle, Communication Satellites: International Organization for Development and Control, 55 Calif. L. Rev. 431, 440–42 (1967).

[30] Statement of Dr. Harold L. James, Chief Geologist, U.S. Geological Survey, Department of the Interior, in H.R. Report No. 999, at 118.

For authoritative discussion of various of the factors important for policy see 23 UN GAOR, Report of the Ad Hoc Committee to Study the Peaceful Uses of the Seabed and the Ocean Floor Beyond the Limits of National Jurisdiction, Annex 1, Report of the Economic and Technical Working Group UN Doc. A/7230 (1968).

[31] Mero states that "Very little is known about the fifth region, that of the hard rock underlying the soft ocean-floor sediments." Mero, The Mineral Resources of the Sea 1 (1965).

attracted the major attention as potential sources of mineral ores. But even in this instance information does not appear to be very firmly based. The manganese nodules, for example, are estimated to exist in almost astronomical quantities, so large that if generally exploitable they would still be forming at a rate that would exceed their consumption. But it is important to note that even these estimates are speculative.[32] Sampling to date is apparently rather widely spaced and the methods employed are relatively crude. In addition, even if manganese nodules are in fact widely distributed over the floor of the oceans, it does not necessarily follow that their composition is uniform and some evidence suggests that in fact differences occur in regions of the Pacific Ocean. Mero's study breaks the Pacific Ocean down into four regions in accordance with the high incidence in such regions of iron, manganese, nickel and copper, and cobalt.[33] Since the number of samples was extremely small in terms of the vastness of the Pacific such a classification would appear to be extremely tentative and variations might well exist within the regions. Still other differences in the nodules could be important for determining value, including variability in size and density of occurrence in the area. External factors might also be significant and would have to be assessed with respect to any proposal to operate in a locale. Water depth, currents, variations in bottom topography, surface wave conditions, weather, and distance from land might all bear upon decisions to operate in an area. But the important point is that the weight to be given to such factors is not now known and probably cannot be known without investigation of particular sites.

Although most of the furor over the prospect of realizing wealth from the deep ocean centers upon non-fuel minerals, the possibility of discovering new sources of fuel minerals should by no means be overlooked. We now have very little basis for estimating the realism of this possibility, but recent statements by knowledgeable persons suggest that it would be unwise to neglect it. Dr. Harold James, Chief Geologist of the Geological Survey, in the U.S. Department of Interior recently noted:

The question has been raised many times as to the possibilities of oil and gas in the deep ocean. We can't answer this question at the present time. It will require a great deal more bottom exploration and drilling before we can even get a hint as to what the real potential is. I suspect that there are real possibilities, and I think one would be very foolish to discount them.[34]

[32] Id. at 175.
[33] Id. at 225 ff.
[34] James, H.R. Rep. No. 999, at 119.
In August 1968 the Glomar Challenger, a research vessel operated by the Scripps Institution of Oceanography of the University of California, and Global Marine, Inc., discovered a show of oil at a water depth of 11,753 feet in the Gulf of Mexico. The site of the find was the Sigsbee Knolls which are reported to be about midway

Another expert, Dr. Hollis D. Hedberg, is reported to have urged investigation of the possibility of locating petroleum reserves beyond the continental rises and out into the abyssal plain.[35]

The above comments about resource characteristics are obviously both extremely brief and general and are made with the realization that in the real world calculations about exploitability will be made in light of the very concrete characteristics of a particular mineral in a specific context. Though it is probably true that, speaking so generally, our ignorance of ocean minerals is vast indeed, it is also most probable that interested business firms have highly detailed information and projections regarding some minerals in some places. Prediction of future developments surely is more reliably based on this latter type of information than on very general assessments of knowledge, but for obvious and good reasons the interested industrial groups do not share such information with outsiders or the public generally.

2. *Participants*

Identity of participants who will probably be directly engaged in ocean mining activities appears to be significant in terms of their number and certain important characteristics.

A strong likelihood exists that for a considerable period after deep ocean mining becomes a reality the entrants into this field will be relatively few. Most observers agree that initial ventures into ocean mining will probably require large capital investments, on the order of $100 million or more.[36] Additionally the enterprise must possess, or be able to command, the even rarer combination of technological skills that are required both in deep ocean operating capabilities and metallurgical processing. In all likelihood these requirements place severe limits on those who will be able to participate in exploration. Initially, at least, operators will be drawn from a few of the developed states, which is itself a small group of states, where there are large private sources of capital and skill or where the state itself may possess the requisite assets.

If this projection proves accurate, several implications for choice of policy may be drawn.

between Louisiana and the Yucatan Peninsula. See 28 Offshore No. 10, p. 33 (Sept., 1968). It should be noted that the Gulf of Mexico is geologically midway between the true oceanic basin and the continental land mass.

[35] 9 Ocean Science News, No. 17, p. 1 (April 28, 1967). Mr. Willard Bascom states that "There is, in my judgment, fairly good evidence that there are oil deposits in quite deep water" but that retrieval of oil "at great depths" is "quite a long ways off into the future." Statement of Willard Bascom, President, Ocean Science and Engineering, Inc., Washington, D.C., in H.R. Report No. 999, at 132.

[36] Brooks, Low-Grade and Nonconventional Sources of Manganese 99 (1966); Mero, op. cit. supra note 31, 268–70; Brooks, supra note 27, at 11.

Assuming, first, that no international or other initiative were taken, the few who are capable of exploitation would reap all the benefits and any distribution of them to non-participants would depend on individual national decisions just as it now does.[37] Second, the possibility of such a situation underlies the attitude of the states not likely to share in direct exploitation that some means should be found for a wider sharing of some of the benefits of ocean mineral exploitation. Third, among non-participants generally are those states whose economies may be more or less seriously affected by the development of a competing source for certain minerals. The net result of these considerations is to suggest the desirability of some mechanism, and a variety of these are easily imaginable, by which the fruits of ocean mining may be made available, in one way or another, to a wider grouping of states than those who actually exploit the resource. Special consideration should be given to the remedial measures required for those developing states from which ores are now obtained in order to prevent serious detrimental effect to their national economies.[38]

It is not to be expected that participants, however small the group, will be limited to private entrepreneurs. Rather it is likely that actual operations will be undertaken by nation states, private groups, and entities composed of both groups. Any community policy that aspires to wide and lasting acceptance must be broad enough to embrace activities pursued by any and all these groups and to countenance the institutional innovations found necessary to achieve rational, orderly production. In particular, such policy must take account of the potential hazards that may attend a competitive struggle between public and private groups, recognizing that the interests of the former may well be broader, on critical occasions, and their resources sometimes substantially greater.[39]

A policy encouraging institutional innovations for exploiting the ocean should not embrace such experiments as attempts to create new political units or "states" whose territory consists solely of installations in or on the sea and whose sole, or primary, purpose is the conduct of mining

[37] The phrase "all the benefits" is not meant to suggest vast riches. To the contrary, the returns from deep ocean mining will probably be quite limited for a period of years, if not decades.

[38] With respect to manganese, Brooks observes that "several countries gain a significant proportion of their foreign exchange from manganese mining," mentioning Ghana, Morocco, Gabon, Guyana and Brazil. Brooks, op. cit. supra note 36, at 114. The impact of retrieving other minerals from the ocean has not, apparently, been investigated.

[39] Private groups may also be used to gain public ends, of course, and sometimes could employ greater assets in such a contest than public groups. Certain states, however, if sufficiently motivated, are in a position to be able to devote far greater resources to ocean mineral development than any single private company or combination of companies unless the latter received government subsidy.

operations. At the same time, private groups should remain free to identify themselves, through the device of incorporation, with such political units as they may choose. There is no discernable reason, at present, why there should be any new restrictions on this method of identifying the national character of a particular enterprise.[40]

The fact that few participants can be expected has another implication for policy which while delicate should nevertheless be confronted. It does not seem improbable that the few states now capable of working in the deep ocean environment may seek special influence on the decision process by which allocation of rights and determination of the important features of the regulatory process will be made. The fact is, as noted below, that some of these same states have many interests in the deep ocean, some closely related to military security, and it would not be surprising if this were reflected in a desire to be assured that an ocean mining regime were compatible with such interests. It may well be that the special influence mentioned may inhere in the few states concerned because of the normal structure of influence operative in the community of states. If additional assurances are desired, due account of them might well be an important consideration in the composition and procedures of an eventual institution for regulation of mineral exploitation.[41]

3. *Objectives*

Any effort to project policies for encouraging ocean mineral development involves consideration of a variety of objectives or goals of those who engage in exploitation. That wealth will be a major goal of some is hardly subject to doubt and the impact of this is widely regarded as a major determinant for policy, even if it seems to offer different guidelines to different people. The assumption is generally made, and soundly it is believed, that if effective exploitation is to be encouraged it is necessary to assure those whose major (if not sole) objective is operating a profitable enterprise that the conditions requisite to such an opportunity can be established and maintained to their reasonable satisfaction.[42] This was one of the major policy considerations underlying the community decision, made express in Geneva in 1958, to confer limited sovereign rights upon coastal states over

[40] However, if there is to be a system for limiting the claims of any one group it will clearly be necessary to prevent evasion by the device of incorporation, shielding the identity of those in effective control.

[41] This thought perhaps found expression at the conclusion of the First Committee debate on the Maltese item at the 22d General Assembly in the statement by the U.S. representative that it would continue to be necessary to defer to the views of a "significant group" of states. See text infra at note 173.

[42] That such an objective may well conflict with others seems manifest and it is partially this kind of obvious conflict that accounts for concern over such generally

the adjacent continental shelf; such an allocation of competence was thought to encourage exploitation since it permitted coastal states to secure investment through the normal operation of national legislation. So clear was the need for some arrangement that many states had already adopted legislation which would provide the climate necessary for development of the shelf.

If every major participant in this aspect of ocean exploitation were similarly concerned over production of wealth, the task of devising a suitable legal framework would be considerably less complicated. But preoccupation with production of wealth as an objective should not obscure the distinct possibility that other objectives are involved in deep ocean mining or that some states believe other objectives are involved. Of the alternative objectives power is probably of the most significance. If influential states perceive that access to deep ocean minerals has, or could have, important consequences for power position, either their own or for potential opponents, this could have deeply unsettling effects upon efforts to arrive at an international system of regulation and to maintain such a system. One rather obvious illustration of potential difficulty is in the employment of deep ocean areas for military purposes. Apprehension that military activities during peacetime could be prejudiced by an international institution for ocean mineral operations might complicate agreement on such an institution unless its structure and authority were designed to take this factor into account.[43] This factor cuts both ways, however, and there might be similar apprehension lest a laissez-faire system of unilateral claims have deleterious impact on military measures.

A more direct, if speculative, impact of power considerations arises from concern over the mineral resources themselves. It is certainly no news to observe that the supply of certain minerals has been, and is, regarded as critical for national security purposes.[44] Should ocean mining appear to play a role in providing some states with such supplies, or even if it appears that this might be the case, decisions could be made that either frustrate agreement on an international regime or substantially disrupt its operation. The fact that ocean mining ventures are likely to be conducted by groups with greatly disparate perspectives and resource bases could present special

worded proposals as the principles recommended by Malta at the 22d General Assembly. See, e.g., statement by Robert A. Frosch, Assistant Secretary of the U.S. Navy for Research and Development, that in his opinion the Maltese resolution, and certain phrases therein, were what he would propose if the aim was to "slow down the exploitation of the seabed for the longest possible time . . . ." H.R. Rep. No. 999, at 206.

[43] This factor is mentioned further infra p. 78 ff.

[44] With respect to the United States, see Landsberg, Fischman, and Fisher, Resources in America's Future, Chapter 21 "Nonfuel Minerals" (1963). For manganese, see Brooks, supra note 36, at 33 ff.

opportunities for discord should one such group, whether public or private, seek to use its resources to undermine a cooperative arrangement. For example, should an auction system be employed for allocating exclusive rights, it might be dislocated considerably if a group decided to engage in pre-emptive bidding. Other possibilities are imaginable, if not likely, such as a relatively sudden increase in production of certain commodities which would significantly lower prices to the detriment of other producers.[45]

That the above observations are speculative does not diminish their relevance or importance. Indeed the very uncertainty of the power implications of developing ocean minerals could weigh heavily in determinations by states of the interests they have at stake in seeking to establish a legal structure for ocean mineral operations. The effect of this could be to prolong the process of deciding upon such a structure and to affect the substance of decisions about it when and if they are made. One obvious possibility could be a desire to insulate this particular use of the ocean from power calculation so that no participant is in a position to gain, or to lose, from manipulating the ocean mineral situation to its exclusive benefit. Another is that if an international structure is created, the attempt may be made to permit quick escape from its requirements should it turn out to work to the power advantage of one or a few participants or to the great disadvantage of a few.[46]

There is, perhaps, need for but brief mention that in undertaking ocean mineral exploitation for their various objectives, states must take account of the fact that similar objectives may be sought by themselves, or by other states, through other activities on land as well as at sea. The balance of benefit or loss implicit in this problem should obviously be given careful consideration both in establishing a structure for regulation and in assuring that the decision-making process is capable of responding as this balance changes through time.

4. *Situations*

The timing of the development of an ocean mining industry is a crucial consideration, although different conclusions are drawn from the common assumption that we are some years, perhaps a decade or more, from initial

[45] Economists and businessmen alike call special attention to the importance of the magnitude of production. See Brooks, op. cit. supra note 36, at 103–08; Bascom, H.R. Rep. No. 999, at 127.

[46] Certainly every effort would be made to anticipate this contingency and to provide against it. The point of the text remark is that if an agreement is concluded under conditions of high uncertainty about future developments, such as now prevail regarding the deep ocean floor, participants will demand relatively easy and quick denunciation of it. This would not represent a drastic departure from usual practice in this regard.

efforts. Despite the seeming attractiveness of the large surficial deposits, and the assurances by some that mining them is both a feasible and economic proposition,[47] there is now no deep ocean mining industry and it is wholly unclear when one will develop. Presently the extraction of ocean mineral resources takes place in relatively shallow waters adjacent to land masses and, except for oil and gas which are produced on a sizable scale, is a very minor part of total world mineral production. In 1966 it was calculated that there were 276 ocean mining operations with an annual production of $700 million, which may be compared to the total world production, estimated at $700 billion.[48] In contrast, oil from offshore areas was reported, in mid-1967, to be 16 per cent of total world production[49] and this share seems very likely to increase annually since offshore exploration activities are rapidly spreading throughout the globe. Perhaps some notion of the difficulties involved in extracting minerals from the sea, which account for the lack of ocean mining ventures, is suggested by the assertion by Willard Bascom (apparently in 1966) that "To this moment (as far as the author knows) there has never been a profitable mining operation in an oceanic offshore area."[50] Perhaps it is understatement to add that "This inhibits mining companies who are otherwise interested in exploring the seafloor."[51]

The absence of current deep ocean mining operations, or even of a profitable operation in relatively shallow ocean waters, does not, of course, signify that there is no interest in deep ocean minerals. One well-informed commentator, Dr. David Brooks, now classifies certain deposits as "resources" in the sense that their potential availability is being taken into account in management decisions and may already have an influence on the price of certain commodities.[52]

---

[47] Dr. John Mero recently repeated earlier optimistic statements: "More interesting, however, are the results of engineering calculations which indicate that these nodules can not only be mined with present day technology, but that it would be highly profitable to use these nodules as a source of nickel, cobalt, manganese, copper, and possibly many other metals." Mero, Mineral Deposits in the Sea 12–13, Paper Presented at the American Bar Association National Institute on Marine Resources, June 10, 1967.

[48] Romanowitz, Cruickshank and Overall, Offshore Mining Present and Future with Special Reference to Dredging Systems 6 (Paper Presented at NSIA/OSTAC Ocean Resources Subcommittee Meeting, San Francisco Area, April 26, 1967).

[49] Weeks, Offshore Operations Around the World, 27 Offshore, No. 7, p. 41 (June 20, 1967) (Annual Drilling and Production Report).

[50] Bascom, Mining the Ocean Depths, in H.R. Rep. No. 999, at 120. In 1967 Mr. Bascom repeated this observation: "So far as I know, there has never been a successful, what I'd call, ocean mining operation." Supplement to Proceedings of OECON, supra note 17, at 73.

[51] H.R. Rep. No. 999, at 120.

[52] Brooks, supra note 27, at 10.

Two major inter-related factors appear to be inhibitions upon expansion of hard mineral production efforts into deep waters. First, as noted above, there is no experience whatsoever in operating mining systems in deep water and the experience gained in shallow waters of 200 feet or less is likely to be difficult or impossible to transfer to work in deeper regions. Hence it is necessary to develop and to perfect the systems required for extracting and lifting material from the depths to the surface. Some work has been done on this and the task is not, apparently, regarded as a tremendous technological obstacle.[53] However, the next step in the operation, the processing of the ores retrieved, especially of manganese nodules, does pose serious difficulties because the problems of fine grain size and chemical composition are most complex and have not been resolved. Brooks has suggested, however, that recent studies "give grounds for hope that relatively simple processes may make a multi-product operation feasible".[54] Such a cautiously phrased expression of optimism perhaps suggests the degree of complexity involved in resolving the problems of processing ocean manganese nodules.

The cost of ocean mineral production relative to that on land is almost universally considered to be the most significant single factor affecting the decision to venture into this environment. Political considerations aside, exploitation of these resources does not seem likely to develop until it is less costly, or more profitable, to secure supplies from this source than from land.[55] Although the quantities of potentially useful metals on the seabed are widely believed to be gigantic, and to dwarf every present estimate of land reserves, the fact is that the latter reserves, on a world-wide basis, are quite large and presently available at a lower cost.[56] It is well known that mining and other companies have made calculations about the profitability of ocean deposits and have reached the conclusion not to develop them at this stage. Willard Bascom reports that:

In one exercise we did, we did a study for a bank of mining some manganese deposits on the Blake Plateau, which is water only about 3000 feet deep off the coast of the United States. For a rough approximation we determined that for a capital investment of about $50 million one could set up a system which would bring in essentially an unlimited quantity of manganese deposits on which

[53] Brooks, op. cit. supra note 36, at 96 refers to the optimistic attitude of a number of business firms. It is generally thought, however, that development costs will be high.

[54] Brooks, supra note 27, at 8. See also quotation from Bascom in text at note 57; World Ocean News, Dec. 1967, p. 9.

[55] It may be just as costly, or perhaps more, to retrieve a particular material from the ocean floor but, as noted in the text below, savings on other parts of the operation may still permit a greater profit from the entire operation.

[56] Mero, op. cit. supra note 31, at 276–77.

our total mining recovery and ferrying the material ashore, for this the total costs were about $5 a ton. Nearly $25 a ton would have gone into the processing of it, and I couldn't see us being on the wrong side of the business.[57]

Other companies have reached similar conclusions.

It does not seem possible to make any reliable projections about when deep ocean mineral production will become economically feasible. The many imponderables affecting future prices are too difficult to measure and to project to permit such an exercise. Those who have studied the problem in detail are also unable to express any firm conclusions in terms of timing developments. Dr. Brooks, who is relatively optimistic, offers no answer to this question:

Despite all of these qualifications [the obstacles yet to be overcome], investigation of as much cost information as I could obtain led me to conclude that deep sea manganese nodules are the only potential resource that might be exploited in the near-to-middle term future and that to a considerable extent they already influence mining decisions. This does not mean that recovery of manganese from the oceans is today competitive with recovery from high-grade ore deposits of the conventional type. Until deep sea mining is actually attempted, the question of competitive standing must remain unresolved. However, it does mean that research on possible exploitation of deep sea nodules has gone far enough to make them the lowest cost alternative resource of any size and hence far enough to put a firm ceiling on the long-run price of manganese—and perhaps of cobalt and nickel as well. The price cannot rise higher than the cost of production of the nodules. Indeed, future prices could well be lower than today's prices, if deep sea mining becomes a reality.[58]

One other economic consideration requires mention and that is that cost-price relationships could conceivably be calculated in terms of unique national or industry needs rather than by more general world considerations. Some of the recent bids for offshore oil leases in the United States are suggestive of this type of calculation since the cash bonus offered to obtain the case virtually equalled expected revenues from production.[59] Dr. H. W. Menard refers to this possibility as follows:

It appears that nodules can be mined by surface ships using suction dredges, but the investment would be large and the venture marginal, considering the present glut of most of the pertinent metals and the fickleness of the sea. A mining company with adequate reserves might have little interest in mining the sea floor. Nations with industries based on these reserves might have no reason to subsidize the mining of the sea floor. However, mining is not carried

[57] Bascom, H.R. Rep. No. 999, at 128.
[58] Brooks, supra note 27, at 10.
[59] United States offshore development might also illustrate the text statement. Some expert observers entertain considerable doubt whether offshore oil production in the Gulf of Mexico or in California is justified by economic considerations and find more satisfactory explanation for such production in political factors.

44

out as a unique activity separated from all other aspects of the economies of individual countries or the finances of individual companies, and resources and industries are not uniformly distributed throughout the world. Several major manufacturing nations, notably Japan and Great Britain, have hardly any resources of several important metals. Both have major merchant navies and a nautical tradition. We may anticipate that at some time one or both of these nations may find mining of the sea floor beneficial for the general economy, even though the mining by itself may be marginal. Take, for example, the present situation in the shipping industry. Large numbers of very large ships are idle. Would it be more profitable to use them for a marginal marine mining operation or to let them sit?[60]

The considerations adduced by Dr. Menard are seen in sharper focus when account is taken of the important place of transportation costs in determining delivered prices of certain commodities. When analyses are made in particular contexts, it may well turn out that for certain states, now dependent on distant sources of certain bulk materials, the higher costs of marine mining are more than offset by lower transportation costs if, and when, marine sources can be identified which are closer to significant markets. It would be greatly surprising if situations of this type did not arise. Again, the point is, as already emphasized, that *general* calculations of feasibility are not necessarily reliable indicators of the future course of operations.

The uncertainty which surrounds projections is not dispelled by the additional consideration, to which little attention seems to have been paid publicly, that political factors (both domestic and international) may affect the course of events. If it is true, as many suggest, that a more reliable legal framework than afforded by existing international law prescriptions is needed *before* private industry is willing to make the heavy investments required for ocean mining, then the attitude of influential states toward the timing of decisions on such a framework is extremely pertinent.[61] It is not unrealistic to expect that states will approach this matter cautiously, in the hope that the pattern of future developments and their impact on power relationships will come into better focus with the passage of time. In the United States, where the matter of deep ocean minerals has already stirred controversy, it is clearly apparent that responsible government officials feel constrained by their uncertainty about the implications of deep ocean mining.[62] It may be that the United States, with its extensive commit-

[60] Menard, Marine Geology of the Pacific 189–90 (1964).
[61] For example, if this hypothesis were acted upon, major states with relatively large reserves of minerals might seek to hinder the development of the essential legal system.
[62] See, generally, testimony by U.S. officials in H.R. Rep. No. 999 and Hearings, supra note 23.

ments in ocean research, development and programs, is not overly uncomfortable in such conditions of uncertainty, and can contemplate their continuance without apprehension. Other states, for different reasons, may be positively unwilling to join in making decisions until the significance of ocean mineral development can be assessed more clearly in terms of their own interests.

Still another possibility exists that political calculations may hasten, rather than defer, the initiation of ocean mining projects. Considerations of economic efficiency may weigh less than some of the current dialogue would suggest, and operations could conceivably be initiated in advance of a favorable economic climate. Such contingencies add even more uncertainty to an already confused situation.

That deep ocean mining efforts may still be at least a decade away, or will occur at some unknown future date, is the basis for some recommendations that now is the time to make certain decisions about allocation of competence over the deep sea bed. The argument is made that *because* there are, presently, no mining ventures, and therefore no vested interests which might be expected to arise after operations begin, now is the time to decide that the deep sea bed is beyond national appropriation by any means whatsoever. Support for this position is sought in the analogy of outer space, and it is urged that states should follow their own example by accepting certain general principles as applicable to an environment in which their intrusion has been relatively slight.

The major difficulty with this supposed analogy is, of course, that the ocean is already very intensively employed by states for a number of purposes and weighty, if not vital, interests are already implicated.[63] And it is the apprehension of undesirable impacts on those interests that appears to counsel caution and deliberateness in establishing new international prescriptions. In addition states, or at least some of them, are fully aware of the rapid pace of technological developments affecting effective access to the deep sea and are also cognizant that these interests, as they are now conceived, may require redefinition or complete revision as they enter and utilize this environment with more confidence and facility. In such a context it is hardly surprising that there would be hesitation in accepting principles that are so very generally formulated that their future implications cannot be realiably ascertained.

[63] It needs to be noted also that the Outer Space Treaty and the Antarctic Treaty hardly provide guides for a situation in which it is expected to find valuable resources. The Antarctic Treaty appears to assume that just the opposite situation pertains in the Antarctic and the Outer Space agreement fails even to address certain, perhaps not too remote, questions about allocation of use of scarce resources. See Taubenfeld, A Treaty for Antarctica 296–97 (Int'l. Conc. Pamp. No. 531, 1961) and Vlasic, The Space Treaty: A Preliminary Evaluation, 55 Calif. L. Rev. 507, 512–13 (1967).

5. *Conditions*

The question is: what conditions may need to be established to encourage and protect the initial ocean mining activities and to maintain their viability through time. In terms of most of the contemporary discussion, the major controversy is over the alleged need to devise a system for assuring that a venture will have exclusive rights to a large enough area and over a sufficient time period that the entrepreneur will have an opportunity to realize a return on investment. It is useful to consider separately the requirements for the initial ventures and those for the long-term.

Practically all commentators on this subject appear to share the belief that in the beginning there are likely to be very few deep ocean mining operations, primarily because the capital requirements are so large and because the capabilities for a successful effort are not widely distributed. But this shared expectation does not at all lead to concurrence upon the need for an international organization to allocate exclusive rights for the initial participants. Some contend that for the pioneering enterprises there is nothing required for protection beyond that which states are able now to furnish under generally accepted principles of international law;[64] others argue that conflict is likely even among the first entrants and that exclusive rights must be assured through an international system.[65]

In part this difference in view may be explainable in terms of different assumptions made about the extent and availability of ocean mineral deposits. One such assumption is, for example, that manganese nodules are very common on the ocean floor, and that despite differences in topography, currents, climate and distance to port, there are likely to be a fairly large number of similarly productive and feasible mining sites. Under these conditions it may be questioned whether there is a need to allocate exclusive rights in order to avoid conflict over the same mining site. The few original entrants can rather easily be scattered over the several desirable locations, without much, if any, occasion for seeking access to adjacent areas that might cause trouble. It is urged, too, that if controversy does arise those involved are likely to reach an accommodation without undue difficulty. The contrary assumption, for which there now appears to be some, if inconclusive, evidence, is that some parts of the ocean are likely to be more valuable than others in terms of composition of the mineral deposit and in other important ways bearing on costs.[66] These differences in value could

[64] Ely, The Laws Governing Exploitation of the Minerals Beneath the Sea, supra note 27, at 376–77; Ely, American Policy Options in the Development of Undersea Mineral Resources, supra note 27. See also discussion in 2 First Conference on Law, Organization and Security in the Use of the Ocean B30–B33 (1967).
[65] Christy, supra note 27, at 241–42.
[66] Brooks agrees that some sites will have greater value than others but that the

47

lead, some believe, to competition for sites that is not amenable to resolution by any doctrines that we now dispose of, other than accommodation through joint ventures or some form of negotiation and payoff. Accordingly, some authoritative means for allocating secure and exclusive rights is required.

It should be stressed that the conclusions some urge on the basis of the first assumption above that desirable sites are not scarce do not avoid, indeed they may intensify, the difficulties of misallocation of resources that could arise because entry is not limited. Economists have pointed out than when investment costs are high and operating costs are low, as is likely to be the case with at least some ocean mining, the incentive is for the operator to increase his scale of production.[67] Even when only one operator so behaves, the increase in production may be such that the price of commodities will be affected. When more than one enterprise enters the field, this problem becomes crucial.[68] Thus, even at the beginning of the ocean mining business there may be a need for establishing limitations on entry, even if exclusive rights to sites are not necessary to avoid conflict. Of course provision for exclusive rights alone would also fail to deal with this problem, unless one of the criteria for allocation included factors relating to scale of production.

The above considerations appear as equally relevant when consideration is given to the production of fuel minerals. Indeed petroleum companies may be even more insistent on the need for exclusive rights since it seems wholly unclear whether petroleum and gas will be as ubiquitous under the deep seas as is commonly assumed to be the case for manganese nodules and the minerals contained therein.

Little empirical data exists regarding the attitude of those who might reasonably be expected to engage in ocean mining toward the choice between the laissez-faire and international systems, at least for the short run. It is probable that views differ regarding the need. One ocean miner, active in shallow waters, has stated that he thought "it would be possible somehow to obtain adequate rights to go ahead if you were anywhere near striking distance of the economics of it".[69] Mr. Northcutt Ely, an American attorney who has addressed this problem, believes that exclusive rights are required but that in the beginning national flag protection is satisfactory

resource "is probably large enough to accommodate the first several operations without conflict." He adds, however, that the situation could change as others enter. Brooks, supra note 27, at 16.

[67] Id. at 11–12a; Jacob, Book Review, 14 UCLA L. Rev. 382, 387 (1966).

[68] Christy and Brooks, Shared Resources of the World Community, in 17th Report of the Commission to Study the Organization of the Peace 135, 156 (1966); Brooks, op. cit. supra note 36, at 103–06.

[69] Bascom, H.R. Rep. No. 999, at 128.

48

for that task.[70] The general belief, to the extent a conclusion can be drawn, appears to be that an assurance of exclusive rights is needed, but there is very little information available regarding views of potential exploiters on how this might be achieved.

For the long run, after the initial ventures are undertaken, there appears to be more widespread consensus that a system of international decision-making is required to assure protection of ocean mining. Even proponents of a national flag method envisage the eventual need for international allocation and regulation of rights as entrants become more numerous. In addition there is the problem, which may be intrusive even very early in the game, of the magnitude of production. Some form of international agreement placing limits on production, or on new entrants, would appear to be essential if reasonable profit levels are to be maintained. It merits speculative mention, in this connection, that those who now support the national flag approach may have this latter problem firmly in mind. If limits on entry are required, those who are already in business have, at the least, the argument that their investment deserves preference in arrangements for limiting either production or new entrants.

In appraising the above alternative approaches, consideration should be given to the possibility that we are not confronted with mutually exclusive courses of action.[71] Preference for an international system in the long term is not necessarily inconsistent with an evolutionary situation which in its initial stages permits unilateral claims by states—perhaps supplemented by international agreement on dispute settlement procedures and on issues of accommodations with other users—and which then develops into a full-blown international system, as experience accumulates the background of information and acceptable practices upon which international regulation can be founded. Indeed it may be that the widespread assumption that initial investors need a "guarantee" of rights is incorrect; they may in fact be willing to begin operations with only the contingent protection afforded by the state of nationality. Should such be the case and should relative costs make the oceans appear attractive in the near future, in less than

---

[70] See sources cited supra note 64.

[71] In this connection reference should be made to Professor Goldie's proposed scheme of regional agencies for recording claims which he believes would avoid the conflict that he expects to arise over creation of an international agency with power to grant rights of access to resources. He states: "... the main policy goals of secure titles, limited access to a resource to insure the prevention of over-capitalization, overproduction and congestion, and the avoidance of 'first-come first served' tactics and the ensuing conflicts, could be gained if regional agencies (with, necessarily, a central index in the United Nations Secretariat) could be established to carry out *evidentiary* (notice) and *recording* functions." Goldie, supra note 27, at 280. It is unclear how this system would operate to provide limitation on entry unless states reached further agreement on the matter.

ten years, the pressure toward unilateral claims would probably be difficult to resist.[72] So long as these claims are made in a way that does not prejudice the development and operation of a subsequent international system, there might be no substantial reason for objection. Exploitation, if this is the goal we prize, need not be postponed until the international mechanism is established. It is, finally, by no means beyond the realm of imagination that the experience gained from widespread exploration and from a few initial mining ventures is necessary for devising an acceptable international system.

It should be stressed, in view of the above remarks, that very substantial weight should be placed upon the goal of establishing an effective international structure, especially for sharing the benefits of exploitation, and that steps toward its development should be pursued with vigor. The short-term practicality and desirability of honoring limited unilateral claims, should this turn out to be necessary in order to realize some benefit from exploitation, should not be permitted to obscure this goal nor to inhibit implementation of it.

6. *Outcomes*

The consequences of ocean mining for states generally, and certain of them in particular, have been alluded to in various parts of the above discussion. It is desirable to emphasize by this separate treatment that these consequences may well differ considerably for all concerned as one or another legal framework is adopted. If the national flag approach, which permits states to carve out areas of limited assertion of rights over the seabottom, is employed either deliberately or by default, the benefits of exploitation are likely to accrue solely to those who engage in it and, as is normal, to the state of incorporation or the flag state. Such an approach carries with it also the risk that the exploiters, if they turn out to be excessive in number even at the beginning, will suffer very considerable loss. But if successful, even over a short period of years, the gains beyond return on investment will not be distributed to the general community of states.

The alternative system of international allocation of rights carries with it, in most formulations, implications not only for protection of exclusive rights but also for a sharing of the benefits. Proponents of this approach contend that if, as they believe to be the case, ocean mining sites can be regarded as having value and if a market mechanism can be created to reflect that value, the general community should be able to benefit by its

[72] Prof. Jacob makes the flat prediction: "Taking into consideration the time schedule on which international agreement must inevitably proceed, it is clear that we will soon enter an era of deep ocean mining based on claims of free access to a free good." Jacob, supra note 67, at 388.

realization. Thus if a bidding system is established for allocating exclusive rights the bids will reflect the market value of a particular site.[73] The proceeds realized by auctioning off the sites would accrue to the agency established to carry on this function and they might be disposed of for the benefit of states generally. They might, for example, be devoted to any of several readily imaginable, non-political, international purposes.[74] Such a system, it should be emphasized, would not necessarily diminish the income generated for the entrepreneur by the mineral production effort itself—although a tax on such income might act as a substitute for the bidding mechanism and may be preferable to the latter—but would permit the economic rent inhering in the mining site to be distributed to the international community.

Since it is likely that an international agency approach will receive serious consideration for adoption, special note is due that a considerable variety of alternatives are available for its structure and functioning. Although not all elements are of similar significance, it is plain that arrangements may be made to vary in a number of ways regarding membership, and termination thereof, the general and specific objectives sought, the distribution of authority functions within the agency and among the agency and various external groups including states, the assets to be conferred upon the agency, the operating procedures permitted it, and the scope of its authority. The important point in this connection is that these elements can, and should, be chosen and combined in ways that alleviate, or lessen, the apprehensions of states about the agency approach. This implies the need, not addressed in the present paper, for realistic assessment of anticipated difficulties as the agency operations begin and continue, coupled with structural and functional arrangements that permit the difficulties to be resolved, or for a procedure to that end, without the demise of the organization itself.

Trend in Decision

In terms of established principles of international law, the questions that attract most attention in the present context are whether a state or other group could lawfully exploit the mineral resources of the deep ocean and, more significantly, whether such principles would provide adequate protec-

[73] For the most detailed available public discussion see Brooks, supra note 27, at 27–32 who refers to and draws upon Mead, Natural Resource Disposal Policy—Oral Auction vs. Sealed Bids, 7 Natural Resources J. 194 (1967).
[74] A major criticism of some proposals for U.N. control of ocean mineral resources stems from the failure to take account of the political difficulties and consequences involved in strengthening the hand of the General Assembly as it is now constituted. See Burke, supra note 27, at 11.

tion to such an enterprise. The latter query perhaps is most fruitfully considered as two, rather different, questions: (1) assuming no practical need for asserting an exclusive right (since conditions of exploitation and marketing afford sufficient assurances), would adoption of past decisions provide protection and (2) if exclusive rights to an area were required, can their protection be secured under prevailing prescriptions.

First, there does not appear to be a serious question that any state or group can make use of the ocean floor, as for mining, so long as the activity is carried on with reasonable regard for the interests of others.[75] If the latter condition cannot be satisfied, as is conceivable in some circumstances, a mining venture or any other unreasonable activity would be in violation of international law. The question, then, cannot be answered in the abstract for any specific operation, but in view of the vastness of the ocean it seems highly probable that a mineral extraction enterprise could be carried on profitably in complete compatibility with other uses.

As indicated, appropriate response to the question of the protection available for the operation requires consideration of what is meant by "protection". If all that is required is the normal protection afforded a national flag vessel operating, however slowly, upon the high seas, there are ample principles available to accomplish that task.[76] If the mining operation is conducted from a mobile surface platform, the latter could easily be assimilated to a ship, if indeed it were not already so regarded, and the usual international law principles made applicable. According to such principles no state, other than that of registry, is authorized to exercise any authority over the vessel except in the instances of violation of international law. Since extraction of minerals is wholly in accord with international law, interference on account of such activity alone would not be countenanced. More positively, the vessel is subject solely to the control of the state of registry. For most maritime states, vessels of their registry are entitled to the protection of internationally prescribed principles for safety of life and operation at sea, including such as may be especially applicable to slowly

[75] This statement is based on the current general expectation that this region is open for use just as the water volume and surface above it, so long as such use is reasonable with respect to the interests of others. It may be recalled that the International Law Commission, in commentary upon Article 27 on "Freedom of the High Seas" noted that its list of freedoms was not restrictive and after observing that there were other freedoms, specifically declared that it "has not made specific mention of the freedom to explore or exploit the subsoil of the high seas." Report of the International Law Commission to the General Assembly, [1956] 2 Y.B. Int'l. L. Comm'n 278, U.N. Doc. No. A/CN.4/SER.A/1956/Add.1. The Commission did, of course, list one freedom pertaining to the ocean bottom, cable-laying, and this also is enumerated in Article 2 of the Convention on the High Seas.
[76] To avoid misunderstanding the text references to high seas are to regions beyond that claimed as "continental shelf".

moving vessels.[77] In sum, if exclusive rights are in practical effect available without reference to international legal principles, there is an adequate legal framework otherwise for the pioneering ventures. It may be noted, incidentally, that it is open to question whether these arrangements would effectively preserve the community interests in all contexts.

The more crucial question, of course, concerns the problem of providing assurance of exclusive access to an area of the seabottom. In most general statement the query is whether it is consistent with free access to the ocean for any lawful use to claim an area of exclusive rights for purposes only of mineral extraction. Is it not a contradiction to seek to justify unilateral establishment of an exclusive prerogative by invoking the ancient doctrine of freedom of the seas? Such argument would emphasize, probably, that exclusive access to one small, almost infinitesimal, part of the enormous quantity of surficial manganese deposits is completely compatible with free access to the remaining part and that if "free access" is to have any meaning at all with respect to mineral resources it must imply the establishment of exclusive rights to one part of the resource, leaving the remainder of the areas open to other exploitation. The latter position would be buttressed by appeals to the standard of reasonableness in the exercise of freedom of the sea, contending that a reasonable exercise of freedom in this context requires as a necessary condition of any activity that each user have exclusive access to a definable portion of the resource. Conversely, it might be urged, an attempt by another state to intrude into a modestly conceived exclusive area for minerals would be an unreasonable exercise of freedom since, in the view of practically all observers, the recognition of such exclusivity is the fundamental condition for a successful operation. Actions which substantially preclude such an operation cannot be regarded as protected by the doctrine of freedom of the seas. All of this would be underlain by repeated emphasis upon the vastness of the resource and of the ocean above, and upon the accompanying freedom of opportunity to gain comparable exclusive access to another part of the resource.

Arguments such as the above are no more cogent than the assumptions underlying them, of course, and it seems realistic to assume that some deposits of some minerals may well be relatively small in size or unique in favorable location. The bald question then is whether previous decisions countenance appropriation by the first discoverer or exploiter.[78]

---

[77] Rule 4(c) of the Regulations for Preventing Collisions at Sea is directed specifically at certain categories of vessels whose functions call for special rules. One such function is that of "underwater operations", which would appear to embrace mining operations. 6 Knauth's Benedict on Admiralty, 1966 Supplement 291.

[78] The question might not arise, of course, since under these circumstances economic considerations may preclude more than one entrant. Furthermore, as already suggested, the location of a deposit may deter other entrants, or make one system of national

Another set of principles which might well be invoked to justify exclusive appropriation of limited areas of the seabottom for mineral extraction are those that derive primarily from exclusive appropriation of land resources. The principal doctrine available, at least arguably, is that of effective occupation. Professors McDougal, Lasswell and Vlasic in their recent magnum opus on space law offered the following:

The sum of all this historic practice of the general community in the allocation of the major land masses of the earth would, thus, appear to confirm that the effective occupation which has in common consensus been regarded as necessary to legitimize exclusive appropriation has been a very comprehensive process, embracing a wide range of activities which have extended through a substantial period of time. This process has most often been considered to include both an expression of intent to appropriate, the *animus occupandi* as exhibited through symbolic ceremonies or other public notification, and an actual occupation, a *corpus occupandi* established by putting people into the area and exploiting its resources, with an accelerating integration of the area into the authoritative processess—political, economic, and social—of the claiman-state.

The comprehensiveness in occupation and intensity of activity required have observably varied in some measure with the physical characteristics of the area being claimed and other features of the context. Thus, though the introduction of some nationals or other agents of the claimant-state into the area claimed has usually been regarded as essential to effective occupation, the most intensive settlement has been required only in temperate zones. The few exceptions which have been made to the requirement that representatives of the claimant-state be introduced into the claimed area have related principally to barren areas, largely devoid of resources and publicly claimed over a long period of time without protest by other states. The very recent settlement with respect to Antarctica suggests, further, that in contemporary expectation, when areas are of genuine concern to many states, intensive settlement and development, however difficult or uneconomic, cannot safely be omitted. The most fundamental policy established by the general community with respect to the modalities for acquiring unappropriated resources, when it permits them to be subjected to exclusive appropriation, would appear, accordingly, to be that of encouraging peaceful use and development by protecting priorities only in such use and development, and not in mere egocentric claim.[79]

With suitable interpretation and modification, either of these sets of decisions could be used to justify the acquisition of ocean mineral resources, but care should be taken in relying on the doctrine of effective occupation as it has been previously employed. Of course, as an initial observation, it is clear that this doctrine thoroughly begs the question of whether these resources should be open to exclusive acquisition, for, as Professors McDou-

law decisive for regulating entry. If a location is favorable because of cheap transportation to a single market, the law of the state in which the market is located could be employed to regulate access to the resource.
[79] Law and Public Order in Space 866–67 (1963).

gal, Lasswell and Vlasic have so eloquently demonstrated, effective occupation is merely a modality for acquiring what is generally regarded as subject to exclusive appropriation.[80] The major difficulty with invoking effective occupation to justify a claim to mineral resources is that the doctrine connotes, in terms of past decisions, incorporation of an area within national territory.[81] Employment of the doctrine in this sense is neither necessary nor desirable, but if offered only to support the authority necessary to encourage mineral exploitation it could provide a basis for protecting and promoting mineral exploitation in the deep ocean floor. From broad community perspectives this use of previous decisions, however authoritative and reasonable their extrapolation, has shortcomings.

Lest it be overlooked, it deserves emphasis that no principle above outlined as potentially available to uphold exclusive appropriation of a portion of the deep sea bed is relevant to one of the major anticipated problems. Excessive production because of entry of producers with strong incentive to operate at a large scale has been identified as a probable difficulty for ocean mining. Recognition of unilateral claims to exclusive rights to various areas does not at all provide a way out of this situation. If entry is severely limited by extra-legal factors then, of course, there would be no initial need to provide for this by means of legal prescriptions.

In addition to principles derived from previous decisions about ocean and terrestrial resources, suggestion is now commonly made that decisions about polar areas and outer space merit emulation in the present context. Unfortunately these suggestions are rarely accompanied by details about what is particularly relevant in either the decisions, or the environmental context, for ocean mineral development. The fact is, quite plainly, that both the Antarctic Treaty and the Outer Space Agreement are built on the assumption that no resources are available from these areas in the foreseeable future and that their principal use is for other purposes. No such assumption is realistic in regard to ocean minerals and it may also, therefore, be unrealistic to attempt extrapolation of principles from one environment to another without giving thought to the differences involved. Indeed so far as resources are concerned the Antarctic Treaty contains little to extrapolate except possibly the decision to "freeze" territorial claims for a period of years. Even this, however, if useful at all in regard to the ocean, would probably require modification; it would certainly need supplementation in the ocean context. In other respects the Antarctic precedent is without much value, except for the spirit or attitudes implied on the part of participating states, since no one expects that the deep ocean bed

[80] Id. at 788.
[81] Id. at 844–67.

can be left, as was the Antarctic, completely without policies and principles for guiding resource development.

The Outer Space Treaty provides little more positive guidance than the Antarctic. It is true that the prohibition of national appropriation has potential for use in the ocean situation, but if so used there will be need for additional prescriptions establishing the conditions under which various forms of exploitation can be undertaken. On this aspect of the matter the Outer Space Treaty is wholly silent except for the most general, question-begging injunctions about conformity with international law and the United Nations Charter. Indeed, with respect to problems involved in use of outer space, one prominent observer commented recently that the Treaty "seems to have created almost as many legal problems as it appears to have resolved."[82] If deep ocean exploitation is anywhere as imminent as many believe, a repetition of such a form of creativity may serve either to discourage rather than promote ocean development or to burden developers and states with unwanted problems. Since we are not likely to gain experience under the Outer Space Treaty for a very considerable period, states whould be well advised to approach the legal problems of the ocean without the encumbrance of supposed analogies in the treatment of outer space.

The only occasion thus far for consideration of these issues by international decision-makers came when the Permanent Mission of Malta to the United Nations, in August, 1967, proposed the following item for inclusion on the agenda of the General Assembly:

Declaration and treaty concerning the reservation exclusively for peaceful purposes of the sea-bed and of the ocean floor, underlying the seas beyond the limits of present national jurisdiction, and the use of their resources in the interests of mankind.[83]

In an accompanying brief memorandum it was recommended that immediate steps be taken to draft a treaty embodying four principles:

(a) The sea-bed and the ocean floor, underlying the seas beyond the limits of present national jurisdiction, are not subject to national appropriation in any manner whatsoever;
(b) The exploration of the sea-bed and of the ocean floor, underlying the seas beyond the limits of present national jurisdiction, shall be undertaken in a manner consistent with the Principles and Purposes of the Charter of the United Nations;

---

[82] Gorove, The Outer Space Treaty, Bull. Atom. Scientists, December, 1967, p. 45. Professor Vlasic and others have called attention to the inadequacies of this agreement in providing guidelines to resource use. Vlasic, supra note 63, at 512–13.
[83] Request for the Inclusion of a Supplementary Item in the Agenda of the Twenty-second Session, U.N. Doc. No. A/6695 (1967) (see Annex, p. 209).

(c) The use of the sea-bed and of the ocean floor, underlying the seas beyond the limits of present national jurisdiction, and their economic exploitation shall be undertaken with the aim of safeguarding the interests of mankind. The net financial benefits derived from the use and exploitation of the sea-bed and of the ocean floor shall be used primarily to promote the development of poor countries;

(d) The sea-bed and the ocean floor, underlying the seas beyond the limits of present national jurisdiction, shall be reserved exclusively for peaceful purposes in perpetuity.

The reception of this initiative in the United Nations quickly laid to rest any assumption that immediate action could be taken in the United Nations to approve recommendations for internationalizing ocean resources. Even before the agenda item was assigned to a committee, when the General Assembly was in the process of making decisions on allocation, Malta proposed an amendment, which was accepted, to delete the reference to a "declaration and treaty". Subsequent speeches in the First Committee, and the action taken by that Committee, provide convincing evidence that the original formulation was considered far too ambitious in seeking a decision on matters of great importance about which most states were exceedingly unfamiliar. Rather than risk alienating the states concerned it was clearly thought wiser to recast the item to read "Examination of the question of the reservation exclusively for peaceful purposes. . . ."

Though inconclusive and unproductive of substantive decisions, the debate in the First Committee shed interesting light upon the perspectives of certain groups of states. States with the technological capability for deep ocean work, or at least with advanced technology, reacted with noticeable caution and hesitation. Among this group, the stance of the Soviet Union was remarkable both for its seemingly extreme apprehension lest the decision process move too quickly and for its insistence that preparatory work be done by states and not by any international body or group.[84] The

[84] 22 UN GAOR, Provisional Verbatim Record of the 1525th Meeting, U.N. Doc. No. A/C.1/PV. 1525, pp. 8–21 (1967).

Further discussion of Soviet and American views relevant to mineral eploitation is infra pp. 92–95.

It is also instructive to take note of the voting on the four resolutions which were adopted at the conclusion of the 23d General Assembly in December 1968. The first of these resolutions [Resolution 2467A (XXIII)] established a Committee on the Peaceful Uses of the Sea-Bed and the Ocean Floor Beyond the Limit of National Jurisdiction, and laid down its terms of reference. Although there were no negative votes on this resolution the Soviet Union is recorded as abstaining, as well as some members of the Soviet bloc. Resolution 2467C (XXIII) dealt with the question of international machinery for exploitation of the resources of the seabed and the ocean floor beyond national jurisdiction and requested the Secretary-General "to undertake a study on the question of establishing in due time appropriate international machinery for the promotion of the exploration and exploitation of the resources of this area" and other matters. The Secretary-General's study was to be submitted to the permanent

United States appeared more than willing to have recourse to cooperative study, proposing the creation of a Committee on the Oceans, but also was careful to advise that the "hasty approach would indeed be imprudent, when all deliberate speed, not indefinite delay is called for."[85] The developing states uniformly spoke strongly either in support of an international body to regulate exploitation (and a few mentioned engaging in collective exploitation) or in support of an immediate declaration of the principles contained in Maltese explanatory memorandum. A few developed states concurred in these expressions of preference for internationalization. Varying degrees of alarm were expressed to the effect that unless immediate action were taken to maintain the *status quo,* the more advanced states would have begun activities and taken positions which it will be difficult, if not impossible, to reverse.[86]

The resolution emerging from the First Committee deliberations, and approved by the General Assembly, in no way resembles the recommendations embodied in the original Malta agenda item and supporting memorandum.[87] This divergence probably reflects, as much as anything else, realization that any successful action by the United Nations depends decisively upon the acquiescence of states capable of effective operation in the deep ocean environment. The interventions of the Soviet Union, the United States, Japan, the United Kingdom, Canada, and France—the most prominent of the states active in the ocean—made it abundantly clear that a great deal of preparatory work was required and that prolonged negotiations might well be anticipated, before substantive decisions were attainable. The Soviet Union was especially reluctant, even to expressing grave misgivings about any organized international inquiry. That these attitudes on the part of these developed states weighed heavily in fashioning the outcome cannot be

Committee on the Peaceful Uses of the Sea-Bed, established by Resolution 2467A, and this committee was to submit a report on the same question to the 24th Session of the General Assembly. Again it is instructive to note that on this vital question of establishing international machinery the Soviet Union is recorded as voting against the resolution, as did most members of the Soviet bloc.

For reasons which do not appear in the report of the discussion in the General Assembly the United States is recorded as abstaining on Resolution 2467C (XXIII). See 23 UN GAOR, Provisional Verbatim Record of the 1752d Meeting, U.N. Doc. No. A/C.1/PV. 1752, pp. 13–20 (21 December 1968).

[85] 22 UN GAOR, Provisional Verbatim Record of the 1524th Meeting, U.N. Doc. No. A/C.1/PV. 1524, pp. 19–20 (1967).

Further discussion of Soviet and American views relevant to mineral exploitation is infra pp. 92–95.

[86] It is relevant to recall here that the *"status quo"*, as this writer views previous policies and decisions, *permits* states to begin ocean exploration and exploitation activities.

[87] Text of the resolution is in 22 UN GAOR, Report of the First Committee, U.N. Doc. No. A/6964, 12 December 1967.

conclusively demonstrated, since the most important discussions were not recorded, but it is likely that such speculation is well founded. If all that mattered were counting noses, the very large number of developing states, whose prospects for deep ocean exploitation with their own resources are not especially bright, might have mustered sufficient votes to endorse the Maltese recommendations. Recognition that such an exercise would lack realism is manifested in the great discrepancy between the substance of the Maltese recommendations and the very modest proposal ultimately adopted with the overwhelming approval of the developing states. Quite plainly very considerable concessions were made in order to gain the approval of significant members.

Far from accepting the several substantive principles suggested by Malta, the First Committee even refused, despite the urgings of the United States, to establish a Committee on the Oceans, but instead approved an *Ad Hoc* Committee with a relatively limited mandate to prepare a study which would include:

(a) A survey of the past and present activities of the United Nations, the specialized agencies, the International Atomic Energy Agency and other intergovernmental bodies with regard to the sea-bed and the ocean floor, and of existing international agreements concerning these areas;

(b) An account of the scientific, technical, economic, legal and other aspects of this item;

(c) An indication regarding practical means to promote international co-operation in the exploration, conservation and use of the sea-bed and the ocean floor, and the subsoil thereof, as contemplated in the title of the item, and of their resources, having regard to the views expressed and the suggestions put forward by Member States during the consideration of this item at the twenty-second session of the General Assembly.[88]

So far as mention of principles is concerned the Committee was content to record recognition in the preambular paragraphs of the "common interest of mankind in the sea-bed and the ocean floor" and also "that the exploration and use of the sea-bed and the ocean floor, and the subsoil thereof, as contemplated in the title of the item, should be conducted in accordance with the principles and purposes of the Charter of the United Nations, in the interest of maintaining international peace and security and for the benefit of mankind. . . ." Beyond the arguable reference in mentioning the maintenance of international peace and security, no mention is made of the issue of military use of the seabed nor is there any suggestion of a freeze on such uses or on territorial claims.

It would be a gross mistake to draw the conclusion from this rather limited action that nothing can be expected to emerge from subsequent

[88] Id. at 5.

activities at the United Nations. The evidence is plain that this is merely the necessary initial step in what is likely to be a series over a period of several years. However, as useful as the debates were in clarifying the need for detailed and careful preparation for eventual substantive discussion, and for evidence that there is very considerable pressure for such consideration, they provide, at least to this reader, little indication of the eventual outcome.

Appraisal and Recommendation

There need be little hesitation, after reviewing the foregoing discussion of policies and decisions, in identifying the kind of steps that are now required if *any* viable policy is to be established. Generalized recommendations calling for an international regulatory system, especially if accompanied by very broad arms control proposals, will receive a frigid reception when they are unaccompanied by quite specific indications of the implications of such a system: its impact on national economies, planning and security, as they may be affected by mineral exploitation in the sea. Similarly, proposals that the laissez-faire, or flag nation, system is alone adequate do not appear to be persuasive in the absence of the same type of analysis. If the recognition of the common interest of mankind recorded in the resolution adopted by the First Committee and the General Assembly in 1967 is to have any meaning at all, proponents of various regulatory arrangements, which would allocate authority in very different ways, bear the heavy burden of supplying concrete details of how the arrangements are expected to work. At the present stage of debate only an incurable optimist would conclude that this burden has been discharged. It is this consideration which, in this writer's opinion, most strongly argues for declaration and acceptance of a moratorium on claims, or activities, which might prejudice ultimate resolution of the issues involved. Without a freeze, on territorial claims and on any claims that do not in so many words admit of a degree of modification for accommodation with subsequent international agreements, the situation could by default tend toward permanent adoption of a flag nation system despite the fact that we are now not sure whether this is the more desirable course to take. Such a freeze should not, it need be stressed, foreclose exploratory work for those who care to undertake it nor should it necessarily forbid active exploitation so long as the necessary claims to rights were made on the premise that they would be subject to subsequent non-confiscatory, international decision on procedures for such allocation. Despite the recent request by an American company, addressed to the United Nations Secretary-General, for an exploratory permit for work in an area of the

Red Sea,[89] most observers regard serious mining operations in the deep sea as about a decade away.[90] If the general community of states does proceed with "all deliberate speed" there is still time to reach agreement, one way or another, upon an allocation of competence over ocean mineral resource exploitation which will provide satisfaction to reasonable demands for orderly and effective utilization, for rewards to investment and initiative, and for equity in the distribution of the benefits. If these goals are to be attained, however, the time is past for general exhortation about the virtues of this or that system of regulation and for broadsides about the evils attending other systems; it is now time to do the work required to overcome the obstacles to these goals.

[89] 4 Oceanology, The Weekly of Ocean Technology 48 (Feb. 15, 1968).
[90] Fuel mineral exploration and development might well occur before there is any extensive non-fuel exploitation.

II. Acquisition and Control of Marine Fishery Resources

Claims and Counterclaims

The trend toward expansion of claims by states to exclusive use and control over adjacent fishing areas has continued unabated, or more accurately in accelerated fashion, since the Geneva conferences on the law of the sea. The techniques employed for seeking expansion are primarily three: (1) changes in the means for determining the area of internal waters; (2) extension of the territorial sea; and (3) creation of a special contiguous zone within which the same rights apply as are exercised by the state within the territorial sea. An additional, if only locally important, method is that of asserting that certain animal resources are "natural resources" of the continental shelf which, by treaty, are within the control of the adjacent coastal state.

It would advance the discussion relatively little to offer detail regarding claims by states to establish straight baseline systems for fixing the limit of internal waters. Suffice to say that since the 1950 decision in the *Fisheries* case, a considerable number of states have adopted such a means of delimitation.[91] Because of the differing nature of individual claims, the opposing claims alleging unlawfulness must necessarily vary.

There is no doubt whatsoever that state claims to a particular width for their territorial sea have had a notable tendency to expand over the past 10 to 15 years. Dramatic indication may be seen in comparison of claims made in 1951 with those now. In 1951 a comprehensive study by Dr. S. Whittemore Boggs reported only three states claiming 12 miles: the U.S.S.R., Colombia and Guatemala.[92] As of April 1, 1967, this number had increased to thirty-one, and Colombia had reduced its claim to 6 miles.[93] In 1951 the great preponderance of states were recorded as claiming a territorial sea of 3 miles, with at least forty-five to be noted, not counting colonial possessions. Today the number of 12-mile states exceeds those opting for 3 miles since the latter number has shrunk to thirty. Of the 91 states on which data is available, two-thirds (61) claim more than 3 miles. However, it certainly merits emphasis that of this 61 only seven make claim

[91] The United Kingdom, Canada, Iceland, Yugoslavia, China (Mainland), Indonesia, the Philippines are among states claiming the system.
[92] Boggs, National Claims in Adjacent Seas, 41 The Geographical Review 185, 192–98 (1951).
[93] The text statements are based on the table in H.R. Rep. No. 999, at 161–63, except that the 12-mile group here is considered to include North Korea and North Vietnam.

to more than 12 miles and that each of these greatly exceeds 12.[94] The major, if not sole, thrust of counterclaim occurs in opposition to these few assertions of authority that greatly exceed a 12-mile limit.

Drawing similar comparisons in relation to special contiguous zones for fisheries is complicated by the lack of reliable data for earlier claims, but it is reasonably clear that such zones were very few in number until recent years. A close scrutiny of Dr. Boggs' 1951 survey discloses only about a half-dozen such claims.[95] That a very substantial shift has occurred in this respect is evident from that fact that at least 35 states now have provisions for exclusive fishing in contiguous zones of various widths. More significant than numbers, however, is the identity of the states concerned since virtually all Western European states,[96] Canada, the United States, Australia and New Zealand now extend their authority over fisheries to regions beyond the territorial sea. With very few exceptions the zones are limited to a width of 12 miles. With the exception of the exaggerated claims to zones of 200 miles, sometimes cast in terms of "sovereignty" over natural resources, claims in opposition to exclusive fishing zones are negligible.

Beyond these claims to exclusive disposition of fishery resources, which mostly relate to areas in relatively close proximity to coasts, the overriding claim to fisheries is inclusive in nature. Each state asserts that its nationals are entitled to have free access to the resources beyond exclusive control without limitation other than that accepted in international agreement. Such counterclaims as exist are devoted to attempts to modify this regime in order to establish some degree of shared authority, through explicit agreement, by which regulations may be prescribed for maintaining the yield of a particular stock or stocks in a region.

Clarification of Policy

The fundamental policy problem is that of securing an allocation of competence among states which promotes the utilization of ocean fisheries as

[94] These seven states are: Argentina, Ecuador, El Salvador, Panama and Peru (all 200 miles); Guinea (130 miles); and Chile (50 kilometers). It should be added, however, that the archipelago states of Indonesia and the Philippines claim extensive areas within their territorial seas and that the width of the latter is virtually irrelevant to the extent of water area within the limit. This is because of the fact that these states are composed of numerous, far-flung islands.

[95] These claims include France, Iceland, Lebanon, Syria, Argentina, Brazil, Colombia, and Ecuador. The list could be expanded a little if claims to sedentary species were included along with those claims put forward in terms of the sea above the continental shelf.

[96] For an account of European events see Johnson, European Fishery Limits in Developments in the Law of the Sea 1958–1964, 48 (1965) (Special Publ. No. 6 of the British Institute of International and Comparative Law).

a direct or indirect source of food, provides for maintenance of supplies (yield) through time, and encourages a rational allocation of effort to fishery exploitation. Three principal means of achieving such an allocation are commonly recommended: expansion of exclusive fishing limits to various, sometimes extremely lengthy, distances from coasts; creation of a single, all-embracing, public international organization to undertake the management and control of all fishery operations outside exclusive areas; and emphasis upon improvement in existing international approaches, especially in the work of regional organizations. Existing literature offers ample discussion of the merits of these various alternatives,[97] hence the following is neither an exhaustive nor an intensive survey of the factors relevant to choice of policy.

The fundamental difficulty for policy, which each of the above alternatives is intended to resolve, arises both because the resource is highly migratory and because the traditional legal framework places most fishery stocks beyond the control of any single authority. At the same time it is widely agreed that in order to attain maximum use of the resource, especially under projected conditions of greater intensity in exploitation throughout the global sea, there is a definite need to establish a system by which effective regulations can be prescribed for maintaining the yield of the species exploited. In addition there is little disagreement about the desirability, assuming it were practical to achieve and did not displace more valued goals, of further limiting effort at exploitation so that the economic return therefrom could be maximized or, at least, improved. Under present conditions there is, in the absence of agreement, no means by which either of the goals can be achieved.

Since no one owns high seas fishery resources in the critical sense of being able to relate the effects of today's fishing activity on the availability and size of fish that is to be taken in later periods, there is an inherent tendency to use too much capital and labor in any operation involving the exploitation of valuable marine resources. In short, effort will always be pushed to the point where total cost of the operation and total revenues received are approximately equal (including in total cost a reasonable rate of return to capital). Any increase in the price of the end products or decrease in costs of production will

---

[97] Johnston, The International Law of Fisheries (1965); Oda, International Control of Sea Resources (1963); Chapman, Fishery Resources in Offshore Waters, in Alexander, ed., The Law of the Sea 87 (1967); Christy, The Distribution of the Sea's Wealth in Fisheries, in id. at 106; Dodyk, International Law of Ocean Fisheries: Prospects and Alternatives (1968) (Study available as Document No. PB 179 427 from the Clearinghouse for Federal Scientific and Technical Information, U.S. Department of Commerce); Chapman, On the Theory and Practice of the United States Flag Ocean Fishing (unpublished paper 1968).

induce more fishing effort even after the point has been reached where further effort produces no increase in output and may actually reduce the catch.[98]

From the physical perspective of population magnitude, the present system permits effort to be increased beyond the point of the maximum sustainable yield, i.e., until the stock or stocks are overfished. As will be indicated below, this description of the legal structure is rough and requires to be modified to take into account modifications through agreement. But the basic proposition of freedom of exploitation holds good, as long as states refrain from agreeing otherwise.

In terms of the basic objectives specified above, the establishment of larger and larger areas of exclusive coastal control has little to commend it except possibly in a very few exceptional situations of limited general significance. Whether these larger areas consist of extensions in terms of 50 miles, of the geological conception of the shelf, or of the complete division of the oceans among "coastal states", the impact is likely to be undesirable for general community goals. Productivity would very probably decrease, when the crying demand is for increase, because the coastal state concerned could not itself engage in full exploitation of the large exclusive area and would be unlikely to permit access to foreign fishermen except under unrealistic, perhaps highly onerous, conditions. The efficiency of existing distant water fishing fleets would almost certainly suffer from the complicated administrative difficulties and outright prohibitions of access which could be expected to attend any such system.

Rational management, in terms even of limits on effort to protect yields, would be virtually impossible to implement for a number of reasons. The migratory character of the major fishery stocks would in most instances preclude management based on the authority of any single state (which means that the present difficulty in this respect would be unresolved) and even the conduct of the scientific research basic to management decisions would likely become more difficult if not impossible to undertake. Such cooperation as has already been achieved in this respect might well suffer a serious setback and the fruits of decades of labor and perserverance be dissipated. For indication of the problems posed by migrating fish, the following description by Dr. W. M. Chapman is enlightening.

The sardine, anchovy, saury, hake, bluefin, and albacore off the coast of Mexico and California typify the complexity that occurs off most coasts. Most of the spawning of sardine and anchovy in this region takes place well to sea offshore

---

[98] Crutchfield, Zones of National Interest: Convention on Fishing and Living Resources of the High Seas 5, Paper Presented at the American Bar Association National Institute on Marine Resources, June, 1967.

both countries, and the fish are available there for fishing, although most of the actual fishing to date is done reasonably close to shore. Presumably the anchovy do not make very long migrations, but the sardine may. The hake spawn in this area also, but apparently move north to feed and grow along the coast up as far as British Columbia. Although generally coastal and demersal, they do not always stay close to the bottom, and may often school at or near the surface. Also they can be readily caught off shore more than twelve miles. The jack mackerel form a large population, which is fished on mostly near the coast, but the spawning area extends at least 1000 miles off the coast, and the fish can be caught out there if large adults are wanted. The saury are found all over the northern part of the North Pacific, and we know nothing of their population structure. It appears to be continuous across the ocean. The albacore spawn thousands of miles from Mexico and California in the west central Pacific, and after coming over to where we can fish them off our coast, go back over to Japan where they can be fished there. The bluefin tuna are commonly caught in the territorial sea of Mexico and California but do not spawn in the eastern Pacific at all. They spawn south of Japan and north of the Philippines, and individuals tagged off Mexico are captured the other side of Japan. Fur seals feed off California and sometimes as far south as northern Mexico. Their nearest breeding ground is the Pribilof Islands in the Bering Sea. Gray whales pass through the territorial sea of southern California proceeding to their calving grounds in the internal waters of the lagoons of northern Mexico; and, having fulfilled this biological purpose, migrate back across the Pacific to the feeding grounds off Kamchatka and the western Bering Sea.[99]

Improvement in the economic returns of a fishery could not be expected from such a regime. It is notorious that progress in this respect is almost completely non-existent even now in fisheries wholly under national control. With more relevance, the division of the ocean even into "national lakes", and certainly anything less, would still fail to comprehend all the fishing effort expended on a particular stock or stocks and it would still be necessary to seek resolution of this difficulty by international agreement.

It deserves stress that these defects attend all recommended expansions of exclusive fishery limits. In particular the recent spate of extensions to twelve miles, a good many of which seek to protect the relatively inefficient inshore fisherman, is widely acknowledged to contribute little to acquiring necessary control over fisheries.[100] And even if further extensions could somehow secure preponderant control, the disadvantages in terms of hindering production and increasing costs would probably far outweigh any exclusive, or even community-wide, advantages that might accrue.

[99] Chapman, supra note 97, at 96–7. See also FAO, The State of World Fisheries, p. 42 (1968).
[100] The hearings in the United States Congress on legislation to adopt a 12-mile exclusive fishing zone are replete with such acknowledgments. See Hearings on S. 2218 before the Subcommittee on Merchant Marine and Fisheries of the U.S. Senate Committee on Commerce, 89th Cong., 2d Sess. (1966).

A good bit of the rhetoric, though certainly not all in view of the appeals of American fishermen, in support of extended exclusive fishing zones emphasizes, and exaggerates, the alleged benefits to developing states in terms of meeting the protein needs of expanding populations. Two major points should be recalled in this connection that are pertinent to assessing the genuine, rather than the spurious, interests of this group of states. Dr. Hiroshi Kasahara has observed that "lack of rigid institutional arrangements due to the common property nature of fishery resources, in contrast to the existence of long-established tenure systems in agriculture, is one of the two obvious factors contributing to the expansion of fisheries in developing countries. . . ."[101] It is at least open to serious doubt whether this advantageous situation could be maintained for the benefit of these states if the ocean were to be compartmentalized by the establishment of enormous, but still numerous, regions to which national laws and administrative structures were to apply. The obstructions to fisheries expansion by developing states which would flow from such an arrangement can easily be imagined. This factor acquires, incidentally, even more serious import in view of the character of the expanded fishing industries concerned. Dr. W. M. Chapman notes:

As these developing countries develop coastal fisheries, they trend almost at once into becoming longer and longer range fishermen as well, fishing off the coasts of other countries as part of their necessary fishery economics just about as naturally and necessarily as the fish migrate for biological necessity. Examples are provided by Mexico, Panama, Ecuador, Peru, Chile, Guayana, Cuba, Senegal, Ivory Coast, Ghana, Pakistan and Thailand.[102]

The losses to such states from interference with the distant fleets could outweigh the gains, if any, derived from the protection of their own near-shore fishermen. If this experience is generalized, and the implications generally understood, it raises interesting conjectures about the positions the developing states might take in determination of community policy toward further expansion of exclusive fishing areas.

In sum the community policies identified above would not be served, and probably would be harmed, by seeking to resolve international fisheries problems by means of large extensions of national jurisdiction.

No suggestion is intended by these rather categorical assertions that the community would benefit from seeking to declare unlawful, or to remove in some other way, those rather limited claims to exclusive fishing zones out to twelve miles. Although the zones contribute nothing of con-

---

[101] Kasahara, Food Production from the Ocean 36, in 1 First Conference on Law, Organization and Security in the Use of the Ocean (1967).
[102] Chapman, supra note 97, at 92.

sequence to resolving any of the real difficulties posed by fishery management, and may not accomplish much for the welfare of the particular states concerned, they do exist, are now very widely accepted, and are likely to continue to enjoy acceptance. However, it is important that these arbitrary, in terms of any valid inclusive or exclusive interests, boundaries should be extended no further. It is better by far to refrain from contributing further to irrationality and to get on with the problem of seeking to increase effective use of these resources for a world which is in desperate need of protein, including that available from ocean fisheries. The disruption and conflict generated by seeking to reverse the moderate claims already made would also inhibit genuine resolution of problems.

At the other end of the spectrum in recommendations are those urging the establishment of a single global authority, probably as an agency of the United Nations, to manage all the fisheries of the world ocean beyond the confines of limited exclusive fishing zones.[103] These proposals are frequently accompanied also by the suggestion that the management goal of such an authority should be that of realizing the maximum net economic yield from the fisheries.[104] Although the major purpose underlying these suggestions is that of providing for suitable management of living resources, a subsidiary objective is often mentioned in an accompanying proposal that the income generated by such a scheme should accrue to the United Nations.[105]

There is a good deal of reason to sympathize with the international agency approach to fishery problems, primarily because it directly meets the difficulty posed by the migratory nature of marine fish. An international organization would comprehend the great bulk of the world's ocean fisheries, at least so long as no further enlargement occurs in exclusive zones. The proposed goal of such a management scheme, that of realizing the maximum net economic yield of fisheries, also has very considerable appeal, especially in view of some demonstrations that, at least in the catching part of the fish business, reduction of effort could increase the net economic yield significantly in some specific situations.[106] Adoption of the global

---

[103] The principal advocate of this approach in the United States is the Commission to Study the Organization of Peace. See the 17th Report, New Dimensions for the United Nations 39 (1966).

[104] Id. at 38.

[105] Id. at 38-9.

[106] The Report of the Second Session of the Committee on Fisheries FAO in 1967, for instance, observes:

"... it was the common conclusion, after a study of three different stocks of demersal fish which are heavily fished in the North Atlantic area, that a substantial cut in mortality would lead after a transitional period of from four to six years,

agency approach might be considered to have the additional advantage of deterring states from seeking to extend the fishery limits further into the sea.

Unfortunately the attraction of these various reasons for favorable appraisal of this international system diminishes rather drastically in light of a number of pragmatic considerations which suggest strongly that such a universalist approach would be counter-productive.

An initial, fundamental, consideration is that knowledge of marine resources, on a global basis, is woefully inadequate. Estimates of total productivity from the ocean vary enormously, yet if the lower ranges in these estimates were accurate, the problem of overfishing (in the biological sense) would loom before us rather quickly.[107] But it is not so much total productivity of which we need greater knowledge and understanding. Rather the greater need exists concerning population dynamics in particular situations. On this score there can be no serious doubt that the levels of expenditure now being made for this purpose are completely inadequate.[108] The importance of this is that such expenditures are, with very few exceptions, made by individual states for their own research efforts and staff.[109] It also is now readily apparent that states have been unwilling to finance research by newly established regional agencies,[110] probably because this is regarded as diverting funds from national agencies. It seems wholly unrealistic to consider that states will be inclined to support a global fisheries agency with the kind of funds that would be required to see that the necessary knowledge of this resource would be generated by the agency. While there may be prospects for improvement in this regard in local situations, the blunderbus world-wide agency approach would face enormous obstacles in attracting support and, in the meantime, would be confronted

to the same or a larger catch being caught by a reduced (by say 20 percent) fishing effort."

FAO Report of the Second Session of the Committee on Fisheries, Rome 1967, 24–29 April 1967. FAO Fish. Rep. No. 46, p. 2. Halibut, salmon, whales, cod and haddock are specific examples of neglect of the costs involved in a fishery. See also Chapman, Problems of the North Pacific and Atlantic Fisheries 7 (Paper Presented at the Annual Meeting, Fisheries Council of Canada, Montreal, May 10, 1967).

[107] Chapman, On the Management of Ocean Fisheries, in Proceedings of the 5th Meeting of the (California) Governor's Advisory Commission on Ocean Resources 77, 83 (1966).

[108] Id. at 80.

[109] Chapman, supra note 107, at 80; Carroz and Roche, The Proposed International Commission for the Conservation of Atlantic Tuna, 61 Am. J. Int'l. L. 673, 696 (1967).

[110] A brief account of international organization effort is in Burke, Aspects of Internal Decision-making Processes in Intergovernmental Fishery Commissions, 43 Wash. L. Rev. 115, 154–69 (1967).

with a gigantic regulatory problem for which it had neither the basic scientific knowledge required nor any reasonably likely prospect of gaining that knowledge.

Objection to the proposed global agency is also founded upon reservations about the usefulness of the goal of maximum net economic yield which is often suggested as the objective such an agency should seek in managing world fisheries. A prime difficulty in this respect is that the objectives of the many fishing states around the world are so varied. Dr. Chapman summarized this situation concisely:

It appears to be a wide-spread goal of nations to optimize their gross physical yield of food from the ocean. This may be for the purpose of obtaining foreign exchange, of obtaining needed animal protein to feed its own population, of protecting its sources of foreign exchange by limiting its imports, to increase the nation's gross economic yield, to accumulate capital, to give useful employment to its people, or to obtain some particular type of fish because of the nation's particular demands. These objectives are not all compatible. Examples can be given for each of these objectives. Objectives of nations in this respect change with changing times and circumstances, and sometimes rather rapidly.[111]

Although conceivably the complexities involved in reconciling diverse objectives under the umbrella of a single "best", or at least "better", yield might be resolved on the more selective basis of a particular fishery or area, there seems ample reason to doubt that such a task can be discharged on an all-embracing, global basis.

Other problems with the proposed goal can also be cited. First, assuming maximum economic yield were somehow acceptable to a sufficient number of states, it would be an enormously complex task to provide for regulations that would approach the end sought. There is every reason to doubt that it is at all feasible to undertake this task now for general application, as some propose. Many fisheries which would be subjected to the proposed system are exploited by a number of states whose economic systems and structure are quite diverse and offer few common denominators for use in constructing a specified economic yield which could be called the maximum for each state.[112] Apart from this there is also the consideration that in many fisheries multiple species are utilized which are differently prized by the various exploiting states. The task of regulating such fisheries in order to obtain the maximum sustained yield from the various species is compli-

---

[111] Chapman, supra note 107, at 85.
[112] See Kasahara, supra note 101, at 27–31 and the discussion at pp. A2–A38; Chapman, supra note 97, at 94.

cated in itself, but to go beyond that to seek economic ends adds much greater complications.[113]

Recently, criticism of the economic yield criterion has called attention to the fact that proponents of it usually are speaking only of the fish-catching end of the fishing industry and do not take into account that the entire enterprise extends from catching to processing to distribution to the ultimate consumer. Dr. Chapman observes:

A fishery must be considered, from the economic viewpoint, in the context of the entire range from the ocean to the consumer of the product. The catching phase is only one part of the business, and profit (or net economic yield) from it is not always the controlling aspect of the fishery's economics. If a fishery is to be viable economically the entire chain from ocean to consumer requires to earn a profit on capital and labor involved (assets employed) equal to what the same capital and labor employed in another business will yield or the capital and labor will go into the other business. It is quite possible that the fishing link in this chain can be run at a net loss and the whole enterprise be economically viable if the profit from another link in the chain is adequate to keep up the profit level of the total. There are a great many variables in this equation that differ with the different fisheries. Only a few can be touched upon here, briefly, as examples.[114]

The notion that the global agency approach would produce income is criticized on a number of grounds, ranging from grave doubt that any would be produced to reservations about providing an independent income for the U.N. as it is presently constituted. The very size and nature of the administrative and regulatory structure of the international agency could mean that costs of operation exceed the income generated by extracting economic rent from fisheries. To the extent income is produced because fisheries are operated to achieve their maximum economic yield, it is also pertinent to note the estimate that probably more than half of world fisheries are now being conducted at levels below that which marks the maximum net economic return.[115] Until the level of effort reaches that which corresponds to the maximum net economic yield there is no need to subject the fishery to regulation, hence no opportunity to realize income.

The issue of an independent income for the U.N. is not really relevant in a discussion of ocean problems. Suffice to note that such income would undoubtedly have to be restricted in terms of the purposes sought in using

[113] Dr. Chapman reviews and illustrates this and comparable problems, in Chapman, supra note 107, at 92–3.
[114] Id. at 88; 1 First Conference on Law, Organization and Security in the Use of the Ocean supra note 101, at A34–A38.
[115] Chapman, supra note 107, at 94.

it, at least so long as disposition would be subject to action by the General Assembly.

The third policy alternative, improving the existing regulatory system for international fisheries, appears to offer more hope for the foreseeable future than the two methods just discussed. Perhaps it is more accurate to phrase it that this alternative seems to be less unsatisfactory than the others, for hardly anyone expresses much enthusiasm for the present method of management. Essentially what is called for by this policy alternative is both improvement in the regional institutions which are the means by which states now seek to agree on conservation policies and prescriptions and the creation of such new bodies as are required to embrace important fisheries which might need regulation in the future. The belief underlying this policy is that it is wiser to build upon existing institutions and that the regional approach offers more hope of adequate surveillance of developing problems and of the necessary selectivity in attempts to resolve such problems. Pursuit of this avenue is further recommended because of the trend now beginning to develop toward efforts at improving existing institutions. Even assuming these are not wholly satisfactory arrangements, it seems wiser to utilize their experience and expertise than to attempt to establish a single gargantuan organization that would seek management of all fisheries on a global basis.

An important part of the approach at improving and revising existing institutional mechanisms should be that of seeking to alter the objectives of management to take greater explicit account of the economic factors relevant to management. The critical comments already made regarding maximum economic yield called attention to the shortcomings of the proposal to adopt this goal for application by a global agency regulating all the fisheries of the world; such criticisms have much less cogency in more selective context. In any event certain aspects of the continuing dialogue about physical and economic goals are worthy of mention as a final observation about policies.

First, there appears to be a failure in communication among those involved. Proponents of maximum economic yield in fisheries regulation often begin by conceding that economic factors are but one element that should be taken into account in choice of conservation policy, but just as often they proceed to elaborate their position as if such criteria were the only ones relevant. Perhaps it is not, therefore, surprising that opposition takes the form of admitting that economic factors are a consideration important for decision but then devotes the greatest part of the rebuttal to arguments against employment of economic factors as the sole criterion for decision. One of the difficulties that may partially account for this rather sterile debate is the dearth of concrete studies into the economic aspects of fisheries. In terms of empirical investigations there appears to be little evidence upon which to base normative guides for conservation policy or guides to practical negotiations about such policy.

Second, the point is usefully made by Professor Crutchfield that the suggestion is not that maximum net economic yield can be employed as an absolute, but that when this consideration is faced explicitly, states may be able to make judgments that permit such degree of approximation as is feasible and negotiable at the moment.[116] The notion is that some improvement in economic yield might be attained as a practical result of regulation if it is consciously sought along with other alternatives. Professor Crutchfield asserts that the gap is so great between the inefficiency engendered by the present lack of management and the gains from introducing direct controls on fishing effort that there is a great deal of room for maneuver in seeking agreement by states for improvement. Even if the optimum cannot be attained, considerable progress is possible. Similar considerations suggest the opportunity of reaching agreement upon a level of yield that is acceptable to the states concerned in a fishery, even if it is not the "optimum" or "best" with respect to any of them.

Third, observation has been made that the criterion of maximum net economic return can be employed not as a goal but as a measuring stick for determining the costs of various alternative goals of the regulatory process.[117] Assuming that some choice must be made between or among various goals or combinations thereof, consideration of economic costs attached to them might make a substantial contribution to defensible or more rational choices.

Trend in Decision

The principal decisions of interest here are those about the lawfulness of establishing exclusive fishing areas, both through the enlargement of the territorial sea and through the contiguous fishing zone concept, and about the management of fisheries beyond exclusive areas in the high seas.

There is no need to recall in any detail the various proposals for the territorial sea and exclusive fishing zone reviewed, but not accepted, at the Geneva Conferences of 1958 and 1960. Although neither conference succeeded in adopting provisions on these matters, there was at least one

[116] Crutchfield, supra note 98, at 6.
[117] 1 First Conference on Law, Organization and Security in the Use of the Ocean supra note 101, at A21–A22.

singularly important consensus clearly revealed at that time. Despite lack of sufficiently widespread agreement on a width for the territorial sea or on details about an adjacent fishing zone, there did appear to be very wide agreement that claims exceeding twelve miles for either purpose were not lawful. Accordingly there need be no hesitation in stating that the various 200 mile claims advanced by some South American states do not accord with customary international law.

As noted above, numerous states have, since the last Geneva conference, unilaterally proclaimed extensions in the territorial sea and creation of new exclusive fishing zones.[118] Since such unilateral pronouncements are an accepted means for creating international law, the question is whether a pattern of any kind has emerged, a trend been initiated, indicating the development or evolution of a generally accepted width for the territorial sea and contiguous fishing zone.

With respect to the territorial sea it appears no longer to be possible to contend, with reasonable justification, that international law does not permit a breadth wider than three miles. Even if state practice has not coalesced, in terms of the views of a preponderant number of states, around a single width beyond three miles, the evidence is quite clear that a very substantial majority of states do not accept restriction to a three mile territorial sea. Insofar as fishery resources are concerned, it does not make much difference what width between three and twelve miles is regarded as acceptable under international law. The reason for this is in the accompanying development of a consensus about the permissibility of an exclusive fishing zone of twelve miles. On this, state practice seems clearly to indicate that such a zone is in accord with customary law. The result is that acquisition of exclusive rights to fishery resources is permissible up to a distance of twelve miles from the base line for delimiting the territorial sea. Contentions that a twelve-mile territorial sea is not in accord with international law must rest on considerations relevant to other issues, hence this controversial matter is not further examined here.

Decisions about authority over exploitation of fishery resources beyond the exclusive fishing area are still dominated by the overriding general principle that states are entitled to free access to such resources unless they have explicitly agreed otherwise. Freedom of fishing is enshrined as one of the four enumerated principles embraced by the concept of freedom of the seas in Article 1 of the Convention on the High Seas. Similarly, the

---

[118] It appears that more states have changed one or the other of these limits than have chosen to retain their limits. To these states must be added the states created since 1958, of whom only a handful have claimed a territorial sea of 3 miles or neglected to establish a wider exclusive fishing zone.

Convention on Fishing and Conservation of the Living Resources of the High Seas in Article 1 affirms the rights of the nationals of all states to engage in fishing on the high seas subject to obligations accepted by agreement.

It is not possible within the short compass of the present discussion to examine the many details of the agreements states have concluded for regulating their fishing activity on the high seas. The following observations concern the general process of decision on this matter and, more specifically, the participants in fishery agreements, the objectives sought, and the authority conferred on intergovernmental agencies.[119]

In overall perspective of the decision process, it is important initially to note that while states have established a number of advisory groups, usually in relationship with FAO, and some intergovernmental commissions with limited authority, the gap continues to widen between the intensity of fishing and the potential occurrence of regulatory problems, on the one hand, and the institutional means for coping with such problems, on the other. With modest exception, virtually all consequential international agreements, which provide for substantive action as distinguished from mere advice, involve a limited number of the developed states exploiting relatively high value species in the northern hemisphere where, until recently, the major fisheries were all located. Yet rapid developments in fisheries, and the potential for conflict over limitations on yield and effort, are occurring in many places throughout the ocean and many of the developing states are heavily engaged in such developments and, hence, in potential conflicts. There is very serious question whether present procedures, or present scientific capabilities, are adequate either to identify emerging problems calling for regulation or to adopt prescriptions suitably fashioned for dealing with the problems.

Two recent approaches are noteworthy as efforts to establish a decision process more suitable than that historically employed which features, primarily, the conclusion of *ad hoc* agreements among states. In an attempt to modify, but not to discard wholly, the slow and cautious route of securing explicit agreement, the Geneva Conference of 1958 concluded a Conservation Convention which provided for special authority in coastal states to initiate conservation measures unilaterally in the absence of agreement by the states affected.[120] Even in this instance agreement must first be sought

[119] The literature cited by Carroz and Roche, supra note 109, provides guidance to the many details of decision in this area. See also Burke, supra note 110. Special reference should be made to the valuable work now underway in FAO in examining the various international institutions engaged in, or related to, fishery management.
[120] For examination of this Convention see McDougal and Burke, The Public Order of the Oceans (1962); Johnston, The International Law of Fisheries (1965); Oda, op.

by the state seeking to initiate conservation measures, but failure does not preclude the adoption of regulations and, under certain conditions, their implementation. Protection of the interests of other states is sought by providing both a set of criteria for determining the permissibility of the measures projected and, of the greatest importance, a compulsory method for making the determination. As commendable as this new procedure appears to be, in terms of *procedure* rather than of substantive policy, the unhappy fact is that the Convention has attracted embarrassingly little support among states and at this stage, ten years after its initial adoption, has played no discernible part in facilitating decisions about instituting conservation measures. Furthermore, although the Convention has not been invoked as yet, there is reason to suspect that some states, or fishery groups therein, may hope to employ the Convention for the purpose of assuring coastal fishermen special exclusive, or preferential, rights to fisheries rather than only for imposing a limit on exploitation.

The second and probably more significant set of activities seeks to work within the present decision process but would attempt to improve its workings by highly conscious, deliberate, and coordinated surveillance of the world fishing scene in order both to apprehend problems in timely fashion and to make improvements in existing institutional structures for fishery regulation. Again without making a detailed survey of events, the above appears to be an accurate description of certain primary functions of the newly created Committee on Fisheries established within the FAO structure.[121] Prime assistance in the accomplishment of these ends is also to be expected from the Advisory Committee on Marine Resources Research, and its Working Parties, which provide advice to FAO and to the Intergovernmental Oceanographic Commission in UNESCO. The major importance of this development within FAO, it seems, is in provision for performance of two vital decision functions: (1) the gathering of intelligence about activities that might occasion need for international regulation or, at least, cooperation, and (2) the appraisal of presently operating institutions to determine their effectiveness and to make recommendation of actions required to remedy deficiencies.[122] Since the Committee on Fisheries is composed of senior fishery officials of many fishing states (some not in FAO), and ACMRR of widely known and respected experts, the essential condi-

cit. supra note 97; Garcia-Amador, The Exploitation and Conservation of the Resources of the Sea (2d ed. 1959); Crutchfield, supra note 98; Burke, Some Comments on the 1958 Conventions, in 1959 Proceedings of the Am. Soc. Int'l. L. 197, 204–06.
[121] An account of the evolution of FAO activities is in Chapman, supra note 106.
[122] See the reports of the first two sessions of the Committee. FAO Fish Rep. No. 33 and No. 46. See also the article by Roy Jackson, Assistant Director General (Fisheries) of FAO, World Fisheries in 1966 and 1967, 6 Fishing News International No. 7, p. 20 (July 1967).

tions for fulfillment of these tasks would appear to be met. It is true, of course, that these FAO activities do not envisage any dramatic change in individual state authority over the oceans, but they nonetheless could have dramatic impact on the decision process by reason of the critical nature of the functions performed. Provision of timely and pertinent information does not alone assure that action will be taken, but it is, at least, unlikely that any remedial or advance action would be taken at all unless such information can be made available.

Turning to more specific aspects of the decision process, it is evident that participation in fishery regulation on an international level is, quite understandably, pragmatic in nature, as states seek to deal with emerging, or suspected, or recognized problems of a particular region or stock. Participation in agreements is usually, but not always, determined by the interest a state possesses in the region or species as identified by the fishing activity of its nationals. Since conditions and interests change over time, sometimes rapidly, agreements need to be, but are not always, designed to permit relatively easy accession by new participants. At the same time recent commentary points out that states party to an agreement seeking common objectives should have a sufficient commonality of interest to support the joint endeavor.[123] Fortunately, political cleavages, representing conflicting interests of various extraneous types, do not appear yet to have been a deterrent to participation in conservation programs.

A major difficulty, already being experienced and likely to get worse, comes from the rapid increase in fishing intensity, especially in relation to the amount of research into the impact of that activity on the species exploited. The question is: when is it necessary to take concerted action to avoid excessive effort and reduction of yield. Because of the nature of the resource and the complexity of developing reliable information about it, appropriate answers to this question demand international cooperation as well as coordination of individual efforts. Fortunately, as already noted, existing international institutions are available for this task and efforts are already underway to deal with this problem.

At the same time, however, it would be unrealistic to overlook that states are by no means displaying any great anxiety about becoming party to the 1958 Conservation Convention which seeks to provide for a means of fishery regulation that does not necessarily depend upon the specific agreement of affected states. Fishing states must, however, accept the basic agreement in substantial numbers before it can be expected to have any

[123] Report of the Advisory Committee on Marine Resources Research Working Party on FAO Regional Fisheries Councils and Commissions 11-13 (Doc. No. ACMRR: 4/67/WP. 27) (14 January 1967).

useful role in resolving the problems of providing acceptable conservation regulations for high seas fisheries. Although this agreement is in effect now, slightly more than 22 states having ratified it, very few of these states engage in consequential fishing activity.[124] Assuming that the Conservation Convention has a useful framework and procedure for resolving fishery conservation problems, and that adequate substantive policies are developed, it still cannot be of consequential help if major fishing states ignore it or if the number of accepting states does not grow substantially. It deserves reiteration that the Conservation Convention does *not* reflect customary law with respect to the authority of coastal states; hence it cannot be invoked by one of the latter against a non-party distant water state.

The extent of participation in this agreement, and other indicators mentioned below, probably accurately reflect the degree of disinterest and inertia among states regarding the ocean fishery difficulties that loom on the horizon. Within the United States, the subject has recently attracted far wider interest than ever before; but so far as high level policy makers are concerned, there is reason to doubt that there is either adequate grasp of the problems involved or the inclination to provide the means necessary to deal with them in time.[125]

Decisions about the objectives of conservation regimes display a rather notable degree of uniformity on the international level. Almost all of the individual agreements establishing intergovernmental commissions, as well as the 1958 Conservation Convention, project the goal of maximum sustainable yield as the end to which regulations are to be directed.[126] Close observers, and participants, in the process of decision on these matters are quite positive in their assertion that the selection of this goal reflects neither parochial bias of scientists toward physical yields as the desirable goal nor a lack of concern over broader social goals.[127] Rather, it is explained, there are insuperable difficulties in accommodating all the various and diverse social objectives sought by states in fishery exploitation, except for the

[124] Of the important fishing states only the U.S., the U.K., Portugal and South Africa are parties. The rest of the parties, with some exceptions, catch only minor amounts of fish and are scattered around the globe.

[125] The first report of the new National Council on Marine Resources and Engineering Development places special emphasis upon providing a solution to the world food problem. The niggardly sums apparently to be devoted to this "solution", in relation to the magnitude of the difficulties involved, suggests that there is less to this emphasis than meets the eye.

[126] The Convention employs the term "optimum sustainable yield" but this is generally understood as referring to the maximum. For critical comments on the term "optimum sustainable yield" and on "maximum sustainable yield" see Crutchfield, The Convention on Fishing and Living Resources of the High Seas, 1 Natural Resources Lawyer 114, 116–17 (1968).

[127] Kasahara, supra note 101, at 27; discussion, id. at A32–A38; Chapman, supra note 107, at 86–7.

general consensus that it is in the common interest to take no more than the maximum the resource will yield on a sustainable basis. Concurrence on this goal both operates to maintain the stock(s) at the highest equilibrium level and facilitates the determination by each individual state of the goal it most prizes within that limit. Achievement of more refined goals is then to be left to negotiation between the particular states concerned.

At the same time, however, there is an easily discernible awareness in international decision-makers of the need for, and desirability of, taking account of economic considerations in selection of alternative prescriptions. In some degree it seems highly probable that these factors already influence international conservation decisions, but there appears to be a growing demand for taking more explicit account of them. A recent FAO staff report offers substantial indication of an attitude that even if found previously is now more evident:

Recently, renewed attention has been drawn to the need for detailed evaluation of the economic consequences of over-fishing. Congestion on some of the most popular high seas fishing grounds has, in some instances, led to international friction. Furthermore, governments and industry are increasingly concerned over the economic waste involved in the employment of more capital and labor than is necessary to produce a given output. The early economic studies demonstrated that an unregulated fishery would not automatically lead to an economic optimum, and that a fishery giving the maximum sustainable yield in weight from a fish stock would in general not give the maximum net profit.

. . . .

The introduction of economic data and analysis will not however provide administrators with ready-made solutions to the complicated problems affecting management decisions. As the biologists can sometimes forecast the effects of alternative methods of regulation on the physical yield of a fishery, the economist may be able to "cost" these methods and thus indicate a preferred line of action from the standpoint of "economic efficiency", in terms of input use of market preference. There may be reasons for making a choice to some degree different because of considerations of political or social acceptability or administrative feasibility. Political factors enter the picture where regulatory action has pronounced "distribution effects", i.e. disrupts the existing equilibrium between groups interested in the fishery. Distribution problems arise in connection with the division of catch and employment opportunities among nations participating in a regulated fishery and, within a nation, the division of such opportunities among different fleets and types of gear. Special problems arise in fisheries in which two or more species are fished simultaneously, in particular if the various groups participating in such a fishery have different preferences for the species caught, because generally the individual species will react differently to a particular regulation method. However, it is possible to determine who, under particular methods of regulation, is a "gainer" and who is a "loser". Clearly, those regulations which promise to result in economic gains for all participants will be preferred to those which are bound to hurt all or some. Clearly also, agreement can be more easily obtained with regard to those regulatory changes that disturb an existing equilibrium less than others. To the extent that it can shed some light on these aspects, economic analysis can make some contribution also toward the solution of the "distribution" question, although the final choice between possible alternatives will be made on the basis of broader policy considerations.

Even where collection of economic information is, however, intended to do no more than to study "efficiency" effects, it will serve useful purposes in the administration of regulatory programs, both in forecasting probable effects, and for taking timely corrective action.[128]

The Committee on Fisheries itself commented in its First Report:

The Committee stressed the unique characteristics of the common property fishery resources of the high seas, and endorsed the general objective of fishing nations to obtain the optimum economic yield from all fish stocks and resources. While techniques for the biological assessment of fish stocks were relatively well advanced (although far from universally applied), the basic concepts of criteria for judging economic returns were still in a relatively early stage of development. The Committee therefore placed a more intensive study of the economic aspects of fishery management high in priority in its future program.[129]

Despite the existence of numerous fishery commissions, it is a mistake to conclude that member states have surrendered any substantial autonomy in decision to these groups or that they are endowed with adequate resources for implementing their objectives. Generally speaking the formal authority conferred on the intergovernmental commissions is severely limited and it is in rare instances that they are sufficiently endowed to adopt prescriptions which become effective against the wishes of a member.[130] Apart from practice, which may indicate a greater level of control, the commissions are usually limited to making recommendations which the members may or may not choose to implement. Such a pattern hardly provides a basis for confidence that states will be willing soon to confer upon an international agency the kind of control required for effective management of fisheries.

Although centralized research activities, under international control, may not necessarily be most fruitful in all situations, it is still notable that very few of the fishery commissions and groups are provided with a staff to carry out this function. This is the more remarkable in view of the widespread, if not unanimous, view that the most successful regimes have been those with a staff for carrying out research independent of national

[128] FAO, Committee on Fisheries, Doc. No. COFI/10/66.
[129] FAO Fish. Rep. No. 33, p. 9 (1966).
[130] Carroz and Roche, supra note 109, at 684–93; Burke, supra note 110, at 154–74.

control. A principal reason for this situation consists of the scarcity of funds for research on a national level, which accounts for the unwillingness to establish an international agency with a need for such funds.[131]

As far as general financial support for the fishery conservation commissions is concerned, it is usually observed to be minimal in relation to the scope and complexity of the problems involved. As noted, this is not accounted for by any animus toward this form of cooperation, but seemingly by the fact that *all* funds for activity in this field are limited on a national basis. Until the problems involved become high priority, or higher than presently, there is little reason to expect change. Within individual states, it is true that officials immediately responsible are aware of the difficulties, but generally these officials are not sufficiently high in the government to effect changes in policy.

Appraisal and Recommendation

Insofar as international decision functions are concerned, the decisions reviewed offer some basis for optimism that impressive gains are being made toward keeping abreast of the regulatory difficulties of marine fisheries. It would be, in any case, premature to offer criticism of the very recent transformation within FAO which is designed to attack these difficulties with a greater sense of urgency and importance than had been attached to them before. Nonetheless it remains to be seen whether the agencies and groups involved can successfully sustain their efforts in the face of the inertia or disinterest which appears to grip important member states at high levels of administration. Although a considerable range of activities is occurring in the development of world marine fisheries as a source of protein, it is plain that at least certain developed states do not place a high priority on this matter, however extravagant the promises in the rhetoric employed for public consumption. And just as food from the sea actually occupies a very minor part in plans for ocean development, little significance appears to be attached to the management problems which exist now and which will multiply as exploitation intensifies. In view of the lead time required for coping with the very costly research effort which must serve as the principal basis for fishery regulations, there is, over all, little reason for encourage-

---

[131] Dr. Chapman perhaps pinpoints the source of this antipathy: "These three quite successful commissions [Halibut, Salmon and Tuna] often have been supported by funding by their member countries on a level more adequate than those governments have funded the research by their own fishery agencies on internal fishery management problems of comparable magnitude." Chapman, supra note 106, at 14.

ment to be found in the niggardly support now made available for this purpose nationally. The time for investing in this effort must, because of the nature of the problem, precede the need for regulation by a long period. In this sense, then, revisions in international regulatory procedures and practices may be rather barren signs of hope, however encouraging they are otherwise.

III. Military Uses of the Continental Shelf and the Seabed Beyond

Claims and Counterclaims

Legal problems arising from military uses of the ocean in peace time are quite common, occurring in every area, from that most immediately proximate to land masses, in ports, to the most remote reaches of the sea, far removed from concentrations of population other than fish. Although some of these recurring problems will be as controversial in the future as in the past, the discussion for present purposes will dwell on points of controversy that are relatively, if not wholly, new because they revolve around present and anticipated uses of the deep ocean floor beyond the continental shelf,[132] and of the shelf itself, which had not previously stirred much concern. Recent policy recommendations, advanced within states as well as in the international arena, focus most sharply on the deep sea bed beyond the shelf, apparently on the assumption, at least on the part of some, that these deep sea regions are not now being employed for military purposes. This assumption is erroneous,[133] but this not only does not vitiate the problem, it serves to intensify concern, add greater complexity, and furnish additional reason for being wary in making policy recommendations.

The precise, but now only potential, exclusive claims to be examined as problems for policy are those to acquire portions of the ocean floor or underlying medium, either as national territory or as subject to some lesser degree of control and jurisdiction. Counterclaims could take different forms but the most important, in terms of current debate, are the demands that the deep sea floor and bed should not be acquired for exclusive use by national appropriation and, in any event, that military use thereof be prohibited either wholly or in important part. With respect to the continental

[132] Unless explicitly noted otherwise, the term "deep ocean floor" is used herein to refer to the surface, the "subsoil" and underlying rock, of the bottom of the ocean beyond the area of the "continental shelf". References to "deep sea bed" are to be understood the same way. Occasionally both terms are employed at the same time to make it even more emphatically clear that every possible region of the bottom of the sea is comprehended.

[133] The text statement is based on the comments of Dr. Robert Frosch, Assistant Secretary of the U.S. Navy, upon paragraph 1 of the Maltese explanatory memorandum which asserted the seabed and floor beyond the continental shelf had not been "appropriated for national use" because this "was not technologically feasible." Dr. Frosch stated flatly: "That is an incorrect statement as a matter of fact. I would prefer to deal with some of the details of it in closed session." H.R. Rep. No. 999, at 206.

shelf, the issue involves whether states generally can employ the region for military purposes and, if not, whether the coastal state itself may lawfully do so.

Clarification of Policy

Considerable difference in substance may be observed in current proposals regarding military use of the deep ocean floor and seabed in terms of the major objective sought and, hence, in the scope of activity affected. As will be seen in the following discussion, the range is from complete prohibition of any military use to the provision of special priority and protection.

By all odds the most comprehensive recommendations for preclusion of ocean floor military operations are those, such as that advanced by Malta at the 22d General Assembly, which seek to reserve the area "exclusively for peaceful purposes," to prohibit territorial acquisition, and to establish an international agency with the crucial task, among others, of so regulating all activities in this region that all states can be assured that no military activities are taking place.[134] Plainly the key element in such a proposal is the phrase "peaceful purposes" since its interpretation would determine the scope of permissible military uses. Insofar as the Maltese proposal is concerned, the reference of "peaceful purposes" is not entirely clear but, judging from elaborations upon it, the intention apparently is to prohibit military installations of any sort, the emplacement of weapons for systems related thereto, the testing of weapons or components thereof, or the storage of equipment. That the object is to preclude *any* military employment of the area is implied, at the least, by the suggested principle that "scientific research with regard to the deep seas and ocean floor, not directly connected with defense, shall be freely permissible and its results available to all."[135] Though usually hazardous, the process of negative implication reasonably yields, in this instance, the conclusion that some scientific research, namely that connected with defense, would not be permissible under this provision or, at the least, would be permissible only under unnamed conditions.

This proposal by Malta, and the parallel one advanced in the United States by the Commission to Study the Organization of Peace,[136] approach

[134] See source cited supra note 83.
[135] This principle was not included among those embodied in the initial explanatory memorandum but was included in Dr. Pardo's statement before the First Committee. 22 UN GAOR, Provisional Verbatim Record of the 1516th Meeting 5 (U.N. Doc. No. A/C.1/PV. 1516) (1 November 1967).
[136] The Commission's recommendations are, if anything, more comprehensive. "The Commission therefore recommends that the General Assembly should declare that the

and perhaps would attain complete exclusion of military use of the region. In contrast, other suggestions which also envisage that the regions of ocean space shall be used for peaceful purposes only would permit a good many but not all forms of such use.[137] Thus, Senator Pell, in a resolution submitted for adoption by the United States Senate, recommends that "The seabed and subsoil of submarine areas of ocean space shall be used for peaceful purposes only."[138] However the remaining paragraphs of the resolution make it doubtful that this injunction is intended as a comprehensive ban on military activities. Paragraph 2 states:

All states shall refrain from the implacement or installation on or in the seabed or subsoil of ocean space of any objects containing nuclear weapons or any kinds of weapons of mass destruction, or the stationing of such weapons on or in the seabed or subsoil of ocean space in any other manner.

If this section may be interpreted as providing a complete specification of activities that are not for "peaceful purposes", then a rather considerable range of military uses, by no means unimportant, are still permissible, such as detection and surveillance systems, countermeasure devices, weapons not designed for mass destruction, and communication and storage facilities. That such an interpretation is reasonably based may be further inferred from paragraph 4 which states that "The prohibitions of this Article shall not prevent the use of military personnel or equipment for scientific research or for any other peaceful purpose." Since this paragraph attempts no distinction between military oceanography and other research, it is a reasonable assumption that it does not seek to prohibit either. Paragraph 4 also makes it explicitly clear that there are other "peaceful purposes" for which military personnel and facilities may be employed. In the formulation in Senate Resolution 186, therefore, "peaceful purposes" does not at all contemplate prohibition of all military uses but rather appears to have the connotation of "defensive" or "non-aggressive" purposes.[139] No novelty attends the observation that prohibition of all military measures except such as are "defensive" is not likely to be regarded as foreclosing many, if any, such measures.

deep sea and the seabed must not be used by nations as an environment in which to install or operate weapons, or for purposes intended to further research on potential weapons or their development." 17th report, supra note 103, at 41. Thus the Commission includes even the water volume within its ban, and would also prohibit certain scientific research.
[137] It is certainly no news that the term "peaceful purposes" lacks in clarity and explicitness. McDougal, Lasswell and Vlasic, op. cit. supra note 79, at 394 ff.
[138] S. Res. 186, 90th Cong., 1st Session, IV, § 1 (1967).
[139] Senator Pell subsequently stated that his concern was "to prevent the creating and the propagation of a new generation of weaponry in which we may well be ahead" and that "the word 'peaceful' could perhaps be changed around to 'defensive' or some other word." Hearings, supra note 23, at 36.

It may be noted, additionally, that Senator Pell's resolution provides in Section 5:

All stations, installations, equipment, sea vehicles, machines, and capsules, whether manned or unmanned, on the seabed or in the subsoil of ocean space shall be open to representatives of other States on a basis of reciprocity.... All such facilities shall be open at any time to the Sea Guard of the United Nations referred to in Article VII of this Declaration.

The initial sentence of Section 5 is drawn, it appears, from Article XII of the Space Treaty and it is therefore pertinent to observe that there is a major, highly significant, difference between this proposed Declaration and the Space Agreement. The latter, in Article XI, provides for notification "to the greatest extent feasible and practicable, of the nature, conduct, location and results" of activities in outer space. In view of the enormous difficulties of detecting activities or objects in the deep ocean environment, the omission of a similar responsibility of notification in the Pell Declaration could diminish considerably the effectiveness of this provision for reciprocal rights of visit.[140] Accordingly, if inspection is an indispensable element of an acceptable arms control scheme, this aspect of the inspection features of the Pell Declaration might be regarded, with justification, as suffering from serious deficiencies.

Furthermore, some doubt, at least, is in order as to whether this inadequacy, if such it is, is remedied by the United Nations Sea Guard which Senator Pell envisages as ensuring observance of the principle reserving the seafloor and subsoil to peaceful purposes. Unless armed with highly sophisticated equipment and skillful personnel, the Sea Guard itself would face grave difficulty in determining what activities were taking place in the deeper regions. Doubt is not dispelled by the circumstance that the Sea Guard would be "under the control and overall supervision of the Security Council," an arrangement which, one cannot help but observe, enables the major deep ocean powers, or any one of them, to be assured of some measure of control over, and protection against, its activities.

Far more limited constraints upon military measures are involved in other proposals which are directed primarily at prohibition of territorial claims on the ocean floor beyond present national jurisdiction. In another resolution, submitted to the Senate by Senator Pell two months earlier than that mentioned above, it is stated:

(3) there is an urgent need for the establishment of an international agreement under which the floor of the deep sea and the resources of the seabed and

---

[140] The qualifying term "reciprocity" also raises questions of effective implementation. See Vlasic, supra note 63, 514–15 for comment on these provisions in the Space Treaty.

subsoil thereof, beyond the limits of the Continental Shelf, will be considered free for the exploration and exploitation of all nations, and are incapable of coming under the sovereignty of any one nation or group of nations; . . .[141]

For a number of reasons, provisions such as this have little adverse impact on military use. First, the declaration that these regions are free for exploitation and exploration of all nations and the supplementary statement that they cannot be subjected to "sovereignty" is not necessarily a comprehensive prohibition of all measures of control and jurisdiction. Military uses of a particular area may be exclusive in nature, but in view of time and other limitations fall short of the assertion of sovereignty. Conceivably, and especially in light of comparable past experience, states might seek to make temporary use of an area for military purposes and to do so in ways that preclude other uses simultaneously. Duration of such activities might vary greatly, from a few hours during the day for several days or weeks to longer periods of several months or a year. In light of these possibilities, the only military uses forbidden by a prohibition of sovereign claims would be those based on explicit assertions of sovereignty or those of such prolonged duration and exclusiveness of authority that a claim to sovereignty could be reasonably implied.

Second, irrespective of the above comments about limited claims to authority, the concept of freedom of exploration and use, without further limitation, appears clearly to envisage the protection of military uses that do not interfere unreasonably with other uses. Far from discouraging measures of a military nature, such a prescription would entail their protection in the same degree, as such activities have been afforded protection in other contexts in the ocean environment.

Third, without necessarily stating it explicitly, the prohibition of the "sovereignty" of any "group of nations" suggests that international control and jurisdiction is either completely precluded or at least would be confined, as are states individually, to lesser forms of authority than "sovereignty" or complete "ownership". Further, provision for freedom of access for all nations seems incompatible with consequential international control over state activities in the absence of further agreement among such nations conferring such authority on an international agency.

In sum, adoption of authoritative prescriptions honoring freedom of use of deep sea areas would, without more, establish a considerable measure of protection for military, as well as other, activities on the ocean floor. This conclusion is buttressed, insofar as concerns Senator Pell's Senate Resolution 172, by the accompanying recommendation that states adopt certain

[141] S. Res. 172, 90th Cong., 1st Sess. (1967).

limited arms control measures involving nuclear and other weapons of mass destruction.[142]

Somewhat more extensive impact upon military uses seems to be sought by proposals which are phrased not so much in terms of "sovereignty" as in forbidding national "appropriation". Thus the explanatory memorandum in support of the Maltese request for inclusion of the seabed item on the agenda of the 22d General Assembly suggested the following treaty principle:

(a) The seabed and the ocean floor, underlying the seas beyond the limits of present national jurisdiction, are not subject to national appropriation in any manner whatsoever; . . .

This formulation, although probably broader than mere references to prohibition of sovereignty, might still invite contentions that temporary exclusive use by one state does not constitute, and cannot fairly be regarded, an attempt to "appropriate" an area. If this type of use were regarded as an "appropriation", the impact of this principle might well be to preclude some effective methods of employing the marine environment for "peaceful" purposes. In and of itself, therefore, this basic principle would appear to leave room for some, perhaps a great many, military uses of the ocean floor.

Senator Pell's S. Res. 186 has a similar version of this formula in the declaration that "Ocean space is not subject to national appropriation by claim of sovereignty, by means of use or occupation, or by any other means." The same contentions regarding temporary exclusive use may be made with respect to this version as with the one discussed immediately above. And, as noted in earlier comment, this particular resolution, in its reference to use of the ocean floor for "peaceful purposes only," does not seem to prohibit all military uses.

Certain other recommendations, either for prohibition of certain military uses of the sea or for some form of international control system for such uses, center around the operations of nuclear submarines and the installation of systems for their detection and surveillance. As is well known, nuclear submarines armed with missiles enjoy a high, but not complete, degree of invulnerability in operation because of the very considerable dif-

---

[142] Paragraph 4 states:

"any such international agreement should incorporate practicable arms control proposals looking toward mutually advantageous safeguard provisions, should encompass the results of an examination of the question of the implacement of nuclear or other weapons of mass destruction on the deep sea floor, and should contribute to a reduction of the world arms race by enjoininig all nations from the stationing of unproven types of nuclear or other kinds of mass destruction weapons on the ocean floor where unique conditions are likely to cause greater risks of accidents; ..."

ficulties in locating them and keeping them under surveillance throughout a cruise. To the extent this invulnerability is preserved, it is widely believed that these weapons systems contribute greatly to the stability of relations between the contending major maritime powers, since each side remains vulnerable if an attack were launched against the other. In these circumstances the successful development of continuous tracking devices that would permit detection of an opponent's submarine force might have a considerable destabilizing effect on the structure of relations. Accordingly there has been some tentative and brief discussion, illustrated by the brief paper by Mr. Donald N. Michael[143] (no doubt there has been far more extensive examination in classified materials), of the desirability of declaring the "deep ocean" to be "off limits" to detection and surveillance equipment. Apparently the assumption is that sooner or later states will be able to detect submarines operating at present moderate depths and that to reestablish their invulnerability they will develop submarines operating at depths beyond such detection capabilities. Mr. Michael concludes:

If the oceans were off limits to such detection and monitoring installations, the relatively high invulnerability of the deep-swimming submarine could be preserved. This might contribute to stabilization of the deterrent postures of those nations with the advanced technologies needed for constructing and operating such submarines.[144]

Elsewhere in his discussion Mr. Michael appears also to envisage outlawing (by the U.N.) of *all* detection facilities in the ocean so that the "deterrent balance" would not be upset by improvements in detection technology.[145]

Some, usually vague, discussion is occasionally devoted to the desirability of establishing either a U.N.-operated detection system or one operated jointly by the maritime powers. The paper by Mr. Michael makes brief mention of this possibility, without offering any detail about it, but believes it to be "moot" whether such a system would "contribute more or less to stability and the maintenance of peace."[146] Professor Goldie has offered similar speculation, based primarily on a supposed need to avoid conflict due to "overcrowding of facilities directed towards the same, or parallel uses."[147]

The possibility of clandestine delivery of nuclear weapons by an "international mischief-maker" has also occasioned reference to systems for locat-

[143] Avoiding the Militarization of the Seas, in 17th Report, op. cit. supra note 103, at 167.
[144] Id. at 169.
[145] Ibid.
[146] Ibid.
[147] Goldie, Military Uses in a Peaceful Regime 9, in Papers Presented at the Law of the Sea Institute, University of Rhode Island, June 28, 1967.

ing submarines. The Committee on Oceanography of the U.S. National Academy of Sciences expressed this as follows:

> Under present international law, a submerged submarine outside territorial waters in peace time is not violating any law or amenity, and is not subject to attack. Thus the probability will become steadily greater in the future that an international mischief-maker will be able with impunity to initiate a nuclear holocaust.
>
> It may then become necessary to make a change in international law which would require a submerged submarine to surface and identify itself on demand or be subject to attack. For enforcement of such an international agreement a submarine surveillance system might be essential throughout the high seas.[148]

In contrast to the above proposals, all of which would place some, if greatly varying, limits on military uses of the ocean floor by individual states, are those which seek quite the opposite and would make provision both for priority and for protection of such uses beyond that now available under customary international law. Professor Goldie has, thus, suggested that as part of a general regime for the ocean (embracing mining and other uses) the demands for certain military use be given a priority over other uses so long as the state concerned gives notice:

> My suggestion is that, on an analogy with the relevant Trusteeship Articles of the United Nations Charter, states seeking to establish fixed defense installations on sea mounts and on the sea bed should give notice to the effect that such areas are taken for defense purposes and are not to be viewed as being any longer within the general regime of the sea bed and its subsoil. Upon such an announcement the state in question may, further, establish security zones.[149]

The procedure should not be mandatory, Professor Goldie believes; but military installations and activities otherwise emplaced or conducted would not have the benefits of the proposed regime and, in particular, would be subordinated to resource exploitation carried out under the general regime he proposes.[150]

It may be seen that this recommendation, as would others, contemplates a change in the present legal framework for military activity, but the change is one which elevates some military uses to an especially protected position and, at the same time, permits any other military activity to be carried on so long as it does not come afoul of other uses. Apparently the suggestion is that rather large chunks of the ocean are to be consecrated to military use only, at the instance of any state so wishing.

Professor Goldie's idea, though seemingly extreme, does seek to confront

[148] NAS–NRC, Oceanography 1960–1970, Chapter 10, International Cooperation pp. 4–5.
[149] Goldie, in Alexander, ed., The Law of the Sea 283–84 (1967).
[150] Id. at 284.

90

a major difficulty, perhaps even *the* difficulty, for efforts to provide an international regime for regulating ocean uses beyond the continental shelf. The major maritime powers will be unwilling to accept an international regime for such regulation unless some means can be devised to accommodate military activities on the seafloor with other uses of that region. This belief assumes, and with reason it is believed, that proposals for complete demilitarization of the deep sea are not likely to be acceptable for the foreseeable future, but that it is possible to arrange such accommodation. The evidence for this assumption derives from the fact that regions of the ocean floor beyond present national jurisdiction are, contrary to the belief expressed by Ambassador Pardo of Malta, currently employed for military purposes; and without very good assurances of dismantlement, and of substitute forms of protection, states are likely to be reluctant to discontinue such uses and the development of others. It seems, furthermore, unrealistic to contemplate an agreement on complete demilitarization at the present stage of technological development, which is characterized by serious difficulty in detecting movement of submerged vessels and the location of objects. Presumably, prohibition of all military use would entail some agreed inspection scheme, hence the problem of satisfactory detection could prove to be a formidable obstacle to agreement.

The evidence that states believe military uses can be accommodated with others in acceptable fashion is not extensive. Undoubtedly, however, considerable and careful thought underlies the following statement by Dr. Robert Frosch, U.S. Assistant Secretary of the Navy for Research and Development:

Future design of sea based deterrents following Polaris/Poseidon may take many forms. Underwater silos, for example, are a possibility. Should that be so it may be that the maritime nuclear powers would like to keep the continental shelves and deep ocean available for some use by such military systems. This, however, would not necessarily be a bar to the use of these areas of the ocean bottom also for exploration and exploitation of natural resources.[151]

Clearly this statement makes no reference to international controls for such exploration and exploitation, but it would seem as likely as not that better arrangements for making any necessary accommodations for avoiding conflicts between military and other uses could in the long run be achieved under some form of unified, and limited, management than if a completely laissez-faire system of development were employed. In any event some method of accommodation is clearly regarded as feasible and acceptable.

For the layman ignorant of present classified military activities in the

[151] Frosch, Military Uses of the Ocean, in Papers Presented at the Second Conference on Law, Organization and Security in the Use of the Ocean p. 4 (7 October 1967).

ocean and of those now on the drawing boards or under exploratory development, there is no point in attempting conjecture about the principles by which states and private groups may make, simultaneously, productive use of ocean floor resources and significant military use as well. One easily discerned characteristic of the ocean environment, its very enormity, suggests, however, that dispersal of military facilities and activities in relation to commercial operations is likely to be an important consideration. Perhaps the reaches of the ocean are so vast that even Professor Goldie's recommendation is capable of implementation, i.e., announcement of the location of an activity in a way that does not disclose precise position. Unless both military and civilian uses of the ocean are extremely common and both require use or occupation of rather extensive areas of the floor, it would appear to be quite some time in the future before occasions for conflict became frequently troublesome. Accordingly it may not be necessary now to contemplate highly refined procedures and techniques for protecting security needs in conjunction with civilian uses.

The high probability that prolonged negotiations must precede any consequential agreement on limiting military uses in the ocean, accompanied by rapid progress toward making effective use of deep ocean regions, occasions anxiety on the part of some that the states with advanced technology may lay claim to some areas of the deep sea bed before diplomacy can succeed in averting such an outcome. Hence, a proposal has been advanced by Mrs. Alva Myrdal to the effect that pending the outcome of negotiations states refrain from "taking any measures with a view to appropriating any parts of the ocean floor or resources on it, and in it, and refrain from activities on the ocean floor for military purposes."[152] The policy underlying the "freeze" on claims is, obviously, that of permitting the development of a regime, by means of negotiation, which will be unencumbered by prior territorial claims and which can, therefore, operate without regard to conditions or qualifications made necessary by prior military occupations of portions of the seabed. However, in the terms suggested by Mrs. Myrdal the "freeze" goes well beyond preclusion of territorial claims, for it extends to any future military activity on the floor even if unaccompanied by, or apparently not even implying, a claim to territory. The importance of this is that in the absence of such terms a freeze on territorial claims alone would have the effect of maintaining the ocean floor as open to free access and use by those technologically capable. Thus, the formula "no appropriation *and* no military use" would appear to constitute a most comprehensive prohibition of military activity.

[152] 22 UN GAOR, Provisional Verbatim Record of the 1527th Meeting 56 (U.N. Doc. No. A/C.1/PV. 1527) (14 November 1967).

The contrary policy to the freeze proposal is, clearly, that of doing nothing about limits on acquisition or on military use while negotiations are underway which might, or might not, proscribe some or all military uses of the seabed. The crucial factor here is what might reasonably be expected to occur if states are thus left to the normal process of unilateral claim and response. Initially there seems little reason to doubt that the two major naval powers, the United States and the Soviet Union, will continue to make use of the seabed for military purposes in whatever manner they find now militarily necessary or desirable, subject to current treaty obligations limiting such use. Under present technological conditions, military uses need carry no implication of territorial claim or other formal assertion of jurisdiction; and it is uncertain, and subject to much doubt, whether either of these states would in the foreseeable future seek to make such a formal claim. The major reason for this inclination, which I assume to be mutual, to refrain from making direct claim is twofold. First, the prime consequence of laying formal claim to the ocean floor would be to destroy the chief advantage presently afforded by the ocean environment, its mantle of secrecy. Second, it is also of great common benefit to these states that they feel free to gain effective access to any portion of the deep sea bed that appears to be useful from a military perspective and it is probably considered unwise to jeopardize this advantage by asserting and recognizing territorial claims. Whatever the "legal status" of the seabed may be thought to be, it is highly probable, indeed virtually certain, that these states share the view that this region is everywhere open to such military activity as they have not already explicitly renounced. So far as the United States is concerned, public declarations are evidence that freedom of access and use is considered to be the most desirable policy and it seems probable that the view is held that such freedom is wholly in accord with international law. Such an attitude does not necessarily imply, it may be supposed, that any and all military uses of the deep sea bed should be countenanced and that there is no room for agreement on prohibiting certain particular uses.

In sum, the common interest of states might well be served by the temporary ban on territorial claims, especially since they seem so unlikely anyway over the near term, but there are serious reasons for questioning whether an interim prohibition of any military use should be preferred. One effect of it could be, and probably would be, to increase rather than decrease tension and distrust between the major powers. There is now, as noted already, very grave difficulty in detection of underwater activities and objects, and it would be virtually impossible to establish a surveillance system which could effectively police the prohibition. In view of the extreme importance the big powers attach to improving their detection capabilities, there would be a strong incentive to continue to use the ocean floor for this purpose. The fact that neither side could have any adequate assurance that the other was actually observing the prohibition would alone provide this incentive. Furthermore, if one side was observing the ban and then somehow discovered that the other was not, the consequences for public order could be very serious indeed.

An additional major cause for doubt is simply that there is no firm basis for the assumption that the ocean floor ought not be the locale for *some* military use. If there is validity in the widespread belief that the existing deterrent system works to reduce the likelihood of a major nuclear war, then it is extremely ill-advised to take actions which could lessen the effectiveness of that system. Whether the temporary prohibition of military use of the ocean floor would have that effect is conjectural, of course, but certainly that contingency should be examined, as it has not been, before taking action to approve such a ban.

The more difficult question, it seems to me, arises over the medium and longer term, as technological developments open the way to emplacing on or in the bottom installations or structures that serve military purposes but do not require, or could not abide, secrecy. The question is whether it is in the common interest to forbid these as well as the clandestine uses. An answer requires consideration of the factors relevant to the various proposals outlined above which involve partial or complete, and permanent, prohibition of military use of the seabed. The better general community policy, it seems to the writer, is to seek agreement on such specific pro-hibitions, whether of overt or covert activities, as would raise the level of security among states, and to avoid efforts at complete prohibition except as this may be involved in, and contingent upon, complete and general disarmament. In practical effect such a recommendation would mean that major attention be devoted to specific arms control measures and to the means by which permissible, or nonprohibited, military activities may be made compatible with other productive uses of the ocean bed. Attaining agreement on these particular subjects might, and hopefully would, contri-bute to the alleviation of the suspicion and distrust that block agreement on broader disarmament measures.

Judgment about the particular types or kinds of military activity that can be proscribed, or limited in some acceptable way, is so entertwined with technological and security considerations that outside observers are not likely to contribute much, except accidentally, to discussion of such issues. By way of illustrating this point, reference may be made to proposals to prohibit the emplacement of nuclear weapons on the ocean bed. It is not immediately clear what purpose this might serve by way of reducing tension or minimizing the possibility of conflict. While this proscription, if effective, might eliminate a possible source of radioactive contamination from the ocean environment, the point has been made that perhaps stationing such weapons in such remote places is preferable to placing them close to concentrations of population.[153] Whether the latter is the only alternative and whether contamination is really a problem in these circumstances are matters that require an awareness of scientific and technological factors before informed judgment can be made about the costs and benefits derivable (and who incurs the costs and enjoys the benefits) from such proposals.

Insofar as clandestine activities and facilities are concerned, the feasibility of inspection schemes, mentioned above in relation to a temporary ban, and the price to be paid for violations of community proscriptions are rather obvious considerations relevant to acceptability.[154] Unless inspection is not only feasible but sufficiently effective to minimize the risk of evasion, states may be unwilling to forego the relative security of their unilateral measures. Similarly unless the price of apprehended violations is made sufficiently high, states may not be deterred from attempting such measures. If either of these conditions is not satisfactorily met, prohibition could well be illusory and might heighten rather than diminish tension. Again, the important factors for making choices appear to be primarily technological in nature. One such factor that could turn out to be immensely important concerns the technology for putting installations *beneath* the bed of the sea.[155] When this capability emerges, if it has not already, large manned stations can

---

[153] Statement by Dr. Robert A. Frosch, Hearings, supra note 23, at 39.
[154] See the discussion in 2 First Conference on Law, Organization and Security in the Use of the Ocean C31–C32, especially the remarks of Dr. John Craven.
[155] The technological requirements for such an enterprise are now under active investigation. For a description, see Austin, Rock Site—A Way into the Sea, 13 Sea Frontiers 342 (November–December, 1967). In comment upon this article the weekly *Ocean Science News* stated: "Deep ocean sub-seafloor military bases of the 70's are being investigated right now under The Deep Ocean Technology program of DSSP....
".....
"The Navy's interest, however, is not primarily ocean mining or geothermal energy. The Navy is thinking specifically in terms of sub-seafloor military bases operating surveillance gear, manning missile stations, and providing logistic support and staging areas for the undersea military forces of the future. It is talking only secondarily about such facilities on the continental shelves. It is far more interested in the deep ocean—and the 'deep ocean' in this context ballparks out at about 6000 feet, which not at all coincidentally is the depth of the higher peaks of the Mid-Atlantic Ridge and at which many of the guyots of the Pacific Ocean top out." 10 Ocean Science News, No. 3, pp. 1–2 (January 18, 1968).
About two weeks later, the editor of Ocean Science News made the following "oversimplified prediction":
"In the years 1971–73, the U.S. Navy will place a one-atmosphere permanent manned habitat on the ocean floor at a depth of 6000 feet and service it with yet-to-be designed and built deep submersibles—a scale model of just such a seafloor base is currently undergoing towing tests in San Diego. A whole network of deep ocean

be placed far beneath the seafloor and their detection may well be exceedingly difficult even if present systems are vastly improved. Of course the same can be said for similar installations on the land mass, so this problem is not unique to the sea except in the sense that the water layer compounds the detection problem. The subfloor stations also have one advantage so far as regulation is concerned in that it may be far easier to avoid conflict with other uses than it is for installations put upon the seabed.

From a more optimistic perspective it could repay serious study to determine what measures, if any, states might accept for foregoing military operations that are within the state of the art for both sides but, when engaged in by both sides, leave the military balance precisely where it was before.[156] Such activities, if there be any, fail to produce any advantage for any contending group, represent wasted expenditure and might, additionally, impose unnecessary costs in the form of restraints on commercially productive efforts in the region. These considerations seem so obvious that mere mention of them suffices for present purposes. Again, however, the feasibility of inspection schemes should be recalled as a potential obstacle.

When one turns to consideration of limits upon military activities that might be conducted without secrecy, and perhaps must be so conducted for safety reasons, it seems to be highly debatable whether community policy should call for complete prohibition of all claims by states that might pre-empt other forms of use. If, as is assumed, states are likely to insist that the deep ocean regions continue to be available for some military operations, including the movement of submarines, there may well be ancillary activities that can be more efficiently performed on the bottom at considerable depths and which, by themselves, add little to the threat potential of ocean-based weapons systems. If, in addition, these activities threaten but little disruption of other forms of deep ocean use, or can be subjected to regulations which offer such assurance, an attempt to prohibit them would seem unnecessary. Certainly, if the overriding concern is to avoid pre-emption of commercially valuable areas by reason of claims based on military needs, community policy should be sufficiently flexible to accommodate this type of use. If some international regulation is required for this specific purpose, it seems

seafloor and sub-seafloor bases will follow—some hollowed out of the rock of the Mid-Atlantic Ridge and Pacific guyots."

Hull, The Ocean Tomorrow—A Forecast of Things to Come p. 4, a speech before the Law Committee of the Marine Technology Society, January 30, 1968.

[156] For reasons mentioned in later discussion, it is neither feasible nor desirable to attempt to de-militarize the deep ocean environment, and thereby maintain the status quo, by prohibiting scientific research in the region.

reasonable to speculate that the states concerned (both users and non-users) possess sufficient ingenuity to devise an acceptable system.

In this connection it would be singularly unfortunate if military installations for scientific research were sought to be prohibited on the theory, apparently advanced by Ambassador Pardo, that such research is directly connected with defense, and therefore not "exclusively for peaceful purposes." The facts on this score are entirely plain that it is extremely difficult, and probably completely impossible, to separate research results into neat compartments comprised of that directly connected and not directly connected with "defence". In the first place if such research can be identified as *only* for "defence" against aggressive measures, it would appear to fall well within the principles of the U.N. Charter. Secondly, even if "defence" is interpreted to refer to military measures generally, whatever this means, the fact is that the results of military oceanographic research are often highly valuable for civilian applications including, especially, fishing. More significantly, the reverse is also true, for civilian research can and does have significance for military activities.[157] It is by no means unknown that quite innocuous private research aimed at more productive commercial use of the sea has had great value for military purposes. It bears repetition that military activities at sea benefit from the same knowledge and understanding of the environment as is sought for the assistance of commercial operations or for the satisfaction of scientific curiosity. Establishing restraints such as that envisaged by Dr. Pardo might well operate to hinder oceanic endeavors that all would agree are "exclusively for peaceful purposes." This seems to be a disproportionately high price to pay considering the prevailing level of ignorance of the ocean environment.

The realism of this proposed ban on military oceanographic research can also be questioned in terms of its prospects for acceptance. If states do agree upon arms control measures involving the deep sea, they may very well be reluctant to wear, in addition, a pair of blinders so far as knowledge of the deep sea environment is concerned. This is especially true in view of the aforementioned interrelationships between civilian and military scientific research. To place a ban on military research merely invites expansion of "civilian" or "commercial" investigation and the state which failed to do so might suddenly find itself confronting a situation for which it left itself completely unprepared. It appears to be completely unjustified

---

[157] Frosch, National Security 12–15, An Address by Robert A. Frosch, Assistant Secretary of the Navy for Research and Development, at the American Association for the Advancement of Science Meeting on "Marine Science Affairs—Policies and Concepts", New York City, 27 December, 1967.

to suppose that erecting a barrier to "military" scientific research will accomplish much toward restricting further military initiatives in use of the environment. If it had any effect at all, it would probably be more in the direction of curtailing desirable civilian activity in the area.

Other kinds of stations on the bottom of the sea also could well serve military purposes without imposing any consequential restraint on other uses. The important consideration is that the claim to use an area should not be extensive, for as long as only small areas are involved it does not seem likely that any consequential pre-emption of other uses could ensue. The ocean floor, after all, greatly exceeds the total land area of the world and, so far as is known, military stations on land have never operated as a deterrent to resource exploitation.

There is also, of course, the fear that claims for military purposes will lead to a competitive race to stake out more and more and larger and larger areas for such uses; and that, in the end, commercial development will be hampered and, more importantly, the scramble for acquisition of new territory will occasion the use of comprehensive violence. While there is no reason to doubt the genuineness of those who express these apprehensions, there is also little evidence available upon which to ground them other than simple historical extrapolation. Such bases for fear as are cited point to the colonization of the world by Western Europe and imagine a repetition of the struggle and bloodshed that accompanied this process and its dissolution. It is quite impossible to respond to these projections in any rational way and no attempt is made to do so here. Suffice to say that there are so many differences involved in these situations that it seems quite hopeless to base policy on supposed historical analogies of this type.

The final problem for policy, for the present inquiry, concerns access to the continental shelf for military use by states generally and by the adjacent coastal state. All of the various proposals so far made regarding use of the seabed "exclusively for peaceful purposes" have made reference solely to the bed beyond "present national jurisdiction" and this is generally believed to mean the region beyond the "continental shelf". Questions could still arise, however, regarding military installations on the floor of the shelf and, as will be noted below in discussing decisions, proposals were made at Geneva in 1958 for disposing of such questions.

In an earlier publication, with Professor McDougal, we observed:

It would be wholly fanciful to expect that a coastal state would feel bound to stand aside while another, possibly hostile, state erected military facilities appearing above the surface or wholly submerged in ocean areas adjacent to its coast.[158]

[158] McDougal and Burke, The Public Order of the Oceans 724 (1962).

98

Since security considerations were a major force in shaping a community policy which places the shelf under coastal jurisdiction for purposes of resource exploration and exploitation, it seems reasonable to prefer the same policy with respect to emplacement of military installations on the shelf. Accordingly, such activity should be wholly under the control of the adjacent coastal state.

With regard to whether the coastal state itself ought to be permitted to use the shelf for military purposes, the following comments still seem pertinent:

Whether or not the coastal state is authorized by international law to construct military installations on its continental shelf would appear to depend on an analysis similar to that made in assessing the permissibility of structures for exploitation purposes. The most general question is whether it is reasonable that such uses be made of structures on the continental shelf, taking into account the importance of the inclusive uses affected and the significance of the exclusive interest at stake. Without detailed explanation, we suggest that in most contexts such uses should be regarded as reasonable, subject to the requirement of relatively slight interference with navigation.[159]

In view of the probable rapid development of a number of ways of using the oceans in addition to navigation, the final sentence should be modified to read that the military installation should not unreasonably interfere with *any* inclusive use of the shelf region.

Trend in Decision

In addition to the few decisions which directly concern military use of the continental shelf and the seabed beyond, others relevant in varying degree to this issue include those about: (a) military uses of the water column and surface; (b) non-military uses of the shelf and ocean floor; (c) the acquisition of territory generally, and (d) allegedly analogous regions—Antarctica and outer space. For present purposes there is no need to canvass decisions involving military uses in internal waters and territorial sea nor those boundary decisions, such as the limit on the territorial sea, to which military or security considerations are intimately related.

Decisions about military use of the seabed beyond the shelf are few indeed and by far the most significant to this date is embodied in the Nuclear Test Ban Treaty which entered into force in October, 1963. The states parties to this agreement provided in Article 1 as follows:

[159] Ibid.

Each of the Parties to this Treaty undertakes to prohibit, to prevent and not to carry out any nuclear test explosion, or any other nuclear explosion, at any place under its jurisdiction.

(a) in the atmosphere; beyond its limits, including outer space; *or underwater, including territorial waters or high seas;* . . .

Clearly the import of this is that testing of nuclear weapons or devices is forbidden on the ocean floor, although perhaps testing conducted beneath the seabed might not be comprehended if it could be accomplished without effects on the superjacent floor or water.

Although a very large number of states are parties to the treaty, it is obviously important that two fledgling nuclear powers, France and Main land China, have refused to accede and continue to test, the former having conducted numerous tests in the ocean environment in the South Pacific. The question this raises most forcefully is whether nuclear testing is now, or ever was, compatible with customary international law principles applicable to employment of the ocean.

It is well known that nuclear tests in the ocean had been undertaken by the United States, the United Kingdom and the Soviet Union prior to the conclusion of the Test Ban Treaty and that the legality of such military use of the ocean was vigorously disputed, primarily in connection with the high seas activities of the United States which preceded the testing by the U.K. and the Soviet Union. Opposition rested, so far as here pertinent, upon the contention that the tests violated the principle of freedom of the seas because they interfered with free access to the affected areas for fishing, navigation and flight and because such a use amounted to a claim to appropriate an area of the high seas for exclusive use, a claim not admissible under customary international law. The United States, for its part (in contrast to writers), defended the tests on the ground that they did not amount to any claim to appropriate a portion of the high seas or to subject it to U.S. jurisdiction or control and that such a temporary exclusive use for a military purpose was fully accepted and recognized by the international law of the sea in other comparable instances.[160] Commentators supporting the lawfulness of the U.S. tests argued that the ultimate test of legality, in terms of freedom of the seas, was whether this use was reasonable in regard to the weight of the exclusive and inclusive interests involved and urged that when so considered the U.S. tests were in full accord with freedom of the seas.[161] These writers assumed that an explosion of hydrogen

---

[160] 4 Whiteman, Digest of International Law 550 (1965) quoting a "paper prepared for the use of the United States delegation at the Conference on the Law of the Sea held at Geneva in 1958".
[161] McDougal and Schlei, The Hydrogen Bomb Tests in Perspective: Lawful Measures for Security, 64 Yale L.J. 648 (1955); McDougal and Burke, op. cit. supra note

weapons constituted, for all practical purposes, an exercise of jurisdiction and control over the dangerous areas involved. Such assumption rejects, it may be noted, the supposed distinction, advanced by some U.S. government officials, between claims to exclusive use and claims to exclusive jurisdiction and control. The U.S. tests are lawful, it is said by these officials, because they involve only temporary exclusive use, which is lawful, but do not involve any exercise of, or even claim to, jurisdiction over the areas concerned, which is not lawful. All the U.S. has done is to warn people against entering the areas because they are dangerous and this, it is contended, is a far cry from *forbidding* or actively prohibiting such entry.[162] The frailty of the purported distinctions, especially in the context of nuclear weapons testing, seems reasonably obvious and they amply deserve the characterization "nonsensical" which was recently bestowed upon them, "with respect," by a noted British writer.[163] The more realistic position, which it is believed was in accord with customary international law, at least until recently, is that states may assert temporary exclusive jurisdiction or control over portions of the high seas, as an incident to, or supplementary of, an exclusive use of a particular region. Whether or not any particular such claim is lawful depended, in this view, on numerous factors in the context which must be weighed in determining the reasonableness of the measures taken in regard to the interests of others.

The more significant present question regarding potential nuclear testing in the ocean environment, including the sea floor, is whether the overwhelming acceptance of the Test Ban Treaty itself indicates development of a customary international law principle that such a use of the ocean is prohibited. One commentator recently offered one possible answer:

... The Moscow Test Ban Treaty of 1963 may itself have started, or at least acknowledged, a general rule of customary international law dating approximately from 1963 to the effect that all atmospheric tests of nuclear weapons are illegal. The nearly universal acceptance of the treaty indicates an international consensus of overwhelming force in favor of the principles contained therein. Any claim to the contrary must be a claim of special interest against community interest. Additionally, the treaty and subsequent practice under it (i.e., restraint from conducting atmospheric tests and restraint from withdrawing

158, at 771–72; *contra* Margolis, The Hydrogen Bomb Experiments and International Law, 64 Yale L.J. 629 (1955); Gidel, Explosions Nucleaires Experimentales et Liberté de la Haute Mer, in Fundamental Problems of International Law: Festschrift für Jean Spiropoulos 173 (1957).

[162] Pender, Jurisdictional Approaches to Maritime Environments—A Space Age Perspective, 15 JAG J 155 (1961) explicitly distinguishes "activity" from an "assertion of jurisdiction" although he also acknowledges that in some circumstances a particular military operation can in practical effect amount to an excercise of jurisdiction. Id. at 157 n. 21.

[163] Bowett, The Law of the Sea 50 n. 1 (1967).

from the treaty under its withdrawal clause) can be argued to be the equivalent of the practice and acquiescence of states to a rule banning atmospheric nuclear tests even in the absence of a treaty. As in any area in which a customary principle is claimed, the basic importance of the Test-Ban Treaty here is the overwhelming (not necessarily universal) expectation of the peoples of the world about the unlawfulness of atmospheric nuclear testing.[164]

In such a view there is not need to resort to balancing interests in terms of reasonableness, as enjoined by the Article 2 of the Convention on the High Seas, to determine the lawfulness of nuclear weapons tests, since there now exists a customary law principle explicitly forbidding this use ot the ocean and the floor thereof and, thus, in effect declaring that testing is not reasonable.

It should be noted, for fairness of reference, that disregard of the criterion of "reasonableness" has also been urged by those who contend, without reference to the Test Ban Treaty, that oceanic testing violates freedom of the seas and is, therefore, unlawful. The Secretariat of the Asian-African Legal Consultative Committee makes precisely this point in the "Study on the Legality of Nuclear Tests" prepared for the Sixth Session of the Committee in Cairo in 1964:

In *The Public Order of the Oceans,* McDougal and Burke state that "the most relevant standard prescribed by customary international law is that of reasonableness" and claim that "the exclusive use attendant upon weapons testing fully comports with the reasonableness criterion." It is submitted that although it is necessary in some cases to resort to the criterion of reasonableness in matters where rules of international law do not exist, in the present instance this criterion is inadmissible as the rules of international law are quite clear in this matter. Considerations of common sense, reasonableness and good faith or, in short, equitable considerations have often been resorted to supplement or progressively develop established rules of international law. In the present instance, however, the introduction of the concept of reasonableness is quite inadmissible because it would enable states to violate established principles of international law by claiming that their action is "reasonable".[165]

The Study then proceeds to offer the opinion that even if a reasonableness standard were employed it could be concluded that nuclear testing on the high seas violated freedom of the seas. In the view of the Secretariat, the high seas weapons tests caused harm to other users and "The exercise of a right in such a manner as to harm or prejudice the interests of others is unreasonable and incompatible with international law."[166] If one adopts

[164] D'Amato, Legal Aspects of the French Nuclear Tests, 61 Am. J. Int'l. L. 66, 76–7 (1967).
[165] Secretariat of the Asian-African Legal Consultative Committee, A Study of the Legality of Nuclear Tests, in Report of the Sixth Session (1964) held at Cairo 187 (n.d.).
[166] Id. at 188.

these views by the Secretariat as applicable to the seabed, the French tests would violate customary international law if they in fact amounted to a use of the seabed. Similarly, if the prohibition of the Nuclear Test Ban Treaty is regarded as expressing customary law, the French tests cannot be accepted as permissible. And apart from the Treaty, one recent commentator strongly implies that the French tests are unreasonable in terms of the exclusive and inclusive interests involved, and that, therefore, they do not meet international law standards.[167]

Although the above decisions concern the ocean floor itself, they are, quite plainly, very limited in scope. The deliberations of the First Committee of the General Assembly, on the other hand, concerned the entire question of military use of the floor but did not succeed in reaching a decision. As we have already noted in prior discussion, the resolution emerging from the Committee was confined almost entirely to procedural arrangements for beginning the study of the issues raised by the agenda item. Where Malta had proposed immediate adoption of the principle that the seabed and ocean floor "be reserved exclusively for peaceful purposes in perpetuity," the resolution contains only the vaguest and most general of references to the issue. There can be little, if any, doubt that the conservatism of the response to the Maltese recommendations stems in substantial measure from regard shared by many states, for their strategic implications for the maritime powers. States generally appeared to recognize both that the prior agreements on military use in Antarctica and outer space were possible precisely because the major powers were not militarily involved in these regions and that these powers were heavily engaged in use of the ocean, including the seabed, for this purpose. A number of states, accordingly, observed either that the whole issue should be handled by the Eighteen Nation Disarmament Committee or that it must be considered in the context of arms control and general disarmament.

Among the maritime states the Soviet Union spoke more directly than the United States and the others to underscore the sensitiveness of the issue of curbing military use of the ocean floor. Remarking that the "complexity" of the Maltese item was not "fortuitous" because "it reflects the nature and the very content" of the issue raised, the Soviet representative observed:

In this, we have such international and political aspects as the problem of maintaining the ocean bed exclusively for peaceful purposes, and also the problem of whether this can be done, and, if it can, how, on what basis and by means of what resolutions, agreements or treaties.[168]

[167] D'Amato, supra note 164.
[168] 22 UN GAOR, Provisional Verbatim Record of the 1525th Meeting 8–10 (U.N. Doc. No. A/C.1/PV. 1525) (10 November 1967).

If the order in which matters are mentioned indicates their importance, the Soviet Union appears to give first priority to this issue since these were the first substantive comments in the speech. The statement indicates, moreover, the desire to examine whether any agreement at all is possible, what conditions might be acceptable to achieve some agreement, and what means of recording agreement would be acceptable. These remarks hardly constitute the enthusiastic regard for the principle of peaceful use which certain other, primarily developing, states were able to express. Moreover in a subsequent passage the Soviet Union appeared to imply that the question of the ocean bed could not be considered separate from questions of disarmament involved in the total environment of the planet earth, perhaps indicating that progress was possible *only* as part of a general disarmament scheme:

We do not want to preclude the fact that all these matters of course need to be studied. The Soviet Union, like the other Member States of the United Nations, of course, will study all these issues. We can even now say quite definitely that the question of the role of the ocean-bed and its use exclusively for peaceful ends is of great and serious significance in our opinion. We should like to remind the Committee in this connexion that the Soviet Union is unalterably in favour of using exclusively for peaceful purposes all media in which human beings live and act—the spacious oceans and seas, the dry land, outer space and the atmosphere and of course the ocean-bed—and we put forward our proposal on general and complete disarmament consistently seeking for its implementation. The Soviet Union considers that disarmament, primarily nuclear disarmament, would once and for all remove the danger of the ocean floor and the sea-bed being used for military purposes, and would liberate tremendous resources, firstly for the more economically developed countries, resources which could be utilized in order to enhance the wellbeing of the peoples of all countries, by also rapidly liberating the resources of the world's oceans and the ocean-bed.[169]

Although the U.S. made but one direct reference to military matters, and that general and hortatory, this hardly reflects indifference to the issues involved. Indeed the U.S. statement contains more of substance in this regard than might appear to be the case. Thus the quotation from President Johnson which includes the statement that "we must be careful to avoid a race to grab and to hold the lands under the high seas"[170] is followed immediately by the statement:

[169] Id. at 16.
[170] The Presidential statement was quoted by Ambassador Goldberg as follows:
"The premise on which the United States bases its position concerning a future legal regime for the deep ocean floor is straightforward. It was stated by President Johnson on 13 July 1966:
'Under no circumstances, we believe, must we ever allow the prospects of rich harvest and mineral wealth to create a new form of colonial competition among the maritime nations. We must be careful to avoid a race to grab and to hold the lands

This means, in our view, that the deep ocean floor should not be a stage for competing claims of national sovereignty. Whatever legal regime for the use of the deep ocean floor may eventually be agreed upon, it should ensure that the deep ocean floor will be open to exploration and use by all States, without discrimination.[171]

Though usually this declaration is mentioned as important in the context of mineral development, its significance in relation to the military issue is probably more pronounced, at least for the near term. Freedom of exploration and use is presently far more vital in application to military measures than to commercial development, and certainly this noticeable emphasis on the great desirability of freedom of use has special meaning in the context of proposed restrictions on military practices on the ocean floor.

The most important general conclusion, or impression, about the First Committee debate is not so much the caution and hesitancy infusing much of the discussion, but the indication that the acceptability of a regime for the ocean floor will be largely, but not completely, determined by the attitude of the super powers. The Soviet Union's reluctance to accept an international study group and its insistence that this matter was for States to study alone can reasonably be interpreted as expressing a desire to retain maximum freedom of maneuver and, as a corollary, as an indication that any collective decisions must be agreeable to it. The United States, in noting that the resolution finally proposed for adoption fell short of U.S. desires, took occasion to note the importance of a broad consensus because this was a "highly complex field involving important political questions" and because the "future regime of the ocean floor is a matter of concern to all countries, regardless of wealth, technology or geographic location. . . ."[172] The representative added: "This Assembly will accomplish nothing lasting in this field if it should proceed over the strongly held objections of a significant group of its membership."[173] It is perhaps not unfair to recall, in light of this categorical assertion, that a number of delegations

under the high seas. We must ensure that the deep seas and the ocean bottoms are, and remain, the legacy of all human beings.' "
Id., Provisional Verbatim Record of the 1524th Meeting 17 (U.N. Doc. No. A/C.1/PV.1524) (8 November 1967).
[171] Id. at 18. It may be noted that the Ambassador's interpretation is conveyed by repetition of the phrase "deep ocean floor", whereas the President's statement referred, variously, to "lands under the high seas", "the deep seas", and "the ocean bottoms". Neither the first nor the last of the latter terms has any qualifying term such as "deep" attached to it. Hence this repetitive reference to "deep ocean floor" might be intended to exclude floor areas not considered "deep", such as, perhaps, certain seamounts. Or, possibly, the object is to distinguish, by this means, the surface of the floor and the region beneath.
[172] Id., Provisional Verbatim Record of the 1542d Meeting 18–20, (U.N. Doc. No. A/C.1/PV. 1542) (7 December 1967).
[173] Id. at 21.

had previously remarked on the decisive influence the two super powers would exert on the issues raised by the Malta resolution. Although neither the U.S. nor the U.S.S.R. regarded the resolution adopted by the Assembly as entirely satisfactory, the more significant point is that both were unwilling to accept either the original Maltese recommendation or any statement of "principles" to be followed in use of the ocean floor.

Beyond the decisions and actions just discussed, which deal directly with a military use of the seabed (and also of the region above), we are forced to examine what might be considered analogous situations. Among these that which seems most immediately pertinent is the environment above the floor, i.e., the water column and the surface. The discussion above of nuclear testing is, obviously, relevant here since most of the controversy over testing concerned the ocean generally and did not differentiate the different components thereof. Accordingly, the above-mentioned conflicting views of relevant legal principles, primarily the doctrine of freedom of the seas, are of interest in this connection. The attitudes and preconceptions underlying such views could bear upon the lawfulness both of military uses, other than nuclear weapons tests, which assert a measure of exclusivity, and of potential claims to authority over the seabed beyond national jurisdiction.

There can be no doubt whatsoever that the overriding legal principle, reflecting universally accepted policy, governing the high seas is that this region is free for use by all states for all lawful purposes, and that the concept of lawful purposes is conceived to be open and flexible, extending to the conduct of military activities as well as to numerous other types of use. The broad range of permissible uses envisaged by authoritative international principles is given succinct expression in Article 2 of the Convention on the High Seas:

The high seas being open to all nations, no State may validly purport to subject any part of them to its sovereignty. Freedom of the high seas is exercised under the conditions laid down by these articles and by the other rules of international law. It comprises, *inter alia,* both for coastal and non-coastal States:
  (1) Freedom of navigation;
  (2) Freedom of fishing;
  (3) Freedom to lay submarine cables and pipelines;
  (4) Freedom to fly over the high seas.
These freedoms, and others which are recognized by the general principles of international law, shall be exercised by all States with reasonable regard to the interests of other States in their exercise of the freedom of the seas.

The comprehensiveness and generality of this formulation of freedom of the seas are most significant for present purposes and have most important implications for military use of the sea. It is quite plain that freedom of use is not limited to the activities enumerated in Article 2 and that, contrary to the views of the Secretariat of the Asian-African Legal Consultative Committee, freedom is not absolute but relative. Article 2 clearly recognizes that uses protected by freedom of the seas may themselves come into conflict and that no rigid standard prohibiting any and all "prejudice" or "harm" is to be employed for resolving that difficulty. A particular use is, instead, to be measured, for determining lawfulness, by assessing its reasonableness in terms of impact on the interests of others whose uses are also protected by freedom of the seas.

This is a far cry, it should be emphasized, from the interpretation by the Secretariat of the Consultative Committee which would label as "unreasonable" any use which "prejudiced" or "harmed", apparently even in the slightest degree, any other free use of the sea.

The purport of this community prescription, which it may be recalled merely "codifies" customary law,[174] in terms of military use is strongly in the direction of recognizing that occasional instances of temporary exclusive use of the high seas for military purposes may be regarded as lawful if the adverse impact on others is reasonable in the context. That this has been the position of leading maritime states hardly needs extensive demonstration. Both the United States and the United Kingdom, in so many words, and the Soviet Union and others in practice, affirm that naval operations, such as for gunnery and torpedo practice and comparable aircraft ranges, are regarded as fully compatible with freedom of the seas even though they may involve some temporary displacement of, and interference with, other uses of an area. Since these common procedures were widely known throughout the world long before the Geneva Conference of 1958, it is wholly reasonable to consider that Article 2 of the Convention adopted there places the stamp of general community approval upon them. To the extent, therefore, that these general community prescriptions are applicable to use of the seabottom for military purposes, such uses accord with international law so long as they can be considered reasonable in relation to the interests of others making use of the region or the superjacent water. Plainly the factors relevant to reasonableness may vary from context to context and require to be weighed and balanced carefully in each context.

Insofar as current practices in military use of the seabed are concerned, it is quite difficult to derive conclusions because most such uses are not,

[174] The preambular paragraphs to the Convention on the High Seas note the desire "to codify the rules of international law relating to the high seas" and recognize that the Geneva Conference "adopted the following provisions as generally declaratory of established principles of international law."

for obvious reasons, well advertised. Nonetheless, it is known that such use is made[175] and, to the writer's knowledge, there has not yet been an instance of conflict with other ocean uses, most of which would be surface or near-surface operations. As far as we know, therefore, current operations can be undertaken without any consequential interference with other uses and can, therefore, without much question be labelled as lawful.

Such non-military use of the seafloor as there is appears largely to be confined to the laying and maintenance of submarine cables. The Convention on the High Seas, quoted above, explicitly incorporates the laying of cables and pipelines within the freedom of the sea and, simultaneously, makes provision for the accommodation of this use with fishing; conflict between these uses is a quite common occurrence. The principal significance of these decisions, which probably should not be over-emphasized in relation to military use, is that the relatively permanent emplacement of cables and pipelines is not considered incompatible with freedom of the seas, and the other uses protected thereby, despite the general awareness that other uses of the region are, or will be, displaced or, at least, subject to a measure of interference. The judgement thus made probably reflects the belief that the value of free access for this purpose outweighs the rather slight, under current technological conditions, detrimental impact on other forms of employing precisely the same area of ocean floor.

Still another contemporary means of utilizing the ocean floor, properly classified as non-military as a general proposition, is as a place for disposing of solid wastes. Some isolated areas of the deep ocean floor have been the locale selected for depositing dangerous, or no longer useful, materials. In the former category, for example, may be mentioned obsolete ordnance and low level nuclear wastes stored in containers. The latter category includes, no doubt, a large variety of objects for which marine dumping is an economical procedure, such as bulky equipment and miscellaneous solid wastes. Though no formal decisions exist about the lawfulness of this activity, it seems to be so prevalent, especially in the more adjacent regions, that it is common expectation that the activity is a permissible one. The relevance of this, if any, is that a similar more positive use in the form of storage of useful materials might also be considered lawful if, as with any other use, the standard of reasonableness is met.

In final brief reference to decisions about the ocean floor beyond the shelf, there remains to be considered the relevance of general international law principles about the acquisition of territory. It may be recalled that

---

[175] See note 133 supra. Dr. Frosch observed "that the Navy has used the sea bottom for many purposes for many years, and it is incorrect to assume that we are not using the sea bottom." H.R. Rep. No. 999, at 192.

Dr. Pardo, of Malta, expressed the opinion in his initial statement before the First Committee that "Unfortunately the present juridical framework clearly encourages, subject to certain limitations, the appropriation for national purposes of the sea-bed beyond the geophysical continental shelf"[176] and then proceeded to elaborate on the principal means recognized by international law for acquisition of land territory. Dr. Pardo explicitly assumed that "the sea-bed and the ocean floor are land."

The difficulty with this pessimistic appraisal is, of course, that it assumes the very question being asked, namely whether the seabed is subject to exclusive appropriation. All the doctrines Dr. Pardo refers to as means of establishing such an appropriation are built on the premise that the object in question is subject to such appropriation. Insofar as is known to the writer there are no decisions that the ocean floor is "land" or is otherwise an object which states may appropriate by reference to doctrines about acquisition of territory. Indeed, insofar as the continental shelf is relevant in this connection, the states adopting the Convention in 1958 were very careful *not* to premise its allocation among coastal states on any theory of "occupation" of the region. Moreover if one has regard to the unilateral claims advanced by states before 1958, it would be impossible to consider them as based on "occupation" since few, if any, of these states had any capability for subjecting the shelf to effective use or to control it in any way apart from control over surface vessels, and even the latter would be questionable with regard to many of these states. In short, so far as prior decisions about acquisition of territory are concerned, it is extremely difficult, if not impossible, to build plausible arguments favoring the appropriation of the seabed unless, as indicated, the preliminary question is thoroughly begged.[177] Whether the seabed should be subject to appropriation, and how, ought not to depend upon the legal technicalities, sometimes of dubious authority, by which a small group of states sought in the eighteenth and nineteenth centuries to extend their dominion over the entire world.

If this experience from the relatively distant past offers but doubtful assistance, there are those who counsel that more recent events provide a reliable guide. Thus, emphasizing the usefulness of analogies, it is frequently urged that the decisions about military activity in the Antarctic and

---

[176] 22 UN GAOR, Provisional Verbatim Record of the 1515th Meeting 37 (U.N. Doc. No. A/C.1/PV. 1515) (1 November 1967).

[177] The policy underlying the doctrine of effective occupation does, however, have application in this context but that policy does not require that portions of the ocean bottom be subjected to claims to territory. The policy purpose of effective occupation is that of promoting development of land areas by permitting an area to be incorporated within the territory of a state. Promotion of mineral exploitation in the deep ocean environment plainly can be accomplished with lesser assertion of authority, just as was the case with the continental shelf.

outer space are "precedents" for demilitarizing the ocean floor. Article I: 1 of the Antarctic Treaty declares:

> Antarctica shall be used for peaceful purposes only. There shall be prohibited, *inter alia,* any measures of a military nature, such as the establishment of bases and fortification, the carrying out of military maneuvers, as well as the testing of any type of weapons.

Observers not uncommonly are wont to remark that this truly comprehensive ban no more than reflects the strategic judgment that military activity in this inhospitable region is of little benefit and, in any event, that any slight incremental advantage realized from such use would be more than outweighed by the political costs of continued dispute over the region. Scientific research is widely regarded as by far the most important (and perhaps only) use for the Antarctic and it is, therefore, noteworthy that for *this* purpose the Treaty does permit the use of military personnel and equipment. Expert observers express doubt that research could be carried on adequately if such use were not permitted.

Provisions regarding military activities embodied in the Outer Space Treaty are far more modest than those in the Antarctic Treaty and in terms of foreseeable practical effect are probably no more significant. So far as the vacuum of space is concerned the only obligation the parties accept is to refrain from placing in orbit "any objects carrying nuclear weapons or any other kinds of weapons of mass destruction, or . . . [stationing] such weapons in outer space in any other manner." This obligation is perhaps less sweeping than it appears to be. In every other respect, the region of space is as open to military use as it was before; in the words of one distinguished commentator, ". . . the treaty in no way precludes states from continuing their current military space programs."[178]

The familiar refrain "shall be used exclusively for peaceful purposes" is employed in the Space Treaty but, significantly, the reference is solely to "the moon and other celestial bodies". "Peaceful purposes", though given some specification in the form of explicit prohibition of military bases, testing and maneuvers, is otherwise left wholly undefined. It is worth remarking also that the practical consequence of this injunction strikes one as slightly less than monumental when not one astronaut has yet set foot on the moon and when enthusiasm for further space adventures is visibly waning, especially for projects beyond the moon landing.

The final set of decisions to be discussed pertains to military use of the continental shelf and is composed mostly of inferences drawn from actions at the 1958 Geneva Conference. In the most direct action taken at the

---

[178] Vlasic, supra note 63, at 515.

Conference, the Fourth Committee (Continental Shelf) rejected a proposal by India which read:

The continental shelf adjacent to any coastal State shall not be used by the coastal State or any other state for the purpose of building military bases or installations.[179]

The stated purpose of this provision, according to the Indian delegate, was to safeguard "freedom of the seas", although no explanation was forthcoming with respect to how the prohibition achieved that end.[180] The principal emphasis of those in opposition was that in preparatory work for the Conference little or no thought had been devoted to this problem and that it raised issues going well beyond those which were presented by use of the shelf for resource development.

The critical question left unresolved by the vote in rejection of the Indian proposal is whether only the coastal state or all states are entitled to emplace military equipment on the adjacent shelf. It is true that coastal authority over the shelf is limited to "sovereign rights for the exploration and exploitation of its natural resources", leaving the implication that no other activity is subject to coastal control except for those named activities (in Article 5) which might come into conflict with exploration and exploitation. However, at the very least, these sovereign rights, if they are to be made effective, demand the exercise of some coastal authority over *any* activity involving installations on the shelf that might obstruct development of shelf resources. Even assuming, therefore, some foreign military use of the shelf were otherwise permissible, the coastal state would seem to require some degree of authority over the location of bottom-mounted equipment or installations implicated in such use. It is difficult to perceive how the coastal state could effectively implement its policies regulating resource development unless such authority were recognized.

Perhaps the most significant consideration resides in one of the basic policies underlying allocation of certain sovereign rights over shelf resources to coastal states. Whether or not explicitly spelled out at Geneva in 1958, it appeared to be common understanding that safeguarding coastal security was, and is, a fundamental reason for extending coastal authority over shelf resources. However irrational it might appear to be, in view of the freedom of access for military vessels in the waters over the shelf, it seems nonetheless to be the common belief that coastal states would not tolerate the emplacement of installations for resource exploitation which would be under the full control of another, perhaps hostile, state. If it is accurate to ascribe

[179] L Official Records, U.N. Conference on the Law of the Sea 141 (A/Conf. 13/42) (1958).
[180] L id. 85.

this belief to states for this type of installation, it would appear to follow, a fortiori, that states would not abide foreign military installations on the shelf and that such intolerance would be authorized by a basic policy already made effective in the Shelf Convention with respect to less offensive installations for shelf exploitation. In sum if the doctrine of freedom of the seas extends to the ocean bottom, as assumed above, there appears to be reason to believe that it does not extend to freedom of access to a foreign continental shelf for the purpose of military uses requiring fixed installations.

Appraisal and Recommendation

The relatively brief consideration thus far devoted by nationstate officials to the problem of limiting or prohibiting military use of the ocean floor makes it hazardous to assess the course of future events. However, the cool reception afforded the recommendation by Malta that all, or much, military use of this area be banned suggests to this observer that a viable deep ocean regime must permit continuance of some military use of deep sea floor. The critical part the ocean and the subjacent region presently play in the military posture of the major powers, and the uncertain course of technological development permitting new and presently unknown methods of use, combine to make it doubtful that any comprehensive ban will be acceptable to these states. This projection, however, does not at all mean that it is undesirable to continue the quest for means of limiting military activity on the ocean floor. Indeed, if this projection of the likely course of events were accepted as the basis for action, it suggests that priority ought now to be placed on investigating what specific measures states will accept for restraining their use of the seabed for military purposes. In such a quest it would be useful if inquiry could proceed without resort to the ambiguous phrase "peaceful purposes" which lends itself more readily to obfuscation than to clarity in discussion. Additional benefit to serious discussion, primarily through the injection of greater realism, could be obtained if those concerned either refrained from drawing the supposed analogies with the Antarctic and Outer Space treaties, or sought, when making the analogies, to establish that the policies embodied in these agreements are suitable for the very different environment of the ocean floor and seabed. There is no longer any reason, if there ever was, for making the bald and simple assumption that the situations are the same when even casual inquiry indicates that they are not.

One further advantage in focussing study upon specific arms limitation measures is that agreement might more quickly be reached upon the means of accomodating commercial exploitation of the floor and bed with military uses thereof. Preoccupation with the more difficult, perhaps unattainable, goal of complete prohibition of military use might delay dealing with what may well be a most important obstacle to agreement on an international regulatory system for commercial development.

IV. Scientific Research in the Oceans[181]

Claims and Counterclaims

Two sets of problems provide the focus of discussion: the claims by coastal states to exercise exclusive control over scientific research and the potential of international agreements for facilitating research. Claims by coastal states pose the familiar question, in the specific context of research activities, of the scope of authority over vessels, and more recently, objects, in adjacent waters and submarine regions. A most important component of such claims relates to research in the area of the continental shelf. Opposition to these coastal claims is mostly, but not completely, potential in the sense that new practices and instrumentalities for the conduct of research raise, or at least suggest, the prospect of controversy over adapting ancient principles to novel situations.

The potential, or actual in some instances, need for facilitating research by international agreement is most conveniently indicated by reference to the newer instrumentalities of research, especially buoys and submersibles, and discussion of this is largely limited to these matters.

Clarification of Policy

The common interest of states generally is in all probability more easily perceived with respect to scientific research than for any other category of activity in the ocean. The vastness of the sea, the enormous gaps in our knowledge and understanding of the environment and its resources, the scale of the effort required for comprehensive and intensive investigation, the demands imposed by the variability in space and time of the phenomena to be observed, the common expectation that great benefits are available from the sea for all mankind, the great and ever-present impact of the ocean on human activity in even the furthest reaches of the land areas—all these factors in combination strongly and urgently suggest, if they do not dictate, the desirability of a legal framework that supports, and does not deter, discourage, or impede, the utmost freedom in the conduct of scientific

[181] This portion draws heavily upon a study done by the author for the National Council on Marine Resources and Engineering Development entitled "A Report on the International Legal Problems of Scientific Research in the Ocean." The study was submitted in final form in September, 1967, and is expected at this writing to be released shortly. Page references to this study are to the original manuscript. Hereinafter this study is referred to as "Legal Problems of Scientific Research".

research. The specific problem for policy is of course the familiar one of implementing this overriding goal in particular contexts.

The high value placed upon freedom of inquiry in the conception of common interest offered here suggests that the scope, and geographical limits, of coastal authority affecting research should be kept at the minimum consistent with protection of the vital interests of the state. Where generally accepted and extensive coastal authority impinges on the conduct of research, or could do so, desirable policy calls for the conclusion of international agreements to provide a suitable climate for these activities. Insofar as the continental shelf is concerned such a policy envisages the amendment of the 1958 Convention either to remove or to modify the requirement of coastal consent for research "concerning the continental shelf and undertaken there." In other adjacent water areas, such as the territorial sea and contiguous fishing zones, the need is for an interpretation of coastal authority which will preserve the utmost freedom of access for research consistent with the reasonable demands of coastal security.

With respect to promotion of research by means of international agreement, it is familiar knowledge that initiatives in this direction are already underway through the Intergovernmental Oceanographic Commission in UNESCO as well as in the World Meteorological Organization. There are in addition the numerous efforts at cooperative activity occurring under the aegis of the intergovernmental fishery commissions and also through the FAO, its Committee on Fisheries and Fisheries Department. The need for close and continuous international cooperation, preferably structured and organized by explicit agreement, is most obvious in light of the progress in the development of new instrumentalities for research, particularly buoys and submersibles. The concluding section of this discussion devotes more detailed treatment to this subject.

Trend in Decision

There is no doubt whatsoever that the general trend in the actions of states bodes ill for the future effective conduct of fundamental scientific research in the sea. A brief summary of the situation is contained in the 1966 Report of the Panel on Oceanography of the President's Science Advisory Committee, entitled "Effective Use of the Sea":

As this report amply demonstrates, for purposes of scientific inquiry, observation and detailed investigation throughout the area and volume of the vast oceans are required, including the benthic boundary. But for purposes of political authority the oceans are now fragmented into parts, sometimes only vaguely defined, some of which are not accessible for scientific research. Thus, the territorial sea and internal waters of various nations with limits varying from nation to nation and measured by variously determined baselines, are wholly removed from investigation of any kind without prior consent of the nation within whose territory the waters are located. In somewhat similar fashion, certain inquiries of a purely scientific nature (such as geologic surveys, benthic boundary studies, and certain biological investigations recommended by the Panel) cannot be undertaken on the continental shelf without obtaining consent from adjacent nations. It should be emphasized in this connection that the seaward limit of the Continental Shelf is but vaguely defined, according to the presently applicable law, and possibly may be expandable to embrace extremely large regions of the ocean floor. Moreover, if in the future nations are permitted to acquire exclusive use of fishery resources in greatly enlarged ocean areas, such as by claiming all the fishery resources in waters above the Continental Shelf or by some other comparably extensive method, the task of obtaining biological and ecological knowledge of important seafood resources could be frustrated entirely or at least severely handicapped. Neither these resources, nor their proper study, can be compartmentalized within artificially determined ocean boundaries if the information necessary for devising wise programs of control and management for international benefit is to be acquired.[182]

The following account of decisions offers support for the conclusions in the PSAC Report.

1. *Internal Waters*

This area of water, located most immediately adjacent to the land, is within the full control of the coastal state and virtually any activity in the conduct of scientific research requires the consent of that state. The only possible exception to this might be the conduct of research while in the exercise of the right of innocent passage which, if the Territorial Sea Convention

[182] Pp. 91–92. The concern expressed in this report is shared by other states as indicated by the establishment by the Intergovernmental Oceanographic Commission of a Working Group on Legal Questions Related to Scientific Investigations of the Ocean. The task of this Group involves:

(a) Considering legal aspects specifically related to scientific investigations of the nature and scientific investigations of the resources of the ocean, including those related to the use of various means of collecting ocean data, with a view to indicating legal principles which should facilitate and guide such research, carrying out this work in coordination with the activities of the group of experts established at the 6th Meeting of the Bureau and the Consultative Council to prepare documentation concerning the legal aspects of the use of ocean data stations;

(b) Preparing documentation concerning the effect of the law of the sea on scientific research and proposals relating both to the contribution of scientific knowledge to the development of the law of the sea, and to the participation of the IOC in the deliberations of the United Nations and appropriate specialized bodies to assist them in taking proper account of scientific interests and scientific knowledge in the consideration of the further development of the law of the sea;

Resolution V-6, adopted at the Fifth Session of IOC, in Report of the United States Delegation to the Fifth Session of IOC, p. 28.

applies, could be available in certain such waters.[183] Because of this comprehensive coastal control, the extent of the region of internal waters claimed by states could be important for research. Unfortunately the evidence is abundant that over the past 15 years or more, states have been active in expansion of internal waters either in particular areas or along the entire coastal water boundary and in some states agitation continues for outward revision of these territorial delimitations. These revisions are, or could be, important not only because they may embrace waters formerly considered as high seas, but because the baselines which form the outer boundary for internal waters are also employed as a basis for delimiting the outer boundaries of other regions of coastal authority which could affect research.[184] Thus, the impact of expanding internal waters could be cumulative, with undesirable effects even on research in a location far removed from internal waters.

By international agreement embodied in the Convention on the Territorial Sea states have established that some of these revisions are to be considered lawful, but in the nature of the case these judgments must be reached in each specific instance of claim.

2. *Territorial Sea*

Coastal states exercise sovereign authority over the territorial sea subject to the right of innocent passage for foreign vessels and it is generally understood that all scientific research in this region requires the consent of the coastal state, unless such research can be undertaken in a way compatible with innocent passage. As noted above in reference to internal waters, the broad scope of coastal authority over research in the territorial sea places special importance on claims to the breadth of that area advanced by individual states. Obviously the wider the territorial sea the more restraint placed upon access to the sea for research purposes. The trend in this respect is, manifestly, expansive, and while most states establish a modest limit of six or twelve miles, a few go far beyond that.

In the next section we shall note that some new issues may well emerge regarding coastal control over research, requiring either modified interpretation of international law principles about such control or the conclusion of international agreements to protect research.

[183] Article 5(2) establishes a right of innocent passage in certain instances of use of a straight baseline.
[184] The baseline for the territorial sea, which encloses internal waters, is also the beginning point for delimitation of contiguous zones and in some circumstances of the continental shelf.

3. Contiguous Zones

In the contiguous areas the most important trend affecting research is the recently developed expectation that the establishment of exclusive fishing zones contiguous to the territorial sea accords with international law. Accordingly states with such contiguous zones may be expected to assert some degree of control over fisheries research conducted in the zone, perhaps to prohibit such research entirely or to impose conditions on access for such purposes. So far as is known, no particular usage has evolved in state practice regarding the scope of "fisheries research" that might be affected by coastal authority.

4. Continental Shelf

Surely the most important decisions about research since World War II are those included as part of the Continental Shelf Convention which introduce restraints on scientific research that were previously unknown in international law. The relevant provisions are Articles 5(1) and (8):

> 1. The exploration of the continental shelf and the exploitation of its natural resources must not result in any unjustifiable interference with navigation, fishing or the conservation of the living resources of the sea, nor result in any interference with fundamental oceanographic or other scientific research carried out with the intention of open publication.
>
> 8. The consent of the coastal State shall be obtained in respect of any research concerning the continental shelf and undertaken there. Nevertheless the coastal State shall not normally withhold its consent if the request is submitted by a qualified institution with a view to purely scientific research into the physical or biological characteristics of the continental shelf, subject to the proviso that the coastal State shall have the right, if it so desires, to participate or to be represented in the research, and that in any event the results shall be published.

Article 5(1) obviously places very high value upon the goal of safeguarding scientific research from the intrusion of activities in resource exploitation on the shelf, but it seems equally obvious that Article 5(8) could impose restraints upon the conduct of certain research, namely that "concerning the continental shelf and undertaken there." A principal question concerns the interpretation states place upon this phrase. It is unknown whether or not a consensus has developed since 1964 on the scope of the consent requirement in terms of the type of research affected, but some states apparently adopt a restrictive interpretation. The United States, which has many scientists at work on shelves around the world, apparently considers, without objection by other states, that coastal consent is needed only for research involving physical contact with the ocean bottom. A pamphlet prepared by the U.S. State Department states:

Research on the continental shelf includes the removal of shelf samples (such as by coring and dredging) and of living resources which are unable to move at the harvestable stage except in constant physical contact with the shelf. Research on waters above the shelf or on swimming creatures is not affected.[185]

The words "on the continental shelf" refer, it is believed, to research involving physical contact with the shelf.

The most important query is whether Article 5(8) has had undesirable consequences. A recent report offered the following comments which are pertinent here:

Turning to the impact of Article 5(8) on research, the important factors appear to be the extent to which outright refusals have occurred, administrative inconveniences, and the degree to which the consent requirement (and procedures associated with it) have deterred proposed research undertakings. The evidence (from the State Department) is that refusals are extremely rare, only one being reported during the last five years, and that just this summer by the Soviet Union. My own inquiries through personal contact with ocean scientists led me to believe that more than one refusal had taken place.

The factor of administrative delay and the inconvenience of making a clearance request is difficult to measure without direct interviews with the scientific community affected. Dr. Schaefer observes that:

"It would appear that any honest scientist, engaged in fundamental research with the intention of open publication, should have no hesitation about this procedure. The difficulty, of course, is that obtaining permits from governmental authorities is usually a time-consuming process, this militating against rapid exploitation of scientific opportunities as they arise in the mind of the investigator. Equally serious is the uncertainty in being able to forecast the time required for obtaining permission from any particular State. The scheduling of large, expensive research vessels, so as to obtain the optimum scientific benefit for the funds expended is already a difficult enough problem, without throwing in this new element of uncertainty."

Insofar as is known there is no data on the extent and significance of these difficulties.

Very little data seems to be available upon the impact of Article 5(8) in deterring research. One scientist stated to the author that he had projected a ten-nation continental shelf survey to be accomplished in two summers of work but had dropped the project because he felt that it would take too long to secure the necessary clearances. The frequency of this occurrence is not known. There is reason to believe, however, that the whole problem of clearances may in practice be resolved by scientists and laboratories through the simple expedient of considering the research operation as one which clearly does not fall within Article 5(8). Unless there were very close scrutiny of activities

---

[185] Interagency Committee on Oceanography, U.S. Oceanic Research in Foreign Waters 7 (ICO Pamp. No. 25, Jan. 1966) (hereinafter referred to as U.S. Oceanic Research).

aboard the research vessel, this method would probably have a very high chance of success. To force adoption of such subterfuge hardly seems a satisfactory or desirable method of operation and it may be that some scientists cavil at this step, preferring to undertake research that actually does not require clearance.[186]

The above comments deal with the requirement for consent as a matter of international agreement, but it is important to note that at least two states, the U.S. and the Netherlands, take the position that scientific research on the shelf is subject to coastal authority by virtue of customary law. The U.S. State Department view is recorded in the pamphlet quoted above:

Although many nations have not become parties to the Convention, permission must be obtained to do research on the continental shelf from all nations.[187]

The following remarks are directed at this statement and the view of the Netherlands government.

The only basis for this assertion seems to be that the consent requirement is within coastal authority under customary international law. It could be, and apparently is, argued that the extension of "sovereign rights for the purpose of exploring and exploiting the natural resources of the shelf" is part of customary international law (as well as provided for in the Convention) and that the accoutrements or ancillary rights recognized in the Convention are also a part of customary international law. The weakness in this argument is that control over research *as formulated in the Convention* does not necessarily follow from recognition of rights over natural resources.

Recent Dutch legislation may rest on an even broader claim to authority since it could result in extension of all coastal laws, without restriction, to all installations erected on the Dutch continental shelf. Dutch writers assert that this action "was based on a *new* rule of international law, which may be summarized as being that a coastal state may exercise jurisdiction over all installations erected on the soil of its continental shelf, no matter for what purposes." Although the legislation does not specifically provide for exclusion of installations for research, unless consent is granted for access, the assumption seems clear that Dutch regulatory power extends to exclusion. Certainly the first use of the law was to exclude certain operations on an offshore installation. Insofar as research is concerned, the Netherlands legislation might have considerable justification, at least if based on the Continental Shelf Convention, since it pertains solely to installations erected on the shelf. Nonetheless such stations need not necessarily be aimed at research into the shelf but could extend to other characteristics of the environment. The issue thus raised is whether the coastal state, under the Convention or under customary international law, is permitted to exercise control over access of any kind of installation to the shelf region, especially at all research installations emplaced by another state. It would appear that both the

---

[186] Legal Problems of Scientific Research 53–4.
[187] U.S. Oceanic Research 7.

United States and the Netherlands concur that customary international law permits such control if the installation is for shelf research.[188]

The above brief review of decisions underscores the importance of the limit to be established, if any, on the continental shelf. The present, indeterminate, limit has already been described in a previous section, along with suggestions for revision. Whatever limit may ultimately be adopted, it is clear that the wider it is, the greater the potential impact on research unless states are agreeable to relax the present limitations on research.

5. *High Seas*

Research on, in, and under the high seas is in common understanding protected by the general international law doctrine of freedom of the seas even though no explicit provision records such understanding in the Geneva Conventions. The most specific evidence in these agreements is in Article 5 (1) of the Continental Shelf Convention, above quoted. It may be recalled too that Article 2 of the High Seas Convention refers to freedoms other than those enumerated therein as comprising freedom of the seas and this reference, especially in view of the attitude expressed by the International Law Commission in the report of its 1956 meeting, is generally accepted as embracing the freedom to conduct research. The following "tentative conclusions", contained in the joint UNESCO–IMCO report on fixed oceanographic data stations, are believed to express a generally accurate summary of international law decisions about research by any method or device:

1. Freedom of the high seas includes the freedom of research in the high seas.
2. No state may exercise exclusive sovereign rights of the high seas for the conduct of research by means of fixed oceanographic stations.
3. No state may restrict the reasonable conduct of such research by other governments or by individuals over whom it has no personal jurisdiction.
4. States are under a duty to ensure that such research undertaken by them or by their nationals is conducted with reasonable regard to the interests of other States in their exercise of the freedom of the high seas.
5. A State is permitted by international law to place additional restrictions on the conduct of research on the high seas for its own nationals and vessels, but not for persons over whom the State has no jurisdiction.[189]

The following observations about these conclusions are relevant here:

[188] Legal Problems of Scientific Research 55–6.
[189] UNESCO, Intergovernmental Oceanographic Commission, Preliminary Report of UNESCO and IMCO on the Legal Status of Unmanned and Manned Fixed Oceanographic Stations 11 (Doc. No. NS/IOC/INF/34) (1962).

One caveat may be in order: conclusion 2 refers to a prohibition against "exclusive sovereign rights of the high seas for the conduct of research." Whether or not intended to raise the issue, this reference recalls the controversy generated by the conduct of nuclear weapons tests on the high seas, an activity in which four major states have engaged, and the contention that the pre-emption of ocean areas involved violated the concept of freedom of the seas. This controversy need not be ventilated further at this stage except to note that one consequence of the controversy was that increased emphasis was placed upon the notion that the rights protected by the concept of freedom of the seas must be exercised with reasonable regard for the activities of others also protected by the same doctrine. It appears to me to be implicit in this re-emphasis that some exclusive use of the high seas is compatible with freedom of the seas. Admittedly it is highly subjective to identify such permissible exclusive use as that which is "reasonable," but it is surely significant that the notion of "reasonableness" is now expressly incorporated into Article 2 of the Convention on the High Seas. The importance of this recognition of the standard of reasonableness may be seen in the following section.

The freedom to conduct scientific research on the high seas has, of course, great importance in terms of easy accessibility and movement for scientists, but it has also other connotations that are important in terms of the prospects for regulation. Since each state can prescribe regulations only for its own nationals (including devices sponsored or used by its nationals) the means for a general regulatory system, extending to all participants and subjects, can only be through international agreement. For example, mention has been made of the idea of setting aside certain areas of high seas, including bottom areas, as scientific preserves, to be maintained inviolate and beyond alternation by human intervention. Although it is at least conceivable that this might be achieved, as a practical matter, by one state acting alone, it is more likely than not that satisfactory arrangements must be sought by agreement between participant-states. Moreover, and this is the point, agreement would be required with all states whose nationals might frustrate the scheme, i.e., every important participant who is a potential user of the preserved area would have to be party to the arrangements. The reason for this is simply that unless restrained by agreement no state is obliged in most circumstances to refrain from entering and using high seas areas, except for the necessity of physical accommodation. Hence omission of even one such state could frustrate plans for an international high seas preserve.

Scientific preserves are only illustrative of a potential need for multilateral agreement to resolve particular problems. More prominent attention has been devoted to the problems involved in establishing and maintaining a large buoy network since most, if not all, of such a network would be located in high seas areas beyond the prescriptive control of one state. While an individual state emplacing buoys in the high seas may be competent to enact regulations applicable thereto and is, under normal admiralty jurisdiction, fully competent to apply such rules in the event of infraction, there is reason to doubt whether any such system of unilaterally prescribed regulations could adequately resolve the expected problem.

The main reason for this is, I think, the difficulties of implementing nationally prescribed regulations concerning, for example, responsibility for destruction and theft. Such difficulties include not only detection of infractions but imposition of penalties. To the extent these functions are inefficiently performed one highly important purpose of the regulations, that of deterrence, would be left largely and perhaps completely unfulfilled.[190]

Appraisal and Recommendation

The following discussion includes comments both about potential problems in terms of the decisions above described and about the usefulness of new international agreements on certain topics.

The most important observation in appraisal of the decisions about coastal authority is to note the expansion of that authority in both quantitative and qualitative terms. With respect to the former, the continued enlargements of internal waters and territorial sea signify in practical effect, whatever the lawfulness of any particular enlargement, a shrinking of the region of the ocean within which scientific inquiry may be undertaken without prior restraint. With respect to the latter, the creation, and general acceptance, of contiguous fishing zones and the continental shelf introduce new constraints on scientific research and added difficulties in the administration of such research. Even in the region of the high seas there are proposals, alluded to in the discussion of military uses, for prohibiting certain forms of scientific research.

The problems for the future arise out of both the intensification of activities in research all around the world ocean and the introduction of new types of vehicles, instrumentation, and platforms. Heightened research activity means that the waters and ocean floor adjacent to coastal states will be investigated, as indeed they must be if the comprehensive effort needed for understanding the ocean is to be carried out properly.[191] Accordingly it is to be expected that in the future the occasions for conflicts with coastal authority will be on the increase. The employment of all the novel types of equipment and vehicles means, similarly, that the ancient doctrines of international law relating to coastal authority and freedom therefrom must be reviewed for their applicability in new contexts. That this process of review and application will be unattended by acrimony and dispute is hardly to be expected.

The major recommendation to be offered regarding the scope of coastal authority over research is to call for restrictive interpretation of that au-

---

[190] Legal Problems of Scientific Research 78–81.
[191] Legal Problems of Scientific Research 2–10 notes the requirement of comprehensive investigation in all parts of the world ocean for physical oceanography, marine geology and geophysics and biological oceanography.

thority whenever the opportunity or need for such determination arises. As an indispensable corollary, coastal states must perceive, and act upon, the interest they share with all states, coastal or not, in achieving greater understanding of the ocean and its resources. In accordance with that perception every effort should be made to promote and to facilitate scientific inquiry, including the ready grant of consent for research where even restrictive interpretation of coastal authority indicates such consent may reasonably be required.

The purport of the recommendation just made may be illustrated by reference to three problems: the use of buoys, controls over research in the contiguous fishing zones, and controls over continental shelf research.

As is well known the potential legal problems from large-scale deployment of buoys have already become the object of study by public international groups. The following statements were made regarding research buoys in the Preliminary Report of UNESCO and IMCO on the Legal Status of UnManned and Manned Fixed Oceanographic Stations:

1. The coastal state may exercise its sovereign rights in governing the use of oceanographic research buoys.

2. The coastal state may freely permit or deny permission to employ such devices.

. . .

4. No one may claim an absolute international right to place oceanographic buoys in the internal or territorial waters of any state without the express or implied permission of the government of that state.[192]

The authors of the Report apparently believed that these principles derive from the "basic rules" for territorial waters. The following comment upon the above statements illustrate another derivation, one more solicitous of research activities than of alleged coastal perogatives:

These conclusions (of UNESCO–IMCO), though tentative, deserve serious consideration and constructive criticism. One may assume that on occasion it is desirable or even essential to place buoys within the territorial sea for legitimate scientific purposes, but nothing inherent in the notion of the territorial sea dictates the conclusions reached in the UNESCO–IMCO Report. The reference to "sovereignty" over the territorial sea in Article 1 (1) of the Convention, if considered in isolation and without consideration of other factors, certainly does suggest that a very comprehensive coastal control over buoys is contemplated by present international law, but there are other factors to be weighed that might put the matter in a different perspective.

The legal regime of the territorial sea is not weighted completely in deference to the coastal state and, in fact, certain provisions of the convention on the Territorial Sea seek to accomodate the general community interest in freedom of use of the ocean. Thus the provisions for a right of innocent passage for

[192] UNESCO, supra note 189, at 6.

foreign vessels, according to which these vessels have a right of access to the territorial sea under certain conditions, are an attempt to reconcile the coastal interest in self-protection with the wider community's interest in making efficient use of the sea for transportation. In this instance the "sovereignty" of the coastal state does not mean that the coastal state may "freely" prohibit passage by foreign vessels.

When these basic policies are considered in this new and different context it seems wholly reasonable to seek to make a similar accommodation. The problem here is to evolve an arrangement which preserves in substantial measure the exercise of the freedom to engage in scientific research by means of buoy technology and at the same time permits the coastal state to exercise sufficient authority to protect its legitimate interests. The assumption underlying this approach is that for purposes of research the ocean cannot be fragmented by political boundaries anymore than it can be for making effective use of it for transportation, and that freedom of research ought, therefore, to be accorded protection from unwarranted interference within territorial waters in a fashion similar to that accorded transportation. Because of possible hazards to navigation the coastal state obviously must exercise some regulatory authority, such as specifying reasonable requirements for location, lighting, marking and communications. But this authority need not be conceived or expressed in terms of an absolute discretion to forbid buoy emplacement nor need the regulatory authority be exercised to have that effect in practice.

Under this proposal it would probably be necessary to require notification by the sponsoring agency to the coastal state concerned so that the above problems could be appropriately resolved. Such notification would properly include information on the characteristics of the buoy and associated equipment. Assurance of a right to emplace the buoy might be achieved by requiring reply, specifying reasonable conditions of access, by the coastal state within a specified period.

This problem, if in fact it is one, suggests the more general observation that previous experience in the law of the sea was limited almost entirely to manned vehicles and that considerable care should be taken in drawing upon this experience for use in the context of unmanned objects. What seems to be necessary in this situation, as it always is when new issues emerge, is to place the emphasis upon all of the fundamental policies involved and not upon the details of specific prescriptions.[193]

The question of coastal controls over research in the contiguous fishing zone arises because of provisions such as that found in the law of the United States which prohibits fishing within U.S. territorial waters or within those waters "in which the United States has the same rights in respect of fisheries as it has in its territorial waters or [engaging] in the taking of any Continental Shelf fishery resource which appertains to the United States" except as otherwise provided in the Act or in an agreement to which the U.S. is a party.[194] That this prohibition is intended to preclude fisheries research

[193] Burke, Law and the New Technologies, in Alexander, ed., The Law of the Sea 204, 215–16 (1967).
[194] 16 U.S.C.A. § 1081.

125

by other states in the new exclusive fishing zone is evident from a later provision which establishes a procedure for permitting such research by a vessel "which is owned or operated by an international organization of which the United States is a member." The following observations examine the problem this prohibition raises and the recommendations made are also pertinent to states other than the United States:

One problem of determining the scope of permissible control over fisheries research in an exclusive fishing zone arises because of the need to distinguish research directly relevant to fishery exploitation from research which may have benefit for such exploitation but is aimed basically at other purposes. Although it has been suggested that the control exercised by the U.S. over fisheries research in its territorial sea is now extended to the exclusive fishing zone, it is doubtful if this can be accepted as in accordance with international law without further clarification. Within its territorial sea the U.S. may exercise control over all research however indirectly related to, but valuable for, fisheries. But in the contiguous zone for fisheries the authority exercised must relate to the purpose which the zone was created to serve, i.e., the protection of fishing rights. It would seem apparent, therefore, that the carryover of controls over research relating to fisheries is not co-extensive with those lawfully exercised in the territorial sea. The latter are fully comprehensive; the former are not.

One possible definition of fisheries research is as follows:

Fishery research is the study of the biology, environment, abundance, availability, and exploitation of fish or other aquatic organisms for the purpose of facilitating the utilization of those organisms for sport or commercial purposes.[195]

This formulation would not require consent for research into marine organisms, which still might be valuable for fisheries, so long as that research is aimed at other purposes. The chief determinant of the necessity for requesting consent for research is in this conception one of the purpose of the conduct.

One caveat is already on record concerning such a definition. Dr. M. B. Schaefer writes:

I submit that this definition is not operationally very useful, because of the difficulty of determining the motives of the scientific complement of any particular research vessel. I doubt, therefore, whether I can rely upon it to determine whether or not I should request permission from any given foreign country before conducting any research in biological oceanography, or related subjects, in its exclusive fisheries zone.[196]

Whether or not the definition in terms of purpose is still too comprehensive calls for decision by scientists not lawyers, but even the latter may raise a question about one seeming ambiguity. Exclusive fishing rights in the contiguous zone extend only to fish exploited in the zone. Yet research in the zone could, because of the many interrelationships between conditions and animals in the zone and those outside, relate to exploitation of fish largely, if not wholly,

[195] Schaefer, The Changing Law of the Sea—Effects on Freedom of Scientific Investigation 15 (Paper Presented at the Law of the Sea Institute, University of Rhode Island, June 28, 1967).
[196] Id. at 15–16.

exploited outside the zone. Even the taking of fish otherwise protected in the zone could further research into the exploitation of still other species not so protected. If administratively feasible the distinction drawn on the basis of "facilitating utilization" might be further refined to take account of this possibility.

In any event it is noteworthy that other states do not appear to have adopted specific definitions of fisheries research. This presents an opportunity to take the lead in molding a definition which will be generally accepted. Therefore, should the United States take the initiative in framing a definition, the criteria proposed are unusually significant. In view of the critical importance of fisheries research (biological oceanography) for an increasing food yield from the sea, especially in relation to the insignificant harms that might stem from research in the fisheries zone, such definition should be framed to impose an absolute minimum constraint upon research. It would seem reasonably clear that the exclusive fishing zone makes no contribution whatsoever to fishery conservation, and probably affords very little assistance on economic matters, hence there is very little apparent justification for using the zone to handicap research that could be of enormous value. For this reason it is recommended that the whole question of U.S. controls, and practices, regarding fisheries research off the U.S. coasts and off those of other states, be reviewed and that appropriate scientific experts be consulted for their recommendations.[197]

As far as coastal authority over shelf research is concerned, it is rather obvious that potential difficulties could be averted if states made it a habit to grant consent for such research. However one of the burdens of the consent requirement consists of the administrative procedures required and this can be resolved only through some further action by states. Among the alternatives for agreement are those outlined in a recent paper by Dr. M. B. Schaefer, until recently the Chairman of the Committee on Oceanography of the National Academy of Sciences:

(a) Designation of the International Council of Scientific Unions, or some other suitable international body, to certify bonafide fundamental scientific research agencies and/or expeditions that the coastal State would automatically grant permission to carry on research in waters under its jurisdiction.

This solution seems quite attractive, especially if it is done by voluntary declaration of the coastal States. In this event, the coastal State is not, so far as I can see, abrogating or compromising any of its rights. Since the arrangement would be purely voluntary, the coastal State could withdraw from it anytime that the privilege was being abused.

(b) Bilateral or multilateral arrangements among particular nations.

This approach is perhaps somewhat less satisfactory than the foregoing, because it will doubtless require much more formal arrangements, by way of treaties or other agreements, in consequence of which the establishment of a suitable regime involving many nations will take considerable time, and also because it is more difficult to terminate such formal arrangements if they prove to be

[197] Legal Problems of Scientific Research 32-5.

127

unsatisfactory. However, since this is a familiar procedure among governments, it may be the only practical way to proceed. Surely the establishment of bilateral arrangements with our neighbors who are closely allied with us politically and economically, should be easy to effect, and the system may then be extended.

Alternatively, one might attempt to establish intergovernmental regional agreements, which would allow free access by bonafide research vessels of the member nations. Multilateral regional agreements are, of course, more difficult to consummate than bilateral agreements. One might, therefore, follow the example of the Convention establishing the Inter-American Tropical Tuna Commission, which was entered into initially between the United States and Costa Rica, but was open to adherence by other nations, on the basis of which the arrangement grew to a multilateral one over a period of years.

It is not immediately evident which of the foregoing possible solutions is the most practicable nor, indeed, whether there may not exist some other better alternative. The problem is of sufficient urgency that various possible solutions should be vigorously explored. I urge that the United States take the lead in attempting to arrive at a solution.[198]

As this discussion of shelf research indicates, it is not always feasible to devise, or implement, creative interpretations of local law or of applicable international law principles that will facilitate research, and the obvious route is then to seek new agreements or revisions of old ones. The buoy problem also illustrates this. Thus the interpretation offered above, for easing the use of buoys by one state in the territorial sea of another by establishing a concept comparable to that of innocent passage for ships, does not seem likely to have wide appeal even if it were assured that dangers to navigation were minimal and that the administrative procedures suggested were feasible. For this reason, as well as a number of others, it may be both necessary and desirable to seek to conclude an agreement, perhaps among only a few states initially, by which a variety of problems, including those of deliberate and unintentional access of buoys to territorial waters, can be anticipated and resolved. Other such problems include marking and lighting, a surveillance and reporting system, recovery of missing buoys, thefts and intentional harms, unintentional harms, and jurisdictional principles.[199]

Another matter possibly ripe for explicit agreement concerns the use of non-military submersibles. The following comments are directed at the question of access of these vehicles to various waters.

If submersible use, whether for scientific or other non-military purposes, increases greatly or appears likely to do so, it may not only be desirable but necessary to reach agreement about the conditions of use, including access.

[198] Schaefer, supra note 195, at 22–4.
[199] Recommendations regarding these are in Legal Problems of Scientific Research 100–111.

Whether or not such increase occurs, circumstances might suggest that an agreement on research submersibles would have value.

Again it seems to be worthwhile to raise first the question, without presuming to answer it, whether an agreement on submersible operation could usefully be confined to a few states, as of those in a particular region or those most likely to be involved as users of research submersibles. If a small group of states can be identified whose interests in submersible operations are parallel, if not similar, prospects for agreement might be enhanced.

One actual, and another potential, issue of access deserves consideration for resolution by agreement. The actual issue is whether research (or other non-military) submersibles (or bottom crawlers) must comply with the present requirement for innocent passage by submarines that they navigate on the surface. Since there is a very good possibility that future generations of submersibles will not be designed to operate at the interface at all, it would seem to be required to alter the law to fit their capabilities.

The nature of such alteration, however, is not so easily devised. Simple abolition of the surfacing requirement, for instance, does not appear feasible, in the sense of widely acceptable, since anxiety about undetected adjacent submarines does not seem to have disappeared or to be likely to do so. Apart from these fears, some irrational and some not, there may be, in any case, legitimate concern about safety of operations in the territorial sea if submersibles need not operate at the surface.

For non-military research submersibles, the appropriate solution (as noted earlier) would appear to be that of permitting subsurface operation in the territorial sea, so long as advance notification of transit has been made. While this could conceivably put a bit of a crimp in efficiency of operation of submersibles, it is much less of a crimp than a requirement for surface operation would impose. Furthermore, submerged transit, without notification, could be hazardous from a navigation standpoint and perhaps from others.

The main difficulty with this suggestion of notification of submerged transit is with the scope of such a requirement and particularly whether it should extend to all submersibles or to all of a particular kind or all designated by the flag state. Some states may not wish to provide notification of passage by military vehicles. And, in perhaps a fantasy of speculation, other states might not prefer a notification system limited to non-military submersibles since this, in conjunction with a coastal detection system, could also serve as a means of identifying military submarines. What seems most relevant here is the sophistication of submarine and anti-submarine technologies.

For emphasis it may be noted that the reference to notification is not intended also to connote any need for authorization. Some states assert authority to require both notification and authorization for military vessels including submarines.

The potential issue of access, noted above, arises from possible efforts to extend coastal authority to submerged vehicles (manned and unmanned) in areas beyond the territorial sea but over the continental shelf. Such a claim might be advanced in two different ways (at least), one couched in terms of control over access of submarines to a contiguous zone delimited by a certain breadth in miles and the other put in terms of the use of submersibles over the shelf.

The first of these possible claims might seek to preclude any submersible operation, in the absence of notification of precise location and purpose, on grounds of apprehension to security or to lesser internal value processes. It may be thought, for example, that the advent of cheap and plentiful submersibles facilitates smuggling of high unit value goods. Limits may be established on the time and location of operations in an effort to simplify, or merely to make feasible, surveillance activities. The shelf claim might be aimed only at seeking to prevent unauthorized exploration or exploitation, but here too the coastal state might demand notification by all submersibles since it is unable to determine reliably what is happening below the surface without notification and would be unable to attempt sanctioning measures.

The purpose of mentioning these possibilities here is to raise the question whether an agreement on submersibles operation could either dispose of them before they would otherwise arise or lay a base for one rather than another method of handling the issue. It does not seem to me that the first of these is a feasible objective since there may very well be a legitimate coastal interest in extending authority to a contiguous zone especially for submersibles. Such interests are now well recognized in international law for protection against certain activities of surface vessels and the unique advantages, and problems, of submersibles suggest that similar recognition may be due to coastal interests in this instance. Therefore, the real question is, probably, whether general agreement can be reached on some particular form of coastal authority over submersibles in a contiguous zone.[200]

Widespread use of submersibles is likely to raise other difficulties for which international agreement is highly desirable, including especially, arrangements for safety of operation and for search and rescue services.

Finally, it is increasingly apparent that the whole gamut of research activities in the ocean could benefit by reorganization of the many national and international governmental structures now responsible for such work. One highly influential scientific body in the U.S. has called, for example, for the formation of a world oceanographic organization in order to secure a more coherent framework for the multiple agencies now in operation on an international level. In its most recent report, entitled "Oceanography 1966—Achievements and Opportunities", the Committee on Oceanography of the National Academy of Sciences declared:

There is no formal apparatus in international governmental organization for the coordination of the activities of the several regional intergovernmental oceanic organizations. Although some of the regional organizations maintain liaison in formally with IOC or FAO, a good many of them do not. Indeed, there is only modest informal communication among those that carry out specialized activities in the same part of the World Ocean.

We reaffirm our recommendation for the establishment within the United Nations of a world oceanographic organization to provide a single home for the

[200] Id. at 111–14.

130

various marine scientific and technological activities now lodged in several United Nations specialized agencies. Such a world organization could vastly improve the effectiveness of existing and future oceanographic programs of the United Nations. It could also make possible effective liaison among, and with, all the international and intergovernmental organizations (regional and otherwise)—whether or not they are dependencies of the United Nations. This could lead to more effective and efficient international oceanographic research and development at greatly decreased cost both in money and in the time of overburdened officials.[201]

[201] NAS–NRC, Committee on Oceanography, Oceanography 1966—Achievement and Opportunities 183 (Pub. No. 1492). A similar recommendation has come from the joint ACMRR/SCOR/WMO Working Party on the Implementation of the UN General Assembly Resolution on the Resources of the Sea, 5 Int'l. Marine Science, No. 3, p. 39 (October, 1967).

Comments on Professor Burke's report and general remarks

Remigiusz Bierzanek

Professor of the Warsaw University and of the Polish
Institute of International Affairs

I. General Remarks

In presenting legal as well as political international aspects of the economic and military use of the oceans in the future, two basic facts should be taken into consideration:

a) The present legal status of the high seas as well as of the seabed and sea subsoil beyond the territorial waters and beyond the continental shelf is based on the principle of freedom of the seas. So the recent trends aiming at adapting the existing legal bases to the new technological and economic conditions, as particularly relevant to our subject, should be carefully analyzed.

b) The enormous gaps in our knowledge about the technological and commercial possibilities of the exploitation of the deep sea bed and subsoil don't at the present time permit the Governments to take a clear position with respect to the legal framework of the particular kinds of use of the deep sea bed and subsoil.

It is in the light of these two facts that I should like to give a brief comment on some of the ideas expressed in the stimulating report prepared by Professor Burke (hereafter referred to as "Report").

Is freedom of the seas an obsolete and useless concept in our age of technological and economic progress? Some few writers have expressed opinions that it is.[1] More numerous would like to see the traditional concept of freedom of the seas changed to the effect that the high seas should be considered *res communis*, as this change favours developing more advanced forms of international cooperation in the maritime field, like international agencies or organizations in which decision is taken by majority. However, neither the Geneva Conference of 1958, nor other more recent conferences on the law of the sea, has answered the expectations of those who would like to see the legal status of the ocean based on completely changed principles. The main task of the Geneva Conference of 1958 was rather to adapt the existing legal framework to new economic and technological conditions and particularly to conciliate it with requirements concerning conservation of the living resources and with justified claims of adjacent States. That is why most of the debates in Geneva

---

[1] See UN doc. A/CN 4/3 p. 2. Among writers such opinions are expressed by Jessup, Modern Law of Nations, pp. 27 and 38; Kunz in 'Revue Générale de Droit International Public', 1957 p. 202; Accioly in 'American Journal of International Law', 1956 p. 853.

were concentrated on such problems as width of territorial waters belt, continental shelf and conservation of living resources.

As far as the principle of the freedom of the seas, itself, is concerned, participating in that Conference I was impressed by the vigorous support given to this principle. A very great number of delegates in their interventions, particularly in the Second Committee, declared the attachment of their States to the above mentioned principle, presented contributions of their countries to the historical development of the freedom of the seas, vividly opposed the view according to which freedom of the seas was an obsolete concept, emphasizing that despite its ancient origin it continues to be useful and timely—as has been said by one of the Asian delegates— "like the Ten Commandments and Koran." What practically is more important, the Conference—as a result of debates in the Second and Third Committees—decided to recognize the special interests and privileged legal position of coastal States in protecting living resources on adjacent waters of the high seas, but did not recognize any privileged position of those States in fishing on the same waters, as has been claimed by some Latin American and other delegations. The Conference rejected some proposals concerning the so-called principle of abstention of fishing some particular species (salmon), regarding those proposals as attempts to achieve some kind of appropriation of the high seas by particular maritime Powers[2]— despite the fact that the claims in this respect were based on rather valid and strong economic argumentation (growing productivity of fishing resources) as well as supported to some extent by the FAO committees' reports. Taking a position on that point, a great number of delegates were ready to satisfy all claims justified by changed technological and economic situation, but on the other hand they were very anxious to assure in the oceans equal rights to all newcomers, i.e., to assure that the numerous developing countries do not find in the future, when they are able to extend their activities in the oceans, that the high seas have been appropriated in any sense by the more developed Powers.

Are there sufficient reasons to suppose that the attitudes of the majority of States in this respect have been profoundly changed since 1958? Till now there are no competing claims by States to deep ocean mineral resources and the question of a legal framework for deep sea mining in the oceans remains a hypothetical one. On the other hand, there is certainly now increased awareness that deep sea mining, as far as technological possibilities are concerned, has become much more of a reality than it was

[2] See Gros, La Convention sur la pêche et la conservation des ressources biologiques de la haute mer, RCADI II, 1959 p. 36; Molodcov, The international legal status of the high seas and of the continental shelf [in Russian], 1960 p. 107 ff.; Bierzanek, The legal status of the open seas [in Polish], 1960 p. 91 ff.

ten years ago. This awareness is due mostly to exploratory drillings in the ocean depths. However, even now it is not clear enough what kind of acquisition of the ocean mineral resources will be in the near future economically practicable.[3] As has been stated in the Report, "the deep ocean basins are almost completely unexplored and it is therefore not surprising that there is virtually no knowledge of the structure and composition of the ocean floor (beyond the continental slope) below the sediments. ... The sediments of the deep sea, and especially the surficial deposits, have attracted the major attention as potential sources of mineral ores. But even in this instance information does not appear to be very firmly based." Even if we assume that the above quoted opinion constitutes a little too pessimistic appreciation of the present knowledge of the ocean bed and subsoil, there can be no doubt that our present, very limited knowledge in this respect doesn't permit us to say what kind of exploitation and of what minerals is to be expected in the near future.

From the legal point of view one of the primary questions that hardly can be answered nowadays is the following one: to what extent the future exploitation of the ocean bed and subsoil requires or doesn't require more durable appropriations of some areas with exclusion of the use of those areas by other exploitants, in other words, to what extent the use of the ocean bed and subsoil is to be *usus privativus*. Assuming that resources are very abundant and their exploitation relatively easy (this is supposed to be the case of the surficial deposits of manganese nodules), there seems to be no sufficient reason to limit in any way the States in exploiting them: the flag State approach consequently appears to be probably the best legal regime for such exploitation. On the contrary, if we assume that, as a rule, the exploitation would require appropriation of considerable areas of the ocean bed and subsoil as well as erection of durable installations hampering navigation, or would demand expenditures greatly exceeding possibilities of particular States, it might be very useful and even necessary to look for some new legal solutions to the effect of limiting the extent of the principle of the freedom of the seas now in force. At present, the gaps in our knowledge about the mineral resources in the ocean bed and subsoil do not permit us to formulate proposals concerning the legal status

[3] In contradistinction to the over-optimistic opinion of Dr. Pardo, presented in the First Committee, about possibilities of winning very considerable profits from the exploitation of the ocean subsoil in the next ten years [doc. PV 1515], some writers are inclined to be much more realistic in this respect. Boyer [Le plateau continental: richesses nationales et juridiction, 'Revue de Défense Nationale', 1966 p. 1077]: "Si l'on croit qu'en mer le prix d'un forage de recherche est en moyenne trois fois plus élevé que sur terre et qu'en principe un forage de recherche est en moyenne une fois sur dix productif, on constate que la recherche et la mise en valeur de ces ressources réprésenteront des investissements considerables."

of future deep ocean mining. This seems to be the main reason for the cautious attitudes with respect to the far going Maltese proposals, taken by most delegations of the maritime Powers in the First Committee of the 22nd session of the General Assembly, as reflected in the resolution 2340 (XXII) adopted by the Assembly on December 18, 1967.[4]

But on the other hand there are now sufficient reasons to expect that in the future—sooner or later—some exploitation of the ocean bed and subsoil in some ways certainly will be practicable; and there is a danger that such expectations may result in efforts of particular maritime Powers to assure themselves an especially privileged legal position in the future competition of States by making now some appropriations of the areas of the ocean bed and subsoil. The awareness of that danger as well as the anxiety connected with it certainly is to be found in the Maltese *note verbale* as well as in the interventions of many delegates in the course of debates in the First Committee. It is particularly the expansible definiton of the continental shelf contained in the IV Geneva Convention 1958 that fully justifies the anxiety mentioned above.[5]

To conclude these general remarks: the discussions concerning the legal framework and organizational forms of the future hypothetical types of exploitation of the ocean bed and subsoil seem to be at the present time of a rather limited and mostly theoretical value. On the other hand, there is at present a timely and even urgent question concerning the introduction into the legal framework of the ocean of necessary provisions and institutions to prevent—during the transitory period from now till the moment when deep sea mining will be practicable—any appropriations and special rights which would probably greatly complicate future efforts aiming at proper legal regulation of the exploitation of the ocean bed and subsoil in the interests of mankind and not in the interests of particular States or private agencies.

II. Delimitation of the Area of Special Rights of Adjacent Coastal States

If we accept the idea of the use of the ocean bed and subsoil, declared to be "the legacy of all human beings," in the interests of mankind, the first task consists in maintaining that legacy secured from being diminished in

[4] Doc. A/6695/RES/2340/XXII [see Annex, p. 211].
[5] In this respect Ferron [Le droit international de la mer, Paris 1958–1960 II p. 199]: "Le risque de s'écarter de plus en plus de la notion du plateau continental est grand. Le critère d'exploitabilité peut en effet permettre à certaines nations, dont les techniques scientifiques sont appuyées par des ressources financières puissantes, d'occuper et d'exploiter d'immences étendues de la haute mer jusqu'à faible distance des pays riverains. Le critère d'exploitabilité n'a du reste été admis qu'avec beaucoup de reticences tant à la Commission de Droit International qu'à la Conférence de Genève."

the period before the exploitation. In this respect the provisions of International Law now in force are far from being satisfactory. The IV Geneva Convention 1958 defines the continental shelf as referring:

a) to the seabed and subsoil of the submarine areas adjacent to the coast but outside the area of the territorial sea, to a depth of 200 meters or, beyond that limit to where the depth of the superjacent waters admits of the exploitation of the natural resources of the said areas,

b) to the seabed and subsoil of similar submarine areas adjacent to the coasts of islands (article 1 of the Convention).

This definition is based on the assumption largely spread in the period preceding the conclusion of the said Convention that the exploitation of the mineral resources beyond the 200 meter isobath is hardly practicable, which assumption appears in recent years to be obsolete. There are at present two general trends in the interpretation of article 1 of the Convention. One is inclined to favour the expansive meaning of the definition, putting stress on the words "or beyond that limit, to where the depth of the superjacent waters admits of the exploitation of the mineral resources" and subordinating to them the requirement of adjacency. The other is inclined to accept the restrictive meaning of the said definition, putting stress rather on the term "adjacency" and the 200 meter isobath considered to be the exemplary criterion of adjacency, and subordinating to that criterion the subsequent part of the definition.[6] The definition is often criticised as logically inconsistent on the ground that it unsuccessfully tries to effect a compromise between the need to draw a certain line and the need to make allowance for developing the exploitation.[7]

What is more important from the practical point of view is that a number of States have adopted the expansive interpretation of article 1 of the Convention and have issued permits for activity beyond the 200 meter isobath. In that situation it is urgently needed to fix the boundary of the continental shelf and to prevent any appropriations beyond the fixed line. The solution may consist:

[6] This interpretation has been reflected in the official position taken by some Governments. So France has ratified the IV Geneva Convention 1958 under the reservation as follows: "Selon le Gouvernement de la République Française le terme 'regions adjacentes' se refère à une notion de dépendance géophysique, géologique et géographique qui exclut par elle-meme une extension illimitée du plateau continental" [see 'Annuaire Français de Droit International', 1965 p. 733].

[7] So inter alios Gutteridge, The Geneva Convention on the continental shelf, British Yearbook of International Law, 1959 p. 102 ff; Samuels, The Continental shelf Act 1964, in the 'Developments in the law of the sea 1958–1964', London 1965 p. 156. It has been observed that the definition of the continental shelf contained in the Geneva Convention has not been taken over by the British Act 1964 and that the position of the British legislator in this respect was more flexible [see Devaux-Charbonnel, Le plateau continental du Royaume Uni, 'Annuaire Français de Droit International', 1964 p. 712].

a) in adopting the restrictive interpretation of the definition contained in article 1 of the Convention, according to which the exploitability should not exceed the adjacency, i.e., the 200 meter isobath,

b) in establishing the new criterion of adjacency a little beyond the 200 meter isobath, and in eliminating the criterion of exploitability,

c) in establishing a new boundary of the continental shelf, taking into consideration the needs of reasonable limitation of the expansion by the coastal States as well as some geographical features of the ocean bed.

As far as points b) and c) are concerned, the formal revision of the IV Geneva Convention 1958 seems to be the only procedure to be recommended. In respect to point a), besides the revision of the said Convention, one may apply the other procedure, namely the adopting by the General Assembly of a resolution containing authoritative, restrictive interpretation of the definition of the continental shelf. Up to the present, there has been no such interpretation. However, it should be taken into account that with regard to the last procedure some legal objections probably would be raised, since the resolutions of the General Assembly do not constitute a *lex perfecta*, as is the case with provisions contained in international treaties. Objections of that kind would be certainly less probable if the resolution were adopted by the General Assembly unanimously or quasi-unanimously. On the other hand, the advantage of an authoritative interpretation given by the General Assembly—in contradistinction to the revision of the Convention—consists in avoiding the situation in which States would seek continued expansion of their coastal jurisdiction during the period of the negotiations for the new legal regime.

As far as point b) is concerned, it should be emphasized that each extension of the continental shelf beyond the 200 meter isobath (it is proposed in the Report to go to the 600 meter isobath) would result in considerable diminishing of areas that could be exploited in the future in the interests of mankind.

The maximalist solution mentioned in point c) not only gives the opportunity to halt the continued extension of exclusive rights in the continental shelf by adjacent States, but at the same time makes it possible to replace the functional type of upper boundary of the continental shelf and particularly the unsatisfactory distinction between sedentary and free swimming fish,[8] as established in article 2 of the IV Geneva Convention 1958, by a more satisfactory solution based on the experience in this field during recent years and adapted to the present state of science and technology. It may be added that the solution in this respect contained in the Geneva

[8] See Bowett, The law of the sea, 1967 p. 35; Bierzanek, Les frontières de type fonctionnel, 'Annuaire de l'A.A.A.', 1961 p. 8 ff.

140

Convention was controversial during the course of the Conference as well as thereafter[9] and that the revision of the adopted solution was taken into consideration in the very period of the Geneva Conference.[10]

III. Acquisition of Mineral Resources

With regard to the future international regime for exploitation of mineral resources three possible general solutions are to be taken into consideration:

1. Division of the ocean bed and subsoil among coastal states.

2. Regulation based on the principle of free access of all States aiming at solving of conflicts and at accomodating of exploitation with other uses of the high seas.

3. Establishment of an international agency charged with the duty to exploit directly or to allocate rights among claimants in the interest of all States or in the interest of developing countries.

If no choice is made in the proper time we risk having the first of the possible systems, as in practice there are clear tendencies to adopt the criterion of exploitability in defining the continental shelf, which interpretation gradually will result in division of the ocean bed and subsoil. This solution seems to be particularly disadvantageous not only for the land-locked countries but also for most of the developing countries, which have not sufficient financial means or technological capacity to undertake exploitation of mineral resources. The second solution is most in line with the present legal status of the high seas: however, it seems to be no more advantageous for the developing countries than the first one. The second and the third solutions presuppose an abandoning of the exploitability criterion of the continental shelf by the States.

As far as the third possible solution is concerned it presents a number of legal and organizational problems, some of them unprecedented ones. There are reasons to expect that this solution may result in a more equitable distribution of profits, but—on the other hand—the creation of an international agency still doesn't solve all the thorny questions connected with a more equitable distribution of benefits. In particular serious organizational

[9] Doc. A/Conf. 13/42, p. 38 ff.; It should be emphasized that France has ratified the IV Geneva Convention 1958 under a reservation establishing a different distinction between sedentary and free swimming fish from that contained in the Convention ['Annuaire Français de Droit International', 1965 p. 733].

[10] It is in 1959 that has been said by L. W. Hilbert [Le rôle respectif des considérations stratégiques, des intérets économiques, des idéologies politiques, des facteurs historiques et géographiques dans la formation du droit international de la mer, Rapport présenté au Centre de Recherches de Relations Internationales de l'Académie de Droit International de la Haye en 1959]: "Avec le présent rhytme de la technologie il est peut-être permis de prévenir que les conventions élaborées durant la Conférence de 1958 doivent, si elles seront ratifiées, être amendées après 10 ou même 5 ans."

difficulties should be taken into consideration if the system of direct exploitation by the international agency is chosen; and if we choose the system of allocation of rights to claimants, which seems to be more practicable, we risk having only a small part of the benefits available for mankind, while most of the benefits are likely to be shared by the licenced enterprises of the economically advanced countries taking the risk of exploitation. The choice of the proper organizational and legal structures for the future in this field depends to some extent on the function to be accomplished by the proposed international agency: the said function may consist only in preventing and solving conflicts among States or may be more ambitious, consisting in contributing to create a more equitable system of distribution of benefits among nations.

In contradistinction to the urgent problem of the delimitation of the continental shelf, there is at present no need for Governments to take decisions concerning above mentioned problems. However, it seems useful now to submit legal and economic as well as political implications of different possible systems to a more detailed analysis among experts.

IV. Acquisition and Control of Marine Fishery Resources

Overfishing and the need of conservation create certainly many thorny legal as well as international political problems. It is also true—as has been stated in the Report—that a major difficulty, already being experienced and likely to get worse, comes from the rapid increase in fishing intensity, especially in relation to the amount of research into the impact of that activity on the species exploited. Generally speaking, these problems are being solved, in a more or less satisfactory way, according to principles established in the III Geneva Convention 1958 as well as in other numerous international conventions and agreements. More concerted action in the field of regulation of fishing as well as in the field of research is surely to be recommended—to avoid the reduction of yield. As the problem presents many different aspects with regard to particular species and to particular regions,[11] it is hardly possible to go into these aspects within the limits of a brief comment.

11 See D. H. N. Johnson, European fishery, Developments op. cit. p. 48 ff.; R. W. Johnson, Fishery developments in the Pacific, ibidem p. 133 ff.; Boyer, La conférence de Londres et son contexte politique et économique, 'Revue de Défense Nationale', juin 1964; Carroz and Roche, The proposed International Commission for the conservation of Atlantic Tuna, 'Amer. Journal of Int. Law', July 1967; Gros, La Convention sur la pêche et la conservation des ressources biologiques de la haute mer, RCADI II, 1959 p. 1–89; De Broucker, La Convention sur la pêche de Londres de 1964, 'Revue belge de droit international', 1966 nr 1; Harrington, International issues of Pacific fisheries, 'Dept, of State Bull.', Oct. 3, 1966.

V. Military Uses of the Continental Shelf and the Seabed Beyond

Prohibiting, or at least more comprehensive limiting, of the military use of the ocean floor and subsoil constitutes a corollary of the future exploitation of those areas in the common interests of mankind as well as a corollary of the future concerted international action in this field. Preoccupations with the legal and political problems of the future commercial exploitation of the ocean bed and subsoil should not delay dealing at present with what may become one of the most important obstacles to the use of the ocean resources in the common interests of mankind. From the theoretical point of view, one of the most characteristic features of the development in the exercising of the freedoms of the high seas as areas not subject to the sovereignty of any State is an increasing difficulty in conciliating conflicting interests connected with particular uses of the ocean. While in the past the uses of the high seas by particular States for navigation, for fishing and for military purposes were relatively easy to be conciliated—as the degree of intensity of the exploitation of the ocean was rather low—nowadays the difficulty in this respect has considerably increased; and certainly it will be much more increased in the future as the above mentioned uses of the ocean become every year more and more numerous and intense. The need to establish some priorities among different kinds of use of the ocean will be consequently more and more necessary and probably will constitute the main trend in the development of the legal status of the ocean.[12] In this sense the freedom of the seas is becoming a more and more relative concept, as it is more and more indispensable to give priority to one kind of use of the ocean over another.

Certainly, one of the dilemmas of primary importance in this respect is making decisions on priorities concerning the use of the ocean for peaceful purposes and for military purposes. Till now one aspect of this dilemma has been vividly discussed, namely that of the legality of testing nuclear weapons in the high seas. In the course of the discussion the opinion has been expressed that such testing does not constitute any violation of International Law as it is a "reasonable" exercising of the freedom of the high seas.[13] But this opinion has met vigorous opposition from many international lawyers, representing many countries and different legal systems.[14] In particular,

[12] For more detailed explanations concerning this trend—see Bierzanek, La nature juridique de la haute mer, 'Revue gén. de droit int. public', 1961 nr 2-3 p. 19 ff.
[13] See Myres S. McDougal and N. Schlei, The hydrogen bomb tests in perspective: lawful measures for security, 'Yale Law Journal', 1955; Myres McDougal, The hydrogen bomb tests and the international law of the sea, 'Amer. Journal of Int. Law', 1955 p. 356 ff.
[14] Margolis, The hydrogen bomb experiments and international law, 'Yale Law Journal', 1955; Gidel, Explosions nucléaires experimentales et liberté de la haute mer,

it has been emphasized by some of them that the testing of nuclear weapons in the high seas—when all its direct and indirect effects are taken into consideration—constitutes some kind of appropriation of the vast areas of the ocean for a certain time and that that is why it is incompatible with the freedom of the high seas.[15] The opinion that the testing of nuclear weapons in the high seas is incompatible with the use of the high seas for peaceful purposes was shared by many delegates to the 1958 Geneva Conference and—taking into consideration that the 1963 Moscow Test Ban Treaty, prohibiting the carrying out of nuclear test explosions *inter alia* in the high seas, has gained overwhelming acceptance—indicates the nearly universal consensus about the illegality of this kind of use of the ocean.

Another symptomatic trend in the recent development of International Law consists in efforts aiming at the demilitarization of areas not subject to the sovereignty of any State. There seems to be a strong support of public opinion in favour of a non-spreading of the armaments race to areas till now not submitted to human activity. The 1959 Antarctic Treaty contains provisions according to which Antarctica shall be used for peaceful purposes only and provisions prohibiting any measures of military nature, such as the establishment of bases and fortification, the carrying out of military maneuvers, as well as the testing of any type of weapon. Provisions of the same kind, though more limited in extent, are to be found in the Outer Space Treaty: it has been prohibited to place in orbit any objects carrying nuclear weapons or any kinds of weapons of mass destruction as well as to station such weapons in outer space in any other manner. The analogy between Antarctica and outer space on the one side and the ocean bed and subsoil on the other side is surely not a perfect one; nevertheless the differences in this respect seem to advocate rather in favour of a different system of demilitarization for the ocean bed and subsoil and not in favour of abandoning the idea of demilitarization altogether.

Then, if deep sea regions are now being employed for military purposes, as has been emphasized in the Report, the continuation of that kind of use of the ocean would inevitably result in considerable appropriations of the deep sea bed and subsoil as well as in a military control of those areas by some maritime Powers and in a "race to grab and to hold the lands under the high seas" which would be hardly compatible with the noble idea of the ocean bottom's being and remaining the legacy of all human beings. The danger of having some vast areas of the ocean bed and subsoil appropriated for military purposes or remaining under the military control of

Festschrift Spiropoulos, 1957 p. 172 ff.; Molodcow op. cit. p. 107 ff.; Bierzanek, The legal status op. cit. p. 131 ff; Stefanova, The international legal regime of the high seas [in Bulgarian], Sofia 1965 p. 54.
[15] See Gidel, Explosions op. cit. in conclusions.

some Powers is increased by the fact that the legal status of the continental shelf as determined in the IV Geneva Convention 1958 is far from being satisfactory in this respect. It is true that in article 2 of the said Convention it has been said that "the coastal States exercise over the continental shelf sovereign rights for the purpose of exploring and exploiting its natural resources." So, in consequence, it seems to be clear enough that the coastal States do not have the right to use the shelf for military purposes or for other purposes which are not connected with the exploration of the continental shelf and with the exploitation of its natural resources. Nevertheless, during recent years contrary opinions have been expressed with respect to the interpretation of the said article, and, namely, it has been claimed that the IV Geneva Convention 1958 has extended full sovereignty of the coastal States on the continental shelf and that these States are thereby entitled to use the shelf for all purposes.[16] On the other side many doubts have been raised as to the legal nature of the continental shelf as well as of the natural resources contained in it.[17] To conclude: the proposed demilitarization of the ocean bed and subsoil should cover the continental shelf too, as the present legal status of the continental shelf is not considered to be sufficiently clear in this respect.

As far as the extent of the demilitarization of the ocean bed and subsoil is concerned, different types of demilitarization are to be taken into consideration. The less extended would consist in prohibiting fixed military installations of any sort, in prohibiting the testing of weapons and components thereof or the storage of armaments and of military equipment. The advantage of that type of demilitarization is that it is relatively easy to supervise by other States as well as by international organs. More extended demilitarization would comprise all military activity including scientific research directly serving military purposes.

It is true that progress in achieving a complete demilitarization of the ocean bed and subsoil is closely connected with the demilitarization of the

[16] So the following opinion has been expressed in the US Naval War College—International Law Studies, 1959–1960 p. 65: "Under a strict interpretation of Article 2 of the Convention, a coastal State is granted sovereign right only for the purpose of exploiting the natural resources of its continental shelf. Hence it might be maintained that the State could not build radar platforms, weather stations, or other defense installations because these would not be for the purpose of exploiting the natural resources. On the other side it seems more logical to argue that the right to exploit natural resources carries with it a corollary right to use whatever means are reasonable.... It is a logical step to conclude that a coastal State could establish defense installations on its continental shelf which were in no way connected with its installations used for exploring and exploiting the natural resources."
[17] So Boyer [Le régime juridique de l'exploitation des ressources du plateau continental, 'Le Droit Maritime Français', 1966 p. 198 ff.] opposes the views according to which the continental shelf is a part of the coastal State territory, and according to which the natural resources of the shelf constitute a property of the coastal State.

high seas; and progress in this respect depends on progress in negotiating some general disarmament programs. However, it is desirable and perfectly feasible to achieve some partial solution to the thorny problem of disarmament, consisting in eliminating the ocean bed and subsoil from areas submitted to the armaments race and other military activity. A close co-operation of international lawyers and military experts in determining kinds of military activities to be prohibited with respect to the ocean bed and subsoil constitutes an indispensable condition of the formulation of a more detailed proposal.

The international multilateral convention seems to be the most appropriate instrument for introducing the demilitarization of the ocean bed and subsoil. To restrain States from making appropriations pending the outcome of the negotiations, a resolution of the General Assembly to the effect of "freezing" the situation now existing is surely to be recommended.

VI. Scientific Research in the Oceans

In the field of scientific research in the oceans we are facing two basic facts which should be taken into consideration in formulating recommendations in this respect:

a) There is a general consensus about the desirability of developing intensive research activities in the oceans, which consensus is connected with the common expectation that in the future considerable benefits from the sea will be available for all mankind and with the awareness of serious gaps in our knowledge and understanding of the ocean environment and its resources.

b) The recognition of special rights and interests of the coastal adjacent States by the new International Law has complicated to a certain extent the legal framework of research activities in the oceans as many coastal States have enlarged their territorial sea, have established exclusive contiguous fishing zones to the territorial sea and have expanded their jurisdiction over the continental shelf, which expansion has necessarily resulted in extending the States' control over considerable parts of the oceans. Consequently, as has been said in the 1966 Report of the Panel on Oceanography of the PSAC, "the oceans are now fragmented into parts, sometimes only vaguely defined" as limits of the territorial sea and internal waters vary from nation to nation and are measured by variously determined baselines; and that is why certain inquiries of a purely scientific nature cannot be undertaken in those waters as well as in the continental shelf "without obtaining consent from adjacent nations."

Since the period of the Geneva Conference there has been a common consensus about creating a legal framework that supports and does not discourage or impede the conduct of scientific research. As far as the continental shelf is concerned, rather detailed provisions in this respect have been introduced in the IV Geneva Convention (article 5 (1) and (5)), favouring fundamental oceanographic and other scientific research carried out with the intention of open publication and imposing on States the duty to give their consent with respect to any research concerning the continental shelf or undertaken there. The documents and opinions quoted in the Report do not prove that the adopted system is inherently bad and necessarily should be replaced by another one: refusals of consent are extremely rare, the difficulties which have occurred are connected rather with the restrictive interpretation of the said provisions or with the usually long time-consuming process of obtaining permits.

Nevertheless, the observation made in the Report—that the heightened research activity in the future as well as the introduction of new types of vehicles and instrumentation requires to some extent a new approach to the problem—is certainly just and timely. That is why the first recommendation to be offered in the field of the legal framework concerning scientific research in the oceans should be the preparation of a draft convention containing more detailed provisions in this respect, which preparation should take into consideration the experience of recent years as well as the progress in instrumentation used in scientific research in the oceans. In particular, some system of registration or notification of the proposed explorations of the ocean bed and subsoil would be useful, contributing to remove suspicions about the activity of particular States in different ocean areas. The other recommendation could consist in intensifying international co-operation in the field of scientific research in the oceans: in this respect it would be desirable to consider the possibility of a concerted international action aiming at advancing more rapidly some fundamental research in this field.

147

Ian Brownlie

Fellow of Wadham College, Oxford

My intention is to comment on Professor Burke's stimulating and comprehensive paper as economically as possible and with reference to specific points. However, after dealing in this way with his four divisions of the subject-matter, I shall make some general observations.

I. Acquisition of Mineral Resources

[Pp. 22, 24–25, 27–28, 30.] Reference is made to the exploitability test as the criterion for the outer limit within the terms of the Continental Shelf Convention. There is some doubt whether this is a correct interpretation: the reference to exploitability was intended to cover cases where the 'geological shelf' concept did not correspond with the 'available shelf' intended to be covered. Thus in the case of Chile there is no geological shelf and in the Persian Gulf and the Mediterranean the interior shelf has features distinct from those of the exterior or truly continental shelf. The exploitability criterion was not clearly intended to be a shifting line. Certainly, the matter was a source of division of opinion in the International Law Commission: *Yearbook of the International Law Commission,* 1956, II, 296–7, Article 67 and commentary. It is noted that in any case Professor Burke discards the exploitability test and the present writer supports the view that some relatively objective concept of adjacency is less likely to create confusion and conflict.

Professor Burke in the present connection assumes that the issuing of permits and granting of concessions constitutes a claim to some sort of exclusive coastal control. With respect, this must depend on the circumstances: there may be some presumption that a claim is intended but states are known on occasion to have granted concessions without committing themselves on the issue of submarine boundaries.

[P. 26.] The writer would heartily endorse Professor Burke's statement that: "Those who would, for security reasons, establish a wide limit for coastal control should bear the burden of establishing this need by reference to facts and not to surmises."

[P. 27.] The "buffer zone" suggestion has some merit as a matter of policy but it is not related to any firm legal basis and would allow conflicting grants of concession rights and an awkward "free for all".

[Pp. 28–30 and passim.] In general Professor Burke's perspective for adequate control is the creation of an appropriate limit for coastal claims, and he tends (p. 31) to rule out the possibility of a regime for ocean minerals. However, the long-term solution for controlling exclusive claims, which is at least as attractive as formulations related to "adjacency", may well be the creation of a special legal regime for deep ocean resources. Of course, the analogy with Outer Space or Antarctica can hardly be drawn in a dogmatic way, but there is an overall similarity in terms of the problems of control and the special hazards and difficulties of access to the area of interest.

[Pp. 32 et seq.] Professor Burke's review of general policy alternatives ranges widely and my criticism is directed to his indication of preferences. He stresses the uneconomic character of deep ocean mining as carried on so far. Without challenging his data, one may wonder why private capital, as in the case of space operations, is so anxious to gain free participation. Professor Burke is unfavourable to control by a public international agency because this would place limits on exploitation by private groups (p. 34), and the consortium approach is proposed (p. 34). Yet the value of the consortium approach to space operations has yet to be established and, in any case, in this type of operation the distinction between government and private enterprise is not maintained: the United States has considerable experience in the co-operation of private corporations and government agencies.

[Pp. 47, 55–56.] Professor Burke's reasons for rejecting in general the analogies of Outer Space and Antarctica do not seem at all conclusive. At pp. 47–48 and 53 the paper touches on a problem common to all three arenas: the nature of squatting rights on mineral sites. The rules agreed upon relating to Outer Space do not really take care of the problems by prohibiting acquisition of sovereign rights since the question of first claims will still arise. Professor Burke adverts to the problem in the context of deep sea mining but ends up by proposing an adaptation of the principle of effective occupation (pp. 53–55). The difficulty is that in relation to the subject matter the principle of effective occupation would give uncertain results and create sources of conflict. One may recall municipal decisions on possession and abandonment of wrecks.

[P. 56 et seq.] The writer was somewhat surprised to discover Professor Burke's coolness to the Malta resolution of 1967 since in some essentials the policy it embodied reflects his own basic concern about unlimited claims. Moreover, it is the case that in the Law of the Sea, as in other spheres, lasting legal regulation can only be brought about if the position of the less advanced States is given due consideration. The Malta resolution no doubt employed formulations which were capable of elaboration and improvement: but the overall aim was to prevent yet another set of resources falling to the effective disposition of the technically advanced States, and this seems to be an eminently sane objective. The fact that the Malta resolution was considerably altered prior to General Assembly approval "in order to gain the approval of significant members" is perhaps only evidence of the political power of those members and not of their wisdom or the wisdom of making concessions to their views (see pp. 58–59). It may be that effective limitation on unlimited exclusive claims will now be postponed for some time since environmental studies may take many years to pursue. In the case of Outer Space the necessary legal regime was regarded as a prelude to and a beneficial contribution toward scientific study and exploration. Whilst the writer supports Professor Burke's proposal for a moratorium on "claims, or activities, which might prejudice ultimate resolution of the issues involved," he also feels that Professor Burke is unrealistic if in fact he thinks that States will sit passively whilst those who have the capacity go ahead with active exploitation (cp. pp. 60–61). In the case of Antarctica it was necessary to provide an adequate legal framework within which activity could be classified as non-claim-generating. A mere moratorium on claims accompanied by unregulated exploration and exploitation might not last very long.

II. Acquisition and Control of Marine Fishery Resources

The useful and clear survey of the problems does not call for extensive comment. As Professor Burke makes clear, the agreed goal is the maximum sustainable yield but the methods for preventing overfishing are not yet the subject of agreement. His preferred solution is the improvement of the existing regulatory system and the use of regional institutions. The present writer regards this as the realistic approach but feels that Professor Burke is not convincing when he rules out the "global authority" solution: there is no substantial reason for regarding any of the approaches as mutually exclusive and the creation of an international authority could remain as a long-term objective. It is probably the case that necessary basic research will not be pursued adequately except through an international agency not influenced by the short-term and domestic considerations which affect the work of national agencies.

Incidentally, is it correct to state (p. 63, n. 94) that the claims of Ecuador and Peru to 200 miles are claims to a territorial sea *tout court?* They may in fact be claims to fishery conversation zones: see Garcia Amador, *The Exploitation and Conservation of the Resources of the Sea,* 2nd ed., pp. 73–79.

III. Military Uses of the Continental Shelf and the Seabed Beyond

Professor Burke's examination of the various possible approaches to the question of military uses is most helpful but there is an unfortunate readiness to invoke the *fait accompli* to preclude a regime of demilitarization. Thus, at p. 91, Professor Burke states that proposals for complete demilitarization of the deep sea are not likely to be acceptable for the foreseeable future because the major maritime powers have started on programmes of military uses and are likely to be reluctant to discontinue such uses and the development of others. This reasoning is less than satisfactory and experience in other contexts has been that the *fait accompli* may in fact alert States generally to the *need* for a legal regime rather than the *a priori* non-feasibility of such a regime. Experience relating to the uses of outer space would seem to suggest that the "all or nothing" approach is not very practical, thus confirming some of Professor Burke's reservations, and yet the same experience might lead us to be rather less pessimistic about demilitarization than is Professor Burke. His tendency is to assume, without specific reasons, that the work concerning the "peaceful uses" concept in the context of Antarctica and Outer Space is not of real relevance. On the contrary, the work of the General Assembly's Committee on the Peaceful Uses of Outer Space has considerable relevance. At the least, it would be surprising to find that the major powers were able to overcome their inhibitions in relation to outer space but not in relation to the deep sea. The points about the value of the "unknown deterrent" surely apply with equal force (whatever force they may have) to both environments. Existing developments provide solutions to a number of the problems posed in the paper. Thus Professor Burke (p. 97) states that it would be singularly unfortunate if military installations for scientific research were sought to be prohibited as not being "exclusively for peaceful purposes." Yet the content of the Antarctic Treaty indicates (article 1) that this problem can be the subject of an appropriate formula. The distinction between "peaceful uses" and "military purpose" appears in the Statute of the International Atomic Energy Agency. It is also possible for a concept of peaceful uses to be reconcilable with a carefully defined right of self-defence: see further this writer, *British Year Book of International Law,* Vol. 40 (1964), p. 1 at pp. 15, 20–23.

With respect to the placing of military installations on the Continental Shelf (pp. 98–99, 110–112), Professor Burke implies that this is permitted by the Geneva Convention of 1958: but the text of the Convention itself does not provide a legal basis for this view (see Gutteridge, *British Year Book of International Law,* Vol. 35 (1959), p. 102 at p. 119) and Professor Burke does not provide a clear alternative legal basis.

In his discussion of nuclear testing, at p. 103, Professor Burke has this to say:

> There can be little, if any, doubt that the conservatism of the response to the Maltese recommendations stems in substantial measure from regard shared by many states, for their strategic implications for the maritime powers. States generally appeared to recognize both that the prior agreements on military use in Antarctica and outer space were possible precisely because the major powers were not militarily involved in these regions and that these powers were heavily engaged in the use of the ocean, including the seabed, for this purpose.

The present writer has serious reservations about these propositions. First, he doubts that the major powers were not militarily involved in outer space. Secondly, the experience concerning fishing zones and the three mile rule indicates that the major maritime powers do not always determine the course of developments. Thirdly, there is no presumption that the strategic implications for the maritime powers (viz., United States, U.S.S.R., and, perhaps, the United Kingdom and France) should be taken as a measure for community policies.

IV. Scientific Research in the Oceans

The writer was in general agreement with Professor Burke's position that there should be utmost freedom of access to the deep sea for purposes of scientific research, and wide promotion of scientific inquiry. His comments on the Continental Shelf Convention are most pertinent in this connection. Incidentally, in the context of the quotation relating to buoy technology and the territorial sea (pp. 124–125), the present writer finds it difficult to entertain the view that the coastal state is limited in its legal right to control scientific research by means of buoys. To suggest that scientific research functions as a solvent of well settled rules is going rather too far.

V. General Observations

1. Overall I would think that Professor Burke has successfully canvassed the problems but that, in canvassing solutions to the problems, he is rather too dogmatic in his attitude to the Antarctic and Outer Space materials. The Antarctic regime, of course, has its peculiarities, but it is a useful example of the type of localised regime which applies also in the context of fishery conservation. Such regimes may provide successful interim programmes and valuable experience. Moreover, certain legal problems may occur like those

raised by the Antarctic Treaty, in particular, the extent to which third states are affected.

2. The issue of prescriptive rights looms large if there is no success in creating a special legal regime.

3. The no-appropriation rule, as it appears in the Outer Space Treaty, does not preclude trouble over squatting and possessory rights: see Fawcett, *International Law and the Uses of Outer Space,* 1968, p. 27.

4. The subject matter needs to be related to the studies on activities harmful to the earth's environment: cp. David Davies Memorial Institute of International Studies, *Draft Rules Concerning Changes in the Environment of the Earth,* 1963.

5. Registration and rules of attribution and jurisdiction relating to vehicles and structures will be important short-term issues even if there is no agreement on "territorial" claims to the deep sea.

Wilbert McLeod Chapman

Ralston Purina Company, San Diego, California

Concerning Fishery Jurisdiction and the Regime of the Deep-sea Bed

The deep-sea bed and the resources attached to it, lying on it, and included in and under it, are probably *res communis,* although existing treaty law is far from clear on the point. If this statement is true then it bothers a good many people, and for a good many reasons.

There is no agreed definition as to what is meant by the term deep-sea bed, but it is pretty hard to define it in a manner that would mean it to comprise less than 80 per cent of the land underlying the ocean, or less than 60 per cent of the total surface area of the earth.[1]

To have such an extensive portion of the surface of the earth exist as a public common was not very disturbing to mankind as long as it could not be used by anybody for anything, but that is no longer the case. The deep-sea bed is being used presently for certain quite practical military purposes.[2] Minerals that are becoming increasingly useful to man are known to exist in enormous volume on the deep-sea bed[3] and there is conjecture that under its surface may be others of value. The technology of gathering mineral resources off the deep-sea bed no longer seems to be excessively formidable to acquire,[4] and that of gathering resources from below it no longer appears impossible of attainment.[5] Man has, in person, been to the very bottom of the ocean. The impediment to doing a considerable number of practical things there is chiefly economic, and economic values have a disturbing trait of changing rather rapidly.

The deep-sea bed thus is in the process of acquiring value. Its value for certain military purposes is already adequate to permit its economic use

---

[1] In "The Oceans", Sverdrup, Johnson and Fleming, Prentice-Hall, Inc., 1942, page 21 is given table of percentage area of depth zones in the ocean. In all oceans including the adjacent seas the percentage of area between 0–200 meters is given as 7.6%; between 200–1000, 4.3%; between 1000–2000, 4.2%; between 2000–3000, 6.8%, between 3000–4000, 19.6%; between 4000–5000, 33.0%; between 5000–6000, 23.3%; between 6000–7000, 1.1 %; and more than 7000 meters deep, 0.1 %.

[2] Frosch, R., Military Uses of the Sea, in Papers presented at the Second Conference on Law, Organization and Security in the Use of the Ocean, p. 4 (October, 1967).

[3] Brooks, D., Deep Sea Managanese Nodules From Scientific Phenomenon to World Resource. Proceedings of the Second Annual Law of the Sea Institute 26–29 June, 1967. Feb. 1968.

[4] Mero, J., The Mineral Resources of the Sea 1 (1965).

[5] Craven, J., Papers presented at the First Conference on Law, Organization and Security of the Ocean, 17–18 March, 1967.

for those purposes, and there is general consensus that it is only a matter of time (at least not more than another generation, and possibly only another decade) until its value for some civilian purposes will permit its economic use for those.

The nature of man abhors (as nature abhors a vacuum) something of value not being owned by an individual, or as groups of individuals organized into business, social, or political entities. To have such a large segment of the earth's surface emerging so rapidly from a condition of no value to a state of probable considerable value is likely to be a major disturbance to public order. In a world where the balance between public order and chaos is delicate (if not ephemeral) and in which technology is developed so highly that public chaos could, at the flick of a few switches, make the earth substantially less habitable, such a situation is not tenable. The problem must be solved. The question is only how and when.

Considerable progress has been made in the last few years in solving problems that seemed to be of a similar nature in two instances—Outer Space and Antarctica. As Professor Burke has pointed out, however, the resemblance between those two problems and that of the deep-sea bed are more superficial than real. The growing value of the deep-sea bed sets it apart from the other two in a fundamental manner.

A critical aspect of the deep-sea bed is that the value of its border is growing at an even more rapid pace than is the value of the deep-sea bed. The rapid strides of the petroleum industry out from the shoreline to the edge of the continents (and already slightly over the edge) is only one manifestation of this. The scientific problems related to man living and doing useful work for extended periods of time on bottom covered by at least 200 meters of water have been solved,[6] and the technical problems of him doing so are near enough to solution that they could be got in hand quickly if there were any urgent reason to do so. They are being worked at on a considerable scale now in several quarters.

Out to a depth of 200 meters (and perhaps a little beyond), therefore, the difference in reason for the land and the sea bed being owned or uniquely controlled is more economic and social than otherwise and is rapidly disappearing. This was recognized in the Convention on the Continental Shelf and the diplomatic and political actions antecedent to its development.

The crunch comes in the fact that there is no convenient or readily apparent physical, economic or political line one can draw on the bed of the

---

[6] National Academy of Sciences/National Research Council "Oceanography 1966 achievements and opportunities" a report of the Committee on Oceanography. Publ. 1492, Wn. D.C., 1967.

ocean which will separate the shallow bed of the margin of the ocean from the deep-sea bed in a manner that is agreeable to all.

The physical characteristics of the sea bed are such that the International Law Commission[7] and the 1958 Conference on the Law of the Sea could find no fully agreeable boundary to the continents adequately described by a physical criterion. The geologists and sea-faring people have long had the concept of the Continental Shelf as the rim around dry land covered by 200 meters or less of water. This was too crude a concept to be useful in the Law of the Sea for many reasons. In some places this shelf has large or numerous deep basins contained within it to the extent that such areas can only be described as continental border lands. In other places the continental mass begins to slope off sharply at substantially lesser or greater depth than 200 meters. In some places offshore sea mounts or guoyots rise to within 200 meters or less of the sea surface and are not connected to the continental mass, although they may be reasonably close to it. In some places the continental mass slopes off almost directly from dry land to the deep-sea bed, and in other places the 200 meter deep continental shelf extends out as much as 800 miles seaward of dry land.[8]

It is necessary in such a situation to make an arbitrary decision not related to any other criterion than simply that to which agreement can be had. As of the spring of 1958 the definition of the continental shelf which could be agreed to by the nations was: "the sea bed and sub-soil of the submarine areas adjacent to the coast but outside the area of the territorial sea, to a depth of 200 meters, or beyond that limit, to where the depth of the superjacent waters admits of the exploitation of the natural resources of the said areas." The same definition was applied to the sea bed and sub-soil of similar marine areas adjacent to the coasts of islands.[9]

Since the spring of 1958, science, technology, and the desires and needs of man have marched on at ever hastening pace. It is now generally understood that a very substantial part of the petroleum resources of the world (perhaps as much as half) underly the sea bed[10] and that there is at least a tendency for the petroleum in such fields to be concentrated toward the outer and deeper part of the area. It is uncertain that there are not large

[7] Report of the International Law Commission covering the work of its eight session, 23 April–4 July, 1956. General Assembly Official Records: Eleventh Session. Supplement No. 9 (A/3159) New York, 1956.
[8] Sverdrup, et al., loc. cit.
[9] Convention on the Continental Shelf in Treaties and other International agreements containing provisions on commercial fisheries, marine resources, sport fisheries, and wild life to which the United States is a party. Committee on Commerce, United States Senate, 89th Congress, 1st session, January, 1965.
[10] Fye, Emery, Maxwell and Ketchum, "Ocean Science and Marine Resources". In Uses of the Sea, the American Assembly, Columbia University, 1968 (in press, Prentice-Hall Inc.)

such resources even underlying the deep-sea bed, but that they may be very rich rather well down the continental slope is so certain that licenses to explore and drill for oil and gas in waters much deeper than 200 meters already have been given by nations. Thus the continental slope is in the process of being incorporated into the continental shelf of nations as defined above in the Convention on the Continental Shelf.

As science, technology and their application increase the depth of the superjacent waters which admits of the exploitation of such natural resources, the area and resources over which the coastal state has exclusive jurisdiction—which in practice is hardly distinguishable from sovereignty and ownership—marches steadily down the continental slope toward the deep-sea bed. There is no general geological feature on the continental slope at which the process is likely to halt. The foot of the shelf, where the deep-sea bed begins, is no more regular and clear-cut from a physical standpoint than is the 200 meter isobath edge of the geological continental shelf.

The 200 meter isobath has already lost its legal effectiveness in defining the edge of the continental shelf.[11] There are proponents of various points of depth below that, or various widths, or various combinations of the two measures, as a line at which to stop national encroachment into the purportedly international common. Each of these proposed new solutions suffer the precise fault of the continental shelf boundary recommended by the International Law Commission, and that finally incorporated into the Convention on the Continental Shelf. Any one of them, to be effective, must be agreed to by the nations.

If this agreement is to be reached in a Conference of Plenipotentiaries convened by the United Nations it must be by a two-thirds majority of the nations present and voting. No sovereign nation is likely to consider itself bound by such an agreement until it has adhered to a convention containing it. A resolution adopted in the General Assembly of the United Nations is unlikely to be of consequential effect on the actions of nations respecting jurisdiction over the use of the sea bed. There is no court of resort in such matters generally because most nations have not accepted the full jurisdiction of the International Court of Justice and there has been a general reluctance by nations to use it in Law of the Sea matters. Accordingly treaty law is what really counts. Nations do not like to renege on agreements made in treaties to which they have adhered.

A practical problem, then, is to get a sufficient number of sovereign nations to agree to a definition of the boundary between the edge of the continental shelf and the deep-sea bed so that the boundary will be accepted

---

[11] Henkin, Louis, "Law for the Sea's Mineral Resources", National Council on Marine Resources and Engineering Development, P.B. 177 725, December, 1967.

into international law and be considered by sovereign nations generally to represent constraints against their appropriating the use of the whole sea bed and its sub-soil to their exclusive and several jurisdictions.

It is only at this point that fishery jurisdiction becomes of much importance in establishing a suitable regime for the deep-sea bed. There is little fishing done anywhere on the sea bed at depths as great as 1000 meters; about 88 per cent of the ocean bed is covered by water deeper than that. Enough is known about the distribution of living resources in the ocean that one can predict with considerable confidence that none will be discovered at depths much greater than that which will be of sufficient value for nations to dispute about very vigorously.

Accordingly, if the sea bed issue can be separated from the superjacent water issue, and living resources pertaining to the sea bed and sub-soil be restricted "to sedentary species, that is to say, organisms which, at the harvestable stage, either are immobile on or under the sea bed or are unable to move except in constant physical contact with the sea bed or sub-soil",[12] then the regime of the sea bed can be settled on its own merits, and fishery jurisdiction issues would not need to be considered.

History gives no shred of advice that this separation of issues can be obtained; it gives, to the contrary, much evidence that it cannot.

Problems of fishery jurisdiction were tangled rather inextricably with the developing Law of the Sea and the relations of nations in Europe from at least the 14th century onward and in North America from the 17th century onward in the Atlantic, and from the early 19th century on in the Pacific. All of these activities were related to the liquid ocean, actions on it, and resources in it—not the sea bed (with the exception of oyster beds in the English Channel area).[13]

Although successful drilling for oil in shallow coastal waters (particularly in the Persian Gulf, the Gulf of Mexico, and off southern California) had begun somewhat earlier, it was toward the end of World War II that jurisdiction over the sea bed (aside from the sedentary fishery problem) became a substantial international issue. This was brought to something of a head by the President of the United States issuing two proclamations in September, 1945.[14] One dealt with the jurisdiction over the continental shelf and the other dealt with fishery conservation.

Although the United States had made extensive, and it thought adequate, diplomatic inquiry leading it to believe there would be substantial agree-

[12] Convention on the Continental Shelf, loc. cit.
[13] Heinzen, B. G. 1959 "The Three-Mile Limit in Preserving the Freedom of the Seas". Stanford Law Review, 11(4): 597–664.
[14] MacChesney, B. International law situations and documents, 1956. Navpers 15,031, vol. L1, Naval War College, Newport, Rhode Island, Govt. Printing Office, 1–629.

ment to the proposals contained in the Truman Proclamation respecting the continental shelf, the two issues (fishery jurisdiction and continental shelf jurisdiction) were immediately interwined in proclamations and claims forthcoming during the next few years from several countries in Latin America. The interaction over this confusion of objectives within the Organization of American States was active and by 1954 came very close to resulting in a majority decision at the 10th Inter-American Conference to couple ocean and sea bed into a joint 200 mile rule for the territorial sea for Latin America.

The International Law Commission had begun the study of the regime of the high seas at its first session in 1949. At its second session in 1950 it deliberately decided to deal with that subject fully and set aside consideration of other aspects of the Law of the Sea. At its third session in 1951 it decided to add to this the regime of the territorial sea as well, pursuant to General Assembly resolution 374 (IV). Work on these matters continued at its fourth session, and at its fifth session (1953) the Commission issued revised drafts of articles dealing with (1) continental shelf, (2) fisheries resources of the sea, and (3) the contiguous zone. It also broadened its study once more to deal with other aspects of the Law of the Sea that it had decided to lay aside at its second session.

In 1954 the United States submitted two proposals respecting the Law of the Sea to the General Assembly. One dealt with the continental shelf; and the U.S. rather confidently expected this to be acted on favorably without any considerable amount of interaction. The other was a proposal, in accordance with a suggestion from the International Law Commission, for an International Technical Conference on the Conservation of the Living Resources of the Seas to be convened by the United Nations. It confidently expected favorable action on this also. It expected the two issues to be kept separate and to be acted upon separately. The opposite happened.

A majority of the nations at the 1954 General Assembly were in favor of holding in abeyance action on any part of the Law of the Sea until the International Law Commission could present to it a draft covering the whole Law of the Sea. The reason for this, cogently put by the representative of Iceland, was that the Icelandic desires respecting extended fisheries jurisdiction would fare better in negotiations covering all aspects of the Law of the Sea than they would in negotiations concerned solely with fisheries jurisdiction. A sufficient number of nations held the same view to carry the vote. The General Assembly therefore resolved to ask the International Law Commission to give it a comprehensive study and report on all aspects of the Law of the Sea in one package.

With this decided the 1954 General Assembly voted to convene an International Technical Conference on the Conservation of the Living Resources of the Sea. This was held in Rome in the spring of 1955. Among the general conclusions of the Conference were these two:

81. It was the concensus of the Conference that it was not competent to express any opinion as to the appropriate extent of the territorial sea, the extent of the jurisdiction of the coastal state over fisheries, or the legal status of the superjacent waters of the continental shelf.

82. The question of the special interests, rights, duties and responsibilities of Coastal States in the matter of the conservation of the living resources of the sea was discussed in the Conference. The opinion of the Conference on these matters, and on the question as to whether the Conference was competent to consider them, was more or less evenly divided.[15]

In matter of fact these issues wracked the Conference from the day of its opening until its close. The decision expressed in paragraph 81 was taken by roll call vote which won by a margin of one vote and resulted in the Vice-Chairman of the Conference resigning with a ringing speech of dissent and leaving the Conference with the delegate of another nation. Of the nations left to the end of the Conference three filed reservations as a result of this vote.

At its seventh session the International Law Commission submitted various articles on the Law of the Sea (including the conservation of fisheries) to member nations for comment and after examining replies from twenty-five Governments it drew up its final report on the Law of the Sea at its eighth session (1956) and submitted it to the General Assembly. In doing so it said:

28. The Commission therefore recommends, in conformity with article 23, paragraph 1 (d) of its statute, that the General Assembly should summon an international conference of plenipotentiaries to examine the law of the sea, *taking account of the legal but also the technical, biological, economic and political aspects of the problem,* and to embody the results of its work in one or more international conventions or such other instruments as it may deem appropriate.

29. The Commission is of the opinion that the conference should deal with various parts of the law of the sea covered by the present report. *Judging from its own experience, the Commission considered—and the comments of Governments have confirmed this view—that the various sections of the law of the sea hold together, and are so closely interdependent that it would be extremely difficult to deal with only one part and leave the others aside"* (italics supplied).[16]

[15] Report of the International Technical Conference on the Conservation of the Living Resources of the Sea, 18 April to 10 May, 1955, Rome. United Nations A/conf. 10/6.
[16] International Law Commission, 1956, loc. cit.

The extensive debates on this issue in the 1957 General Assembly[17] substantiated the Commission's view that the various aspects of the Law of the Sea were so interrelated that they required to be considered together. Pursuant to the resolution then adopted the requested Law of the Sea Conference was held in Geneva in the spring of 1958. Most member nations of the United Nations (including land-locked ones) attended. Four comprehensive conventions were adopted (Convention on the High Seas, Convention on the Territorial Sea and Contiguous Zone, Convention on Fishing and Conservation of the Living Resources of the High Seas, and Convention on the Continental Shelf). Two key issues were left unresolved: (a) the breadth of the territorial sea, and (b) the jurisdiction by coastal States over fisheries lying in the high seas.

The fishery issue threatened the success of all four substantive committees of the Conference.[18] Committee Four (dealing with the Continental Shelf) finally got rid of this issue, so it could proceed with its work, by adopting the above noted definition of living resources of the sea bed and sub-soil. It was able to do this not by a margin of even one vote, but because a motion to include shrimp and demersal fishes as resources of the sea bed drew a tie vote and therefore failed of passage. Committee Three (dealing with fisheries) got rid of the issue by referring the breadth of the territorial sea and jurisdiction over fisheries in the high seas to Committee One (the Political Committee). It could then proceed to the satisfactory conclusion of its other very delicate work. Committee Two (dealing with the territorial sea and contiguous zone) did the same. Committee One was not able to come to agreement on these two issues or to separate them, because the fishery interests of the nations could not be composed into a form of words that would attract a two-thirds vote on these two issues together or separately.

After extensive debate in the ensuing General Assembly a second conference on the Law of the Sea was convened in 1960 to consider only these two remaining issues: breadth of the territorial sea, and jurisdiction over fisheries lying in the high seas. The second conference, like the first, became a rather straight-out diplomatic confrontation between the U.S.S.R. and U.S.A., with both prepared to sublimate their fishing interests to what each considered to be its supervening national posture needs respecting the Law of the Sea. Neither could persuade enough allies to subjugate their

[17] Verbatim record of the debate in the Sixth Committee of the General Assembly at its eleventh session, relating to agenda item 53(a), United Nations Conference on the Law of the Sea, A/Conf. 13/19, 3 December, 1967).
[18] United Nations Conference on the Law of the Sea. Official records, Seven volumes, A/Conf. 13/37, Geneva, 24 February–27 April 1958.

fishery interests to the general cause for any proposal to win the necessary two-thirds majority on any proposal dealing with the breadth of the territorial sea or fishery jurisdiction in the high seas, although the United States came within one abstention of doing so at the end in 1960.

An essential point to remember is that the two Law of the Sea Conferences did not resolve the issue of fishery jurisdiction or satisfy those rather numerous nations which felt that they had special fisheries needs. These countries ranged in special need from Iceland (which felt wholly dependent on the yield from its fisheries and wanted to exclude all foreign fishermen from the area of its continental shelf), to Japan (which felt itself critically dependent on the yield of its fisheries both nutritionally and economically and wanted its fishermen to be able to fish anywhere in the high seas). This range of interest in fisheries still exists among the nations.

In the eleven years since the 1958 Conference on the Law of the Sea ended there have been many strong changes in the situation surrounding the voting that took place then. Among these are:

1. Keflavik airport in Iceland is not so vitally important to the NATO alliance as it was then.

2. The political polarization between U.S.S.R. and U.S.A. is not so distinct as it was then, and neither can be quite as sure of voting support on all issues by friendly nations as they could then.[19]

3. A mutual understanding of the awful consequences of nuclear warfare is much clearer than it was in 1958, leaving an impelling desire not to let confrontations arise to be faced on other than the most vital issues.[19]

4. The nuclear powered (and weaponed) submarine, by taking advantage of the opacity of the ocean, has induced at least a temporary strategic stalemate that did not exist so clearly in 1958.[19]

5. The world catch of fish and shellfish in 1958 was 33.2 million metric tons and in 1966 (the last year of record) 56.8. It was higher in 1967, and will be higher in 1968 than in 1967. This rapidly increasing fishing pressure is causing a whole range of new fishery jurisdiction problems as well as exacerbating many of those existing in 1958.[20]

6. U.S.S.R. has doubled its fish and shellfish catch from 2.6 million metric

[19] MacDonald, Gordon J. F. "The Oceans—An American View", Uses of the Sea, the American Assembly, Columbia University, 1968, Prentice-Hall, Inc.
[20] Jackson, R. I. "Trends in World Fisheries". Fisheries News International, London, 6(7): 20–27.

tons in 1958 to 5.4 in 1966[21] (5.7 in 1967). Its fishing vessels now operate on a fully world-wide scale and it is working consciously and vigorously toward another doubling of its catch. This enormous increase in fishing effort is a major force in fishery jurisdiction problems. The fishing interest of U.S.S.R. was strong in 1958. It is much stronger in 1968 and less easy to submerge in other U.S.S.R. interests.

7. Japan has increased its catch from 5.5 million metric tons in 1958 to 7.1 in 1966[21] (7.7 in 1967) and its fishing vessels now fish on a world-wide basis, contributing in a major way (with U.S.S.R.) to growing high seas fishing pressure.

8. Nations that in 1958 were not considered long range fishers have become so and are increasing in number and effort. Among these are South Korea, Taiwan, Greece, Spain, Italy, Kuwait, Israel, Yugoslavia, Poland, East Germany, Bulgaria, Roumania. On a lesser, but developing, scale are Ghana, Senegal, Thailand, Mexico and Canada.

9. The members of the United Nations were 81 in number at the end of 1958[22] and 122 in 1967.[23]

10. The interest of the whole world has been attracted steadily toward the ocean in the last decade.[24] A measure of this is that the U.S. Federal budget for its "National Oceanographic Program" increased by a factor of nearly 10 in the decade after 1958[25] and is still increasing.[26] Other nations (especially U.S.S.R.) have increased their ocean research efforts substantially also. There has been an International Oceanographic Commission in UNESCO since 1960 and it is in the process presently of being strengthened materially. Fishery development and conservation within the United Nations family has been enormously strengthened, particularly through support of U.N. Special Fund since 1958 through FAO, and the reorganization of FAO's fishery work into a Department of Fisheries since 1965. Sea-air interaction research has taken on a new dimension internationally through the World Meteorological Organization. It is not ridiculous to say that man

---

[21] Food and Agriculture of the United Nations Yearbook of Fishery Statistics, 1966, vol. 22.
[22] Every man's United Nations, United Nations, New York, 1959.
[23] Reader's Digest 1968 Almanac and Yearbook, Pleasantville, New York.
[24] "Effective Use of the Sea" Report of the Panel on Oceanography, President's Science Advisory Committee, The White House, June, 1966.
[25] "Marine Science Affairs—A Year of Transition". The First Report of the President to the Congress on Marine Resources and Engineering Development, February, 1967.
[26] "Marine Science Affairs—A Year of Plans and Progress". The second report of the President to the Congress on Marine Resources and Engineering Development, March, 1968.

has learned more about the ocean, its processes, and its resources since 1958 than he had learned about them to that time.

11. The political climate within the United Nations has changed markedly since 1958 with the proliferation of newly independent countries and their induction to membership. As shown in the UNCTAD conference in 1964, and others more recently, these nations of the developing world are quite capable of seizing political initiative in the U.N. on subjects in which the developing world is broadly interested, and not relinquishing it to the great powers or to the affluent nations. The developing world is broadly interested in fishery development and in fishery jurisdiction.

12. The issue of exclusive jurisdiction over fisheries by the coastal state in a zone contiguous to its territorial sea and extending (with the territorial sea) to a distance of 12 miles from the inland waters boundary was one of the most profoundly disturbing issues at both the 1958 and 1960 Law of the Sea conferences. This issue has been pretty well settled by the practice of nations in the intervening years. At least 62 nations now claim a 12 mile breadth for their territorial sea or exclusive jurisdiction over fisheries within 12 miles of their coast.[27] This (as predicted[28]) has had no material effect in reducing fishery jurisdiction problems. At least 12 nations now claim more than 12 miles for territorial sea breadth or exclusive fishery jurisdiction.

A consideration of the effect of these twelve factors (and perhaps some others) on the attitude of nations as they vote on issues respecting the Law of the Sea in the General Assembly, or other forums of the United Nations, must weigh heavily in decisions reached on methods to be used in modifying existing Law of the Sea through United Nations action.

A lesson from the Truman Proclamations, and from the 1958 and 1960 conferences, is that if one nation raises an issue it wants settled by change in law other nations are likely to raise issues they want changed that are inimical to the original. They may have the votes to win. It is the old story of Pandora's box. If the lid is raised things are likely to fly out that may not be wanted, and that may be hard to control.

U.S.S.R. and U.S.A. are much closer together on several aspects of the Law of the Sea in 1968 than they were in 1958 or 1960. In the two previous Law of the Sea conferences each side was able to muster a one-third blocking vote against most proposals brought by the other that it seriously did

---

[27] "Commercial Fisheries Review" vol. 30, no. 4. April, 1968. Bureau of Commercial Fisheries, Department of the Interior.
[28] Chapman, W. M. "The Theory and Practice of the Twelve Mile Fishery Limit". Proceedings of the Sixteenth Annual Session of the Gulf and Caribbean Fisheries Institute, November, 1963.

not want adopted. This is probably the case also in 1968. A more serious question existing in 1968 is whether U.S.S.R. and U.S.A. working together can muster a two-thirds vote to secure the adoption of a proposal not wanted by a considerable segment of developing nations—such as confining a new Law of the Sea Conference to a consideration of problems of the sea bed. This is very doubtful. More nations are interested in fishery jurisdiction matters than was the case during the 1950's when it was impossible to consider continental shelf problems in U.N. forums separately from the fishery jurisdiction issues. Everybody talks about oil riches, but fish and shellfish are still the most valuable product taken from the ocean. In 1964 the value of fish and shellfish catch at the fisherman's level was $6.4 billion; for petroleum from the sea, $3.8 billion; and for minerals $0.3 billion. In 1966 the value of the world catch of fish and shellfish was about $9.0 billion.[29]

Another relevant question is whether U.S.S.R. and U.S.A., as the outstanding elements in the world power structure, can muster a one-third blocking vote against a proposal brought by the developing countries that they jointly do not want adopted. The record of the UNCTAD conferences gives pause for thought. While a good many proposals of this sort could be thought of, a few may be listed by way of examples.

One of the main drives behind internationalizing control of the use of the deep-sea bed has been to provide the United Nations in the long run with funds independent from voluntary member contributions.[30] It is not at all certain that the U.N. members now providing most of the funding want the U.N. to have substantial funding independent from them or that they could block such a proposal brought before a general conference of plenipotentiaries dealing with ocean affairs.

To take a more delicate matter, the whereabouts of nuclear powered submarines is hard to discover after they have gone beneath the surface of the sea and until they surface again, which may be weeks later and on the other side of the world. It would be technically possible to have each such vessel deep in instant touch with a recording computer under U.N. control (through the voluntary action of each such vessel's sovereign) so that its whereabouts could be known in real time. It is doubtful that the owners of such vessels would desire such a registry system to be installed, and if such a proposal came forward in such a conference stopping its adoption might be embarrassing, if not difficult.

[29] Jackson, R. I., May, 1968, Personal communication of FAO data. Two tables are given in which values of estimates arrived at by different means of calculation are set out.
[30] Louis Henkin, "Changing Law for the Changing Seas" Uses of the Sea, the American Assembly, Columbia University, 1968, Prentice-Hall, Inc.

A more realistic third such proposal might be to put all fishing on the high seas under control of the United Nations.[31] The ramifications of such a proposal, including limiting entry into such fisheries, might have grave consequences to the national economics and nutrition of several large countries. Whether they could muster a one-third blocking vote against such a proposal if they desired to do so is a moot question.

A fourth very serious question is just what sort of regime would best serve man's interest for management of the use of the natural resources of the deep-sea bed. Not much is really known yet about their distribution or the means of practically bringing them to use.[32] It is not much more clear now than it was when the International Law Commission considered the issue last (in 1956) what regime other than the exploitability and adjacency criteria it then adopted would be agreeable to the nations, or more desirable. A question does arise as to whether the putative economic interests of a few large petroleum and mining firms is of sufficient importance to the world to move hastily in framing new law touching upon so many delicate aspects of world public order.

If the history of dealing with international aspects of the use of the sea over the past twenty years has anything to teach, it is that problems of this sort and complexity cannot be dealt with satisfactorily in the political atmosphere of the United Nations and, particularly, the General Assembly. The issue of a regime for the deep-sea bed now stands at about the position the issue of a regime for the continental shelf stood in 1947 (when the United Nations was very new). Experience then was that this issue could not be settled separately from other issues related to the whole body of the Law of the Sea. These other issues, and it, had to be removed from the political arenas of the General Assembly to technical bodies (the International Law Commission, the International Technical Conference on the Conservation of the Living Resources of the Sea, several particular advisory bodies, and finally two conferences of plenipotentiaries) before they could be dealt with effectively. This process took a full ten years. At every phase it was interfered with by the issue of fishery jurisdiction on the high seas, and in the end this issue was not sufficiently resolved to insure its stability.

In the intervening decade a whole army of new technical bodies has arisen, or been perfected, in the international field capable of providing technical advice and assistance to the world community in dealing with the technical

[31] Christy, F. T. and A. Scott, "The Common Wealth in Ocean Fisheries". The Johns Hopkins Press, Baltimore, Maryland, 1965.
[32] Walthier, T. N. "Remarks on the Mining of Deep Ocean Mineral Deposits" The Future of the Sea's Resources. Proceedings of the Second Annual Conference of the Law of the Sea Institute, 26–29 June, 1967, University of Rhode Island, Kingston, Rhode Island.

aspects of the exceedingly complex problems related to the improved utilization of the ocean and its management. These include:[33]

1. The Intergovernmental Oceanographic Commission of UNESCO, which has lead agency role in the United Nations family for oceanographic research. Its International Global Ocean Station System (IGOSS) will be an important factor in this whole array of problems. It has working parties actively considering technical aspects of the Law of the Sea as they affect scientific activities on the sea, the mooring of fixed buoys and stations, etc. It relates several aspects dealing with ocean pollution to work among other international bodies.

2. The Department of Fisheries of FAO, which has lead agency role in the United Nations family for fishery development and management. Its Committee on Fisheries, *inter alia,* advises FAO with respect to growing conservation problems in high seas fisheries and means to deal with them. Related organically to FAO Department of Fisheries are the Indo-Pacific Fisheries Council, the General Fisheries Council of the Mediterranean, the Regional Fisheries Advisory Commission for the Southwest Atlantic (CARPAS), together with new bodies in the process of establishment for the Indian Ocean and for the East Central Atlantic Ocean. It works in particularly close relationship with the International Council for the Exploration of the Seas, the North East Atlantic Fisheries Commission, and the International Commission for the Northwest Atlantic Fisheries. It will have a special relationship with the International Commission for Atlantic Tuna and with a new intergovernmental body in the process of forming for the South East Atlantic Fisheries. It is engaged in fishery development projects and studies throughout the developing world supported by U.S. Development Program and International Bank for Reconstruction and Development (IBRD).

3. The World Meteorological Organization has lead agency role in the United Nations family with respect to atmospheric matters. Its World Weather Watch and Global Atmospheric Research Program (GARP) bring it in ever closer relationship with IOC and FAO Department of Fisheries. It deals with the legal problems related to fixed observation stations in the sea, as does IOC.

4. The Intergovernmental Maritime Consultative Organization (IMCO) has purview over international maritime matters and particular responsibilities under treaty in respect of oil pollution.

5. There are three advisory bodies of scientists acting in their capacity as

[33] Second Report of the President, op. cit. supra note 26.

individuals that have broad and active marine responsibilities. These are the Advisory Committee of WMO, the Advisory Committee on Marine Resources Research (ACMRR), of FAO, and the Scientific Committee on Ocean Research (SCOR) of the International Council of Scientific Unions. The latter two are designated as official advisory bodies of IOC.

6. The Division of Resources and Transportation of the Economic and Social Council of U.N. has purview over assisting nations in the development of the resources of the sea bed and sub-soil within their jurisdiction.

7. The International Labor Organization, the World Health Organization, and the International Atomic Energy Agency have special responsibilities respecting international ocean affairs dealing with safety at sea, pollution, etc.

8. The Sub-Committee on Oceanography of the Administrative Coordination Committee of ECOSOC relates together the ocean activities of the specialized agencies of the U.N. family.

9. There are a number of intergovernmental fisheries commissions established under treaty among nations, and not organically related to the United Nations family, that have responsibility respecting particular fisheries. These include: Inter-American Tropical Tuna Commission, North Pacific Fur Seal Commission, International North Pacific Fisheries Commission, Northwest Pacific Fisheries Commission, International Pacific Salmon Fisheries Commission, International Pacific Halibut Commission, International Commission for the Northwest Atlantic Fisheries, North East Atlantic Fisheries Commission, South East Pacific Commission, Black Sea Fisheries Commission and the International Whaling Commission.

10. There are a number of intergovernmental organizations established outside the United Nations structure having other specific responsibilities respecting particular international ocean affairs. These include: International Hydrographic Bureau, International Council for the Exploration of the Sea, Permanent International Association of Navigation Congresses, North Atlantic Treaty Organization, Organization for Economic Cooperation and Development, International Commission for the Scientific Exploration of the Mediterranean Sea, Central Treaty Organization, South Pacific Commission, Colombo Plan Council for Technical Cooperation in South and Southeast Asia, Organization of American States, Inter-American Development Bank, Pan American Health Organization.

The proliferation in the last few years of international, intergovernmental, and non-governmental organizations, bodies and agencies dealing with particular or general aspects of international marine affairs is astounding. The above listing is not intended to be comprehensive. At least twenty-five non-governmental organizations of greater or less importance have been left out. Most of this total volume of organizations of all sorts have been brought into being during the past twenty years while the Law of the Sea has been under such active consideration, and a large number of them are new since the 1960 Conference on the Law of the Sea ended. It is increasingly difficult to see how the multiplicity of interests in the ocean which they represent can be attended to by consideration on a very narrow legal ground of any change whatever in the Law of the Sea.

The great enthusiasm that international activities in and around the ocean have stimulated came to an abrupt head in 1966 when the General Assembly adopted resolution 2172 (XXI) (Resources of the Sea). This requested the Secretary-General to make a comprehensive survey of what was going on about the ocean in the world and make proposals as to what should be done about it. This had an electrifying effect on the ocean community and great activity has ensued, upon which the Secretary-General will report to the General Assembly in 1968. It is expected that he will make some far-reaching proposals.

In the following year (1967) the General Assembly took even more vigorous continuing action by adopting resolution 2340 (XXII) (Examination of the Question of the Reservation Exclusively for Peaceful Purposes of the Sea-bed and the Ocean Floor, and the Subsoil Thereof, Underlying the High Seas Beyond the Limits of Present National Jurisdiction, and the Use of Their Resources in the Interests of Mankind).[34] The extensive debates that took place during the activities leading toward this action were most illuminating as being the first extensive reflection of national attitudes respecting the Law of the Sea since the end of the 1960 Conference. It was noteworthy that, in general, the tensions then existing were still reflected in the 1967 debates. It seemed obvious from them and the action taken by the General Assembly that no precipitate action is going to be taken in this field.

Resolution 2340 established an *ad hoc* committee to cover substantially the same grounds that resolution 2172 had asked the Secretary-General to cover, with particular reference to the sea floor but taking into consideration also the results of activities already under way under resolution 2172 and ECOSOC resolution 112 (XL), as well as documentation to be provided

[34] See Annex, p. 211. For discussions preceeding the adoption of the resolution see "Examination of the question of the reservation exclusively for peaceful purposes of the sea-bed and the ocean floor, and the subsoil thereof, underlying the high seas beyond the limits of present national jurisdiction, and the use of their resources in the interests of mankind," provisional verbatim record of the 1515–1530 meetings of the First Committee, 22nd session, 1–16 November, 1967, General Assembly, United Nations, New York.

by the specialized agencies of the United Nations having particular responsibilities in ocean affairs.

This is an enormous and complex task. The *ad hoc* committee is also supposed to report to the 1968 General Assembly (twenty-third session). It obviously will not be able to produce a comprehensive report in that length of time. It met first in March, 1968, and did nothing more than divide into two sub-committees (each having a representative from each nation comprising the full committee), one of which will deal with the legal aspects of the problems involved and the other of which will deal with the economic aspects. Neither can proceed very far until it gets materials from the U.N. Secretariat working on resolution 2172 and ECOSOC resolution 112 (XL). These two committees intend meeting during the summer of 1968 so as to have some preliminary materials to present to the full *ad hoc* committee before the General Assembly begins in September.

The assessment of all of this activity about the ocean during the past two or three years that can be made from the debates (note 34) leading to the adoption of resolution 2340 (XL), and the activity of national delegations both in and outside the inaugural meeting of the *ad hoc* committee it established, is that the bloom is gone from the rose. The near-hysteria that flooded the international ocean scene at the end of 1966 after the largely unanticipated passage of resolution 2172 has subsided. The enthusiasm that existed in some quarters at the beginning of 1967 for holding another full dress Law of the Sea conference has tapered off. Extensive diplomatic inquiries have indicated such a mixture of views that thought is being given to the old axiom which states that a meeting should never be held until one is reasonably sure what will be decided at it. There is some feeling growing that even if the Law of the Sea as reflected in the four conventions resulting from the 1958 Conference is faulty in some respects, a new conference might produce results that would be even less conducive to public order on the ocean.

Essentially the nations have come face to face with the hard reality of complex international problems arising from increased use of the ocean and found them not easy to deal with. It is obvious that what will now result is a sober, detailed, comprehensive examination of this whole field of problems on a technical level before elements are sorted out that will lend themselves to political or legal treatment. This is probably all for the best as it will draw attention to real problems arising from the increased use of the ocean, as contrasted to those raised by publicists involved in grinding an ax for some special interest, and lead to appropriate activities being eventually recomended for attending to them. Time constants in the international agency field are rather large.

One of the most positive results of this U.N. activity about the sea to date has been a consideration of the scientific implications of resolution 2172 by a Joint Working Party of ACMRR/SCOR/WMO(A.C.). After a detailed report of its examination of the field it made a series of nine recommendations divided into three time phases. They are:

A. *Immediate Actions*

1. that joint working parties on matters of mutual concern be appointed by SCOR, ACMRR and WMO(A.C.).

2. that there be small combined meetings as necessary, on questions of mutual concern, of representatives appointed for the purpose by IOC, the Committee of Fisheries of FAO, and WMO, with participation of such other organizations as are concerned with the questions to be discussed, e.g., the United Nations itself (including UNDP), IMCO, IAEA, IHB, IBRD, etc.

3. that a joint secretariat to deal with questions of common concern be appointed from the secretariats of IOC and/or the Office of Oceanography of UNESCO, of the FAO (Department of Fisheries) and of WMO.

4. that appropriate funds be allocated for the above purposes by the organizations concerned.

B. *Actions to be taken as soon as possible, preferably within the next two years*

5. that at the fifth session of IOC, to be held in October, 1967, consideration be given to the establishment of a budget with funds contributed by the Member States of IOC in accordance with the normal U.N. formula, in an amount sufficient to make a start on the questions of data and information handling, collection and dissemination of oceanographic intelligence, development of standards and intercalibration of methods, and others urgently requiring international action.

6. that provided such an operating budget is established, the staff and services available to the IOC be appropriately expanded by joint action of UNESCO, IOC, FAO, and other interested organizations, it being understood that this may necessitate appropriate changes in the statutes of IOC.

7. that consideration be given to the designation of appropriate international scientific and technical organizations, such as ICSU or its subsidiary bodies, as scientific advisers to the Department of Fisheries, FAO and to the ocean activities of WMO, while retaining the financial support by these agencies of bodies in which scientists act in their individual capacities.

8. that the most urgent consideration be given to an adequate increase in the proportion of the budgets of international agencies devoted to oceanic questions.

C. *Long-term Action*

9. that the member governments of the United Nations family and the various United Nations agencies give early and thorough consideration to the advisability and feasibility of establishing a central intergovernmental oceanic organization to deal with all aspects of ocean investigations and the uses of the sea.[35]

[35] "International Ocean Affairs, A Special Report" Scientific Committee on Oceanic Research, International Council of Scientific Unions, 1 September 1967, La Jolla, California.

Considering the rather far-reaching nature of these recommendations, fairly good progress is being made toward their implementation. Some are moving in the agencies, some are forming parts of the Secretary-General's recommendations to the General Assembly under resolution 2172,[36] and some are being formed into action programs of principal U.N. members. Particularly needed is adequate funding of these international undertakings and the establishment of the central intergovernmental ocean organization foreseen in recommendation 9 so that thrust and force can be given to these international oceanic undertakings.

It is likely that progress on these fundamental underpinnings of international oceanic affairs will have a more far-reaching beneficial effect on the public order of the ocean than will endless legal discussion and political interactions over the Law of the Sea. It is only as knowledge and understanding of the ocean, its resources, its processes, its bed and sub-soil, and the flow of energy through the heat-engine that the ocean and atmosphere comprise is accumulated that wise and mutually agreeable rules for the management of the use of the ocean and its resources can be contrived.

Summary and Conclusions

On the basis of the above comments the following summary and conclusions are made:

1. The deep-sea bed comprises at least 80 per cent of the land surface underlying the ocean and 60 per cent of the surface area of the earth. As far as it falls within a regime of law it is the common property of all nations.

2. The deep-sea bed is in the process rather rapidly of acquiring value. In consequence there are strong moves afoot to assign ownership or jurisdiction over it to a more finite entity than humanity at large.

3. The development of a regime for the deep-sea bed can scarcely be accomplished until the outer boundary of the continental shelf of present law is determined more precisely than by the exploitability and adjacency criteria of current law.

4. There is no clear-cut physical feature that can be used for such a boundary. The boundary must be a term of art agreed to by the nations to have validity in law. It is likely that such a boundary could be agreed to if the matter could be approached by negotiation on its own merits without being tangled up with other aspects of the Law of the Sea.

[36] "Marine Science and Technology: Survey and Proposals", Report of the Secretary-General, United Nations Economic and Social Council, E/4487, 24 April 1968 (see Annex, p. 214).

5. The history of the Law of the Sea over the past twenty years indicates rather strongly that the outer boundary of the continental shelf cannot be determined separately outside the context of the technical, biological, economic and political, as well as the legal, aspects of the entire Law of the Sea.

6. There is no direct connection between fishery jurisdiction and the deep-sea bed, as there are no living resources of consequence on the deep-sea bed. Fishery jurisdiction questions do not fit into any reasonable scope of discussion about the legal questions of the deep sea. Nevertheless it can be predicted with some certainty that the regime of the deep-sea bed cannot be settled without involving quite fully questions dealing with jurisdiction over fisheries lying in the high seas, as was the case with all parts of the 1958 and 1960 Law of the Sea conferences.

7. The key question in dealing with the regime of the deep-sea bed is whether it can be dealt with separately on its own merits. This seems unlikely. If considering it involves opening the entire question of the Law of the Sea, is the probable gain from the standpoint of public order on the ocean likely to be greater than the loss at the present period of time? The debates and actions of the nations surrounding resolution 2340 (XL) of the 1967 General Assembly indicates that the nations are unsure on this question.

8. International, intergovernmental and non-governmental international activity respecting the ocean and its use has increased enormously in volume and complexity since the 1958 Conference on the Law of the Sea. Pursuant to resolution 2172 of the 1966 General Assembly, the Secretary-General is making a survey of what international ocean activity is going on in the world and making proposals on it to the 1968 General Assembly.

9. The strong thrust by some nations in the 1967 General Assembly to establish by resolution a radically new regime for the deep-sea bed which would internationalize it was blunted or broken into a resolution establishing an *ad hoc* committee to examine all aspects of the question. This committee cannot really begin its work until the Secretary-General reasonably well completes his study and reports under resolution 2172 of the 1966 General Assembly, and until it can receive and digest documentation on the subject from the specialized agencies involved. This appears to be a hopeless thing to achieve before the 1968 General Assembly and undoubtedly the *ad hoc* committee will require an extension of time. Otherwise nothing fruitful is likely to come from its deliberations.

10. No great harm should result from this delay. There is no wealth on

the deep-sea bed to be divided among the developing nations; wealth must be created. It will be some years before any revenue to anyone is likely to come from the deep-sea bed, and it is likely to be a generation before this is of sufficient size to bother with. A more appropriate division of the social surplus among the nations should neither await this slow development nor expect to be much aided by it. Only two, and at most five, nations have the technical and economic capability to use the deep-sea bed in the reasonably near future for military purposes likely to disturb public order, and their warlike activities are more apparent and as easily controllable by others in the air and on the surface as they are on the bottom. The only real control available is public opinion pressure and that is no more easily applied in the hidden reaches of the deep than it is in broad daylight where every man can see.

11. In the meantime there is much work to be done in the technical, scientific, biological and political fields before major progress can be anticipated in the legal aspects of ocean affairs. In particular it is necessary to accumulate much more knowledge and understanding of the ocean, its resources, its processes, its bed and subsoil, and the flow of energy between air and water before new rules for the management of the use of the ocean and its resources can be contrived that are much more wise or more agreeable than the ones we have.

12. The Joint Working Party of ACMRR/SCOR/AMO(A.C.) on resolution 2172 (Resources of the Sea) produced a series of recommendations that, if vigorously implemented, would have far-reaching beneficial effects on the public order of the ocean by providing the nations with the knowledge and understanding they need to illuminate their path toward a more full and happy use of the ocean.

Claude Girard

Captain (rtd), French Navy

Military Uses of the Continental Shelf and the Seabed Beyond

Mr. William T. Burke, Professor of Law, has prepared a remarkable study on the "Contemporary Legal Problems in Ocean Development" for the Stockholm International Peace Research Institute. This very detailed study explains and discusses in particular the various points of view and opinions of the people interested in these matters whose ideas tend to establish or perfect the rules of International Law in this respect, in which the interest of Man has only recently arisen.

The aim of this paper, which will cover the legal problems of the ocean from the point of view of Military Uses only, is to establish, from these ideas and opinions, an international regime which takes into account what has been done and what will be done in the near future in the military field.

I. Historical Background

The International Law concerning the regulations applying to the sea was constituted in the course of history according to rules issuing from the application of the basic principle: respect of the freedom of the seas.

In order to satisfy some particular and definite requirements, exceptions to this principle were necessary: in particular, the recognition in favor of the Coastal State of sovereignty rights on an area of three nautical miles in order to assure the security of the Coastal State along its coasts.

Sovereignty rights were conferred upon Coastal States for the following reasons:

- They are required to assure its security.
- The Coastal State can enforce these rights: the distance of three nautical miles from the coast was chosen arbitrarily, but, in fact, represented about the maximum range of the gunnery based on shore.

The principle of the freedom of the seas was, however, prevalent. It was applied whenever reasonable security requirements allowed it. Thus, within this area of three nautical miles, called "territorial waters", the Coastal State must not impede the passage of an innocent ship.

So the seas—about 70 per cent of the surface of the globe—were free. Each State could avail itself of this freedom lawfully if this right were used reasonably, taking into account the interests of the other States, which had the same right in accordance with the same principle.

It must be mentioned that in certain specific cases, in which problems arise from geographical and political conditions, treaties are signed, for instance "Convention des Détroits", in order to reconcile the requirements of the security of the Coastal State and the application of the principle of the freedom of the seas.

It might be useful to stress that some restrictions have been made regarding the principle of freedom of the seas by the exercising of certain special rights beyond "territorial waters": in the case of fisheries, in particular, these rights exist either because they originate in time-old custom or in order to protect fishermen, nationals of the Coastal State. This point has been treated in another chapter of Professor Burke's study.

The principle of freedom was applied, roughly, to the surface of the sea only, for as far as the penetration of the ocean was concerned, it was necessary to solve a number of problems:
- The techniques for penetration were still in an infant stage.
- The environment is physiologically hostile and Man required an appropriate training which needed to be studied and perfected in order to enter into this environment.

As the price to be paid for the penetration of the seas was too high, compared to the advantages one could reasonably expect, Man was little interested in exploration, other than for scientific curiosity or love of risk.

It was, then, unnecessary to seek solutions to legal problems regarding the ocean, the seabed, etc., for the simple reason that interest was lacking. Everything was therefore relatively simple.

II. Recent Developments

Quite recently, a change has taken place: the will of Man to exploit resources and principally to extract oil from wells dug at the bottom of the ocean has been aided and promoted by the development of technology.

At present, Man can see underwater (photography and underwater television); he can work underwater, manually at a depth which is still limited but assuredly greater than before; he can at last consider the use of nuclear power, which, because of its compatibility with the marine environment, opens all sorts of perspectives, both economic and military.

This appreciable increase in the possibilities of penetration of the marine environment has led the States to agree on certain rules or regulations contained in the Conventions of 1958.

It is to be pointed out that, while these Conventions include regulations to be applied to the different sections to be taken in consideration—that is, internal waters, territorial waters and contiguous zone; Continental Shelf; High Seas—the said Conventions only stress that:

a. the contiguous zone adjacent to territorial waters cannot extend beyond 12 nautical miles from the reference line for measuring the width of the territorial waters,

b. the Coastal State has sovereign rights over the Continental Shelf in order to explore it and to exploit its natural resources. The term "Continental Shelf" is used to designate: (1) the seabed and the underlying medium of submerged regions adjacent to the coasts, but situated beyond the territorial waters up to a depth of 200 meters, or beyond that limit, up to a point where the depth of the water allows the exploitation of the natural resources of the said region; (2) the seabed and the underlying medium of similar submerged regions which are adjacent to the coast of islands.

But one might say that up to now, the rights of Coastal States have actually been based on a criterium of accessibility, that is:

– the range of artillery fire from the coast (three miles),

– or the distance of 12 nautical miles, limit of the contiguous zone adjacent to territorial waters,

– or the possibility of penetration: depth of 200 meters or, beyond this limit, to the point where the depth of the water enables the exploitation of natural resources;

and it is no longer possible to use such a criterium to define the zones over which more or less extended rights can be exercised by Coastal States.

Taking into account the developments of techniques, it can be considered that there are no longer any points in the sea where Man cannot penetrate, either in relation to the acquisition of natural resources or in relation to military uses.

It can be said that the taking into consideration of the problems of cost price and return on investments can put a stop to or restrain penetration to acquire natural resources.

As things stand at present, certain points on the seabed can only be reached by using advanced techniques. These are the most costly. In this respect, it is possible to underline a certain similitude of the difference of cost between laboratory and manual techniques and industrial techniques for the production of goods.

If it is taken into account that:

– the depth of 80 per cent of the ocean is over 900 meters and 2 per cent over 6000 meters,

– the recovery of an object at the depth of 900 meters required months of work and the use of considerable means,

it can be said that the expense incurred to acquire resources on the seabed is, at present, such that only States (or national agencies, etc.) capable of undertaking the research and study with a view to perfecting these advanced techniques can consider using them—states or perhaps powerful financial groups.

This being the case, in the near future, only a very restricted group is likely to dispose of the necessary means to exploit the resources of the seabed.

As far as military uses are concerned, it can be said that:

– there is no limit to the range of weapons,

– it is no longer possible to base a criterium on a distinction between strategic weapons and tactical weapons, or offensive weapons and defensive weapons.

Furthermore, the use of weapons generally requires the setting up of quite a system, consisting of installations, devices and measuring instruments.

The working of each of these individual devices could satisfy peaceful aims and purposes, but they can lose this peaceful characteristic with the coordination and convergence of their use in a specific way. That is why, as Professor Burke mentions it, the expression "exclusively for peaceful purposes" is not quite clear.

From the point of view of national defence, if the considerations concerning cost price and return on investments do not carry the same weight as in the case of the acquisition of resources, it can be pointed out that, at present, the cost of the setting up of military means in the ocean is considerable. Therefore, only States capable of undertaking research and surveys for perfecting these techniques can consider such an expense. This depends on how much a national economy can afford for military expenditure.

The development of technology has complicated the matter.

III. Determining a Policy for Military Uses

With the possibilities created by the development of technology for both penetration of the marine world and weapons, the following conception could be adopted:

The ocean

– forms a three-dimensional whole:

    1. bed and underlying medium,

2. waters, and

3. surface;

– and might be considered in a parallel way to:

1. aerial space, for which there are a certain number of rules (flights over the High Seas; local rules concerning flights over a territory; . . .)

2. outer space (Outer Space Agreement).

A. *How does one go about determining a policy for the ocean?*

"A priori" there is no reason why the policy for the military uses of the seas should be the same as for the acquisitions of resources, fisheries or scientific research.

It can be mentioned that the use of certain weapons and armaments— mass destruction devices—may be controlled by agreements on disarmament (eg., Outer Space Agreement).

As far as a ruling from the point of view of military uses of the seas is concerned, certain persons might draw a parallel with international regulations, agreed upon for the surface of the ocean, with a view to insuring the security of navigation and the safeguard of human lives. These regulations could be extended to subjacent waters: rules concerning the routes to be used in very crowded areas, routes which should be used by very large tankers, etc.

These rules are applied to specific cases and experience has proved that in such cases it is relatively easy to reach an agreement. But what is more difficult is the determination of rules liable to be accepted by the States and the aim of which is to limit the scope of their rights in the various fields and over the areas where they can be applied.

B. *Situation*

As things stand at the moment, some restrictions concerning the freedom of the seas, contained in the Conventions of 1958, are in favor of Coastal States, giving them the privilege of certain rights within a certain distance only from the coast:

1. For security reasons, a Coastal State has sovereign rights over its territorial waters, the seabed and underlying medium of these waters,

2. A Coastal State enjoys certain rights over the contiguous zone only,

3. A Costal State has sovereign rights over the Continental Shelf in order to explore it and exploit its natural resources.

If it is considered that the Continental Shelf is the submerged extension of the national territory, the Conventions of 1958 nevertheless determine a limit: the distance from the coast to a point where the depth reaches

200 meters or, beyond that limit, to a point where the depth of the water makes exploitation possible.

As far as military uses of the Continental Shelf are concerned, nothing transpires from the Conventions; and Professor Burke mentioned in his paper the following points as being reasonable:

1. The setting up of military installations on the Continental Shelf should be placed under the control of the Coastal State, in the same way as the Continental Shelf is placed under its jurisdiction only for exploration purposes and the exploitation of its resources.

2. The setting up of such military installations must not interfere unreasonably with utilization of the Continental Shelf.

C. *Remarks on the questions pertaining to the Continental Shelf*

Whether this sovereignty over the Continental Shelf for its exploration and its exploitation could be extended or not to military uses is a question to be debated. Whatever the result of such a debate, a question still arises over the delimitation of the Continental Shelf in the above mentioned field.

The criterium adopted by the Convention of 1958 in this respect is that of the possibilities of exploitation. The development of techniques is such that it is possible to foresee the exploitation of greater depths, and only economic considerations—for instance, cost price—can impede such exploitation works and postpone them.

Which criterium is to be adopted to delimit the Continental Shelf for the above aims (exploration and exploitation of resources, military uses)? Depth or distance from the coast? Neither one of these two criteria seems convenient because the application of either would bring out glaring injustices.

The question is therefore whether a delimitation arbitrarily based but setting this limit at a reasonable distance from the shores of the Coastal State is or is not the way to reach a solution. The arbitrary delimitation might be the result of interregional agreements between States bordering a sea the depth of which is less than 200 meters; in this respect, specific cases can only be resolved by specific solutions.

One can be tempted to push this limit of the Continental Shelf as far as possible from the shores, thinking a security increase for the Coastal State would go along with the extension of the zone where military installations could be set up.

This would be an illusion if the Coastal State did not have considerable means—military or not—for controlling any military installation which another State could set up secretly, to take advantage of a supposed weakness of means of control of the said Coastal State.

Well-known problems then crop up:
– policing,
– proof of infringement,
– punishment of the infringement.

The proving of an infringement: the State must have at its disposal powerful means—and all States do not dispose of such means—to detect military installations set up secretly.

An alternative would be to request an international organization to do the policing and to gather the evidence, but this would mean that the said organization must have equally powerful means.

It seems hardly feasible to ask a group of States, with such important means at their disposal, to intervene; this would be equal to asking a State to be both judge and party.

It might be a good thing to define the Continental Shelf in order, if possible, to delimit the area over which a Coastal State has sovereign rights for the acquisition of natural resources.

In the case of a positive reply to the question whether or not the Coastal State can lawfully use its Continental Shelf for military purposes, it might be necessary to define the Continental Shelf with a definition which would differ from that of the acquisition of natural resources. This debate could entail the examination of the policy to be adopted concerning the waters above the Continental Shelf. It is necessary to continue to study all the aspects of this question and it is only after serious thought that a solution will be found.

It is most important that Coastal States do not put forth occupational claims, either to the Continental Shelf or to the deep seabeds, as long as a solution to the question of the definition of the Continental Shelf has not been found. In this respect, one could think that the occupation of the terrain is less than before a symbol of riches and power of a State. It is doubtful that the implantation on the seabed of manned installations can be compared to that of infantry posts on land, for in such underwater installations man is a prisoner of the environment.

D. *Remarks on questions pertaining to the High Seas and the deep seabed beyond the Continental Shelf*

As far as these areas are concerned, considering the various systems of regulation which have been proposed, it is to be wondered whether the *"laisser-faire"* system is an acceptable solution or not and the best international regime to be applied. As Professor Burke mentions it, there is perhaps no point in dismantling the equilibrium among Nations brought about by the terror caused by the deterrent weapons.

In the *laisser-faire* system, it is unlikely that there will be a race to appropriate submerged territories. The benefit of a secret maneuver would be lost in the case of such an appropriation. It is necessary for States to have free access to any submerged area which is useful to them from a military point of view; it is of no interest to them to lose this advantage by claiming territories. It is in the interest of all States which are Maritime Powers to take advantage of all of the military activities which they have not renounced. In this *laisser-faire* system, all states can enjoy free access to and use of the seas, this being in accordance with International Law. Furthermore, a ban on certain military activities can only be considered if the means of detection are sufficiently acute to enforce the prohibition and this is not the case at present time.

The *laisser-faire* system does not mean that the various States cannot come to an agreement abandoning such or such military activity. An International Committee could be established to draw up a list of all the points subject to total or partial renunciation of their rights. *Ad hoc* Committees could then be given the task of determining and studying, for each of these points, the possibility of an Agreement between States.

If it is not possible to find analogies in the Antarctic Treaty (December 1, 1959), it is nevertheless possible to note that the States agreed to put aside their initial territorial claims—often disputed—and to set aside for scientific research the Antarctic regions, as inhospitable as the depth of the ocean.

The task will no doubt be more difficult for the ocean contributes, from distances greater than before from the coast, more than Antarctica, to the security of the Coastal States, whose duty and lawful right is to ensure their own protection.

A certain amount of goodwill and mutual understanding is necessary to reach acceptable solutions.

It would be an indignity to Mankind if the progress of techniques and means attained by Man, owing to his intelligence and work, only reached the stage of base competition between States, and created "a jungle" instead of contributing to the improvement of humanity.

E. J. Manner

Judge of the Supreme Court, Helsinki

The comprehensive Report prepared by Professor Burke gives an excellent survey of the legal problems, which have recently attained greater actuality, i.e. since the United Nations according to the General Assembly resolution 2340 (XXII) has established an *ad hoc* Committee to study the peaceful uses of the sea bed and the ocean floor beyond the limits of national jurisdiction. This item, which was included on the agenda of the 22nd General Assembly upon request of the Maltese Government, contains or is closely connected with numerous legal problems. The merit of the Report of Professor Burke lies in the fact that he examines those problems in a realistic way taking into account all relevant economic, technical and political factors. On the other hand, as also appears from the Report, there are certain basic problems concerning the legal status and use of the high sea area which obviously need a primarily juridical study and clarification.

As already mentioned, both the Maltese proposal and the study carried out by the United Nations refer to the use of the ocean floor underlying the seas beyond national jurisdiction. There are, however, sea areas which according to present international law are beyond the limits of national jurisdiction, but cannot geographically be counted as oceans. The Baltic Sea is one example of such small and enclosed seas which do not correspond to the concept of ocean, but nevertheless include both high sea and continental shelf areas beyond the territorial waters of their coastal states.[1] The special problems concerning such smaller seas are in no way easier to solve than those referring to oceans. Therefore the present study should also be extended to the bed and floor of high sea areas other than oceans.

One of the main principles concerning the present United Nations item refers to the freedom of the high seas. According to article 2 of the Convention on the High Seas this freedom comprises, for both coastal and non-coastal states, freedom of navigation, freedom of fishing, freedom to lay submarine cables and pipelines and freedom to fly over the high seas. These freedoms and others which are recognized by the general principles of international law shall be exercised by all states with reasonable regard to the interests of other states in their exercise of the freedom of the high seas. In spite of the fact that there is no doubt of the validity of the general

---

[1] On the concept of enclosed sea, see Manner (1960). "Some international legal aspects of the enclosed seas, especially the Baltic Sea, with regard to their protection against pollutive agents". In: IAEA, Disposal of radioactive wastes, Vienna, p. 592.

principle of freedom of the high seas, the general formulation of its definition in the Convention leaves ample room for different interpretations. The claims and considerations connected with the different uses of the high sea areas are as appears from Professor Burke's paper, in many cases based upon inadequate legal argumentation. The discussions at the United Nations General Assembly which led to the adoption of its resolution 2340 (XXII) clearly proved that the majority of states were not ready to accept new rules without a more thorough-going study of their legal premises. From a legal point of view this stand is well founded, because the problems connected with the status of the high sea and its bed still need more study and clarification. The following questions, *inter alia*, should be subject to further examination.

Are the sea bed and the ocean floor beyond the limits of national jurisdiction, because of their depth or of some other reason, in a different position than the surface area above? If this question is answered negatively, it means that there is in principle no difference regarding the status of the bed between the high sea and the more shallow waters of the territorial sea and the inland watercourses. As to the latter areas, their bed and the water and the airspace above, all together form an integral whole, subject to similar legal principles. If, on the other hand, the question mentioned before were answered affirmatively, it would mean among other things that the principle of the freedom of the high seas need not, with absolute necessity, regulate the use of the sea bed in the same way as it concerned the surface of the ocean.

Historically seen the freedom of the high seas originates *i.a.* in principles of the old Roman law according to which the water running in the rivers, the atmospheric air and the open sea were regarded as *res communis omnium*. In its present form, however, the principle of freedom is reborn and has been developed with modern international law. Many different factors, both political and legal, have left their marks on the formulation of this principle. During the present discussion it has been pointed out that the sea bed and ocean floor beyond the limits of national jurisdiction should not be regarded as *res communis omnium,* but as having special status as a common heritage of mankind (Government of Malta). On the other hand there are opinions according to which the same vast areas should remain as *res nullius.* It is sure that the many different problems concerning the use and exploitation of the bed of the high seas and the ocean floor cannot be solved only by referring to the legal status of those areas. A fundamental legal study and, if necessary, also progressive development of new rules *de lege ferenda* concerning this question should proceed simultaneously with the application and expansion of the peaceful uses of the high sea bed and the ocean floor. When compared with legal theories on the right to occupation, mainly applied to national legislation, a distinction may be made between areas regarded as *res nullius* and other considered to be *res communis omnium*. An area regarded as being *res nullius* is in principle subject to occupation, that means to such permanent appropriation which for instance is necessary for the exploitation of mineral resources. But, if an area is permanently appropriated, it is no more object of the old freedom, and in proportion as the occupation is increasing, the freedom of the high seas becomes more restricted. If, on the other hand, the bed of the high sea is considered as being *res communis omnium,* no permanent appropriation is in accordance with the position of those areas. It seems obvious that neither of those alternatives can as such serve as a basis for a future legal regulation concerning the uses of the bed of the high seas and the ocean floor. Therefore the old concepts must be replaced by some new and more appropriate provisions.

When compared with many other uses of the high sea areas, the problems related to fishery resources and the scientific research of the ocean seem not to be the most difficult. In spite of the fact that the implementation of the 1958 Geneva Convention on Fishing and Conservation of the Living Resources of the High Seas has remained defective, the problems connected with its application are mainly of administrative nature and do not in the first place bear upon legal principles. The same applies in the main to the international organization of the research of the high sea areas.

As to the military uses of the high seas there seem to be certain difficulties in pointing out the problems which may attain greater actuality. The oceans of the world have from ancient times been a scene of military operations. Numerous naval battles have taken place both on and under the surface of the high sea. The fact that the modern submarines may reach greater depths or stay a longer time under the surface than their predecessors does not create essentially new legal problems. The same concerns the possibility of launching missiles from warships situated on the high seas. Problems of a new kind and actuality may on the other hand be caused by the new technical possibilities to use the sea bed and its sub-soil more permanently for military purposes. Such military measures may get into conflict with the exploitation of natural resources and with other peaceful uses of the deep sea areas. As already mentioned by Professor Burke, questions concerning the use of the continental shelf for certain military purposes also require further clarification.

The present study deals with sea bed and ocean floor beyond the limits of national jurisdiction. According to article 2 of the Convention on the Continental Shelf, the coastal state exercises over the continental shelf sovereign rights for the purpose of exploring it and exploiting its natural resources. In both those relations the sea bed and sub-soil of the continental shelf are obviously subject to the jurisdiction of the respective coastal states. On the other hand the definition of the term continental shelf contained in article 1 of the Convention is too vague. In addition to the submarine areas adjacent to the coast but outside the area of the territorial sea to a depth of 200 metres, it also includes sea bed and sub-soil beyond that limit to where the depth of the superjacent waters admits of the exploitation of the natural resources of the said areas. As stated by the Belgian Government in its reply to the Secretary-General of the United Nations, "This means in fact that, in accordance with the provisions of the Convention, if there is any exploitation, it must of necessity be on the continental shelf of the nearest state, whether or not there had been any proclamation. Unless the continental shelf is defined more precisely, there is a risk of never-ending disputes about the limits of national jurisdiction." On the other hand this conclusion is mainly theoretical as long as there really does not exist any practical means to extend the exploitation of sub-soil beyond the depth limit of 200 metres.

Professor Burke has in his excellent paper only incidentally mentioned problems of pollution. Without doubt many forms of exploitation of the natural resources of the sea bed and especially its use for military purposes may cause serious pollution problems. It must also be taken into account that the depths of the oceans are already used for the disposal of radioactive and other dangerous wastes. The provisions of the articles 24 and 25 of the Convention on the High Seas, as also the International Convention for the Prevention of Pollution of the Sea by Oil signed in London in 1954, are obviously not sufficient with respect to the new kinds of deep sea exploitation. As to the disposal of radioactive wastes, the efforts of the International Atomic Energy Agency to control such activities, have not led to any final results. Even if already many international organizations are dealing with problems concerning certain kinds of pollution, it seems to be most important that in connection with the present study deep sea pollution should also be taken into serious consideration.

The Maltese proposal as also the whole complex of problems concerning the peaceful uses of the sea bed and the ocean floor beyond the limits of national jurisdiction contain elements which go beyond the old scope of international law as a law of state relations. We are here dealing with the principles and rules *de lege ferenda* which, concerning states and individuals also in their relation to the whole mankind and the international community, may be called by the old name *jus gentium*.

186

R. R. Neild

Director of SIPRI

Alternative Forms of International Regime for the Oceans

It has been suggested by various people that the best solution to the problem of the oceans is an international regime which would own and in some degree manage the exploitation of the mineral resources that may be found beyond the line which, under a reasonable reinterpretation of the 1958 agreement, might be called the limits of the Continental Shelf. Usually only a few forms of international regime are mentioned. For example, it has been suggested that an international agency should grant concessions upon payment of exploration and exploitation levies which would accrue to the U.N. and thus benefit the whole community of nations. (See the recommendations of the Netherlands branch of the International Law Association to the Helsinki Conference of the International Law Association in 1956.) Before making up your mind for or against an international regime it is advisable to consider what alternative forms it might take. I therefore thought it useful to explore this subject on paper. This note, which contains the results, concentrates upon possible regimes for the exploitation of minerals under the ocean bed. The problem of creating an international regime to regulate the exploitation of fish or other natural resources in the oceans themselves is not dealt with; nor is the military problem.

I. The Purposes of an International Regime

There are two main sets of arguments for an international regime: those concerning order and harmony, and those concerning economics and equity.

Order and Harmony

There is now quite a body of opinion in favour of an international regime on the ground that there is no alternative way of ensuring an orderly development of the ocean bed. As Professor Burke has shown clearly in his

I am indebted to Mr. F. Blackaby and Miss M. Kaldor for suggestions and comments made while I was preparing this note.

paper, the view that each nation should simply expand outwards from its own coast until at some midpoint it meets another nation expanding from its coast, is scarcely tenable. The pattern of land masses, islands and oceans in the world is such that no one has found—or is likely to find—a coherent principle on which to draw the lines.

The alternative of a competitive free for all, in which anyone may claim any area beyond a defined Continental Shelf, is not attractive since no company or nation can be sure that its claim to an area of the ocean will be respected and that another enterprise will not move in alongside and trespass on its finds, unless there is some international authority to record and approve claims.

An international regime, which at least registered claims and supervised the game, therefore has clear attractions as a means of avoiding conflicts and achieving security of tenure.

Economics and Equity

The proposition is that outside national borders (including a limited definition of the Continental Shelf) man may find natural resources, such as oil or minerals, which can be exploited economically. One can regard this as the discovery of a gift of nature (or God) to mankind.

In the most general terms the benefits derived from a discovery are a more abundant and hence cheaper supply of the natural resources in question.

In fact there are gains (and some losses) divided between consumers and producers. Consumers and producers are not strictly separate: they may be the same people. Nevertheless, individuals, groups, enterprises or nations have a producer and a consumer interest in a real sense. Moreover, different nations will attach different relative importance to the consumer interest and the producer interest, depending upon their economic structure, including their endowment in natural resources and the social organization of their economy.

From the consumer's point of view, a new discovery of a natural resource means a lower price associated with a wider use of the material in existing uses and in those uses where it can be substituted for alternative materials. The rate of exploration and exploitation of the new discoveries, its efficiency and the pricing policy followed all help to determine the extent and speed of these gains.

Producers face a risky venture. If, as a whole, it is a success, existing land-based producers will lose and some will be forced out of business. Those who make rich finds in the oceans will make abnormal windfall profits or, in other words, "abnormal rents".

The benefits are not likely to be reaped equitably nor necessarily in the most efficient way, if exploration and exploitation is left to a competitive struggle:

a) Those nations, notably the Soviet Union and United States, which command great resources and technical knowledge of the oceans—the latter being partly the result of military interest in the oceans—would alone be able to enter the game and grab the windfall rents. The less developed countries, and probably many of the smaller industrial countries, would be left out.

b) In a competitive struggle people are likely to be secretive about the results of research and exploration. That can entail wasteful duplication of effort.

c) Markets for primary products, including minerals, are notoriously unstable at the best of times. (This is because demand and supply for primary products are both inelastic in the short run: a lower price will not quickly lead people to use more of a material, nor will it quickly lead to a reduction in output; and vice versa.) New discoveries can add to instability. It can be argued that a smooth transition to new, cheaper supplies is more desirable than an erratic one in which the price see-saws and there is much uncertainty. International machinery is about the only way of trying to stabilize international commodity markets.

d) It is also clear that the rate of development of new supplies has an effect on the income of existing suppliers, many of whom are likely to be less developed countries. A competitive struggle may not achieve the ideal rate of development of new supplies. But this is not a very useful statement since it is virtually impossible to define what is the best rate of development.

This means that the main economic argument for an international regime is equity: the main task is to ensure that the windfall rents are properly shared. The other arguments involve the efficiency of development as well as equity (i.e. the effect on the total wealth of the world as well as its distribution—though the two always interact on one another).

If these are the aims or potentialities of an international regime, what are the ways of achieving them?

II. The Form of Regime

Ownership

The first question is, should the international agency that operated an international regime own the ocean bed, at least initially?

It might be thought that you could have an agency which merely recorded and endorsed claims to particular areas that were made by exploring enterprises. But if these claims are made before exploration has been undertaken and finds have been proved, then everybody will rush to claim the right to explore and exploit the whole ocean. The agency is bound to be forced into the position of rationing out exploration rights, in which event it has effectively become first owner, even if it makes no charge for rights. The alternative that the agency should have no influence over exploration but should endorse claims for rights to exploit, when they are made on the basis of proved finds, also seems unsatisfactory. It would mean that there was a completely unregulated free for all in exploration; enterprises undertaking exploration would not have security and there would be risks of conflict at the stage of exploration. For these reasons it seems best that the agency should own the ocean bed and that it should be responsible for disposing of it, by sale or lease.

Area

The next question then is what area should it own. At what point should the Continental Shelf end?

Any answer to this question seems bound to be pretty arbitrary and to be influenced a good deal—but not totally—by what has happened already. The obvious considerations are:

a) The wider the area of coastal claims, the more coastal nations win at the expense of inland nations. In other words, the greater the inequality through accidents of geography.

b) If you have a wide limit to coastal claims, small islands do extraordinarily well—unless the distance over which coastal claims are respected is made a function of the size of the nation or land mass. But it is hard to think of an acceptable formula.

c) As Professor Burke points out, military considerations may tell in favour of wide coastal strip. A Chinese mining operation off the United States might generate tension or conflict.

d) It might be useful to know at what distance free access to the local shore for personnel, supplies and products ceases to be economically important because operations can be supported equally cheaply by ocean-going vessels coming from more distant points. This is one consideration that might help to determine where the line should be drawn—though probably it would give an answer that was further out than that provided by other considerations.

It would be possible to make the agency itself the sole operator, entrusting it with the task of exploring and exploiting the ocean bed. That seems a pretty unrealistic notion now. The political differences between different nations are too great and the experience of international enterprise is too limited. It would be possible to permit the agency to undertake some operations itself, and it would probably be desirable to do so, since it would give it direct experience on the basis of which to conduct its negotiations with others. For the most part, however, the task of the agency should probably be to allocate or sell to others rights to exploit the ocean bed. Presumably these rights to exploit would carry with them the right and need to explore, though the need might not be great if the international agency did a lot of research and exploration centrally.

The next question is would it be better if the agency were to allocate titles to ownership of the ocean bed to different nations (i.e. national governments) in proportion to their population, thus sharing out the oceans in a single once-for-all operation, leaving governments then to dispose of their allocations as they think fit (notably by selling, or leasing them to enterprises at home or abroad which have the resources and technical know-how to undertake exploitation), or, alternatively would it be better to keep ownership in the hands of an international agency, which would provide leases to operating nations or enterprises in such a way that it taxed the rent and disposed of the income in such a way that the inequity was, so far as possible, redressed?

Much the same degree of equity between countries might be achieved by either method. Suppose that leases were auctioned under both systems, in the first case by governments to whom parcels of the ocean had been allocated on the basis of a lottery, in which the number of tickets held by each nation was proportionate to its population (i.e. randomly selected bundles proportionate to population) and in the second case auctions by an international agency. Suppose that in both cases anyone can bid without constraint at the auction and that the terms of the leases (notably the length and the level of annual payment, if any, to be made in addition to the purchase price) are the same. And suppose that in the second case the international agency distributes the income to all nations in proportion to their populations. The only difference between these two systems, so long as the relative size of the populations of different countries remain constant, is that with the first each nation, in its capacity as an owner of the oceans, is running the risk whether it receives rich or poor parts of the ocean, wheras in the second case this risk is removed. This means that the same degree of equity will not quite be achieved: some countries are bound to do worse and others better than they would have done under the alternative system, and the smaller the country the greater this risk, since it will hold fewer parcels of the ocean floor. The extent of the difference would depend on the size of the parcels.

There are several other less easily calculated points which are much more important:

a) There are the obvious arguments for having a continuing international agency, providing leases centrally, so that it can also perform the other functions mentioned earlier—research, stabilization of markets and influence over the rate of development—as well as possibly dealing with other ocean problems, such as military uses, fisheries and pollution.

b) There is the question whether the bargaining power of the strong powers against the weak would be greater under the first basis or the second. How great would their bargaining power be in a system where they had to compete in buying leases from many different countries? The population of the super powers is not very great. China and India would hold a large part of the ocean. On the other hand, how far would the strong countries manage to dominate an international agency, settling the terms for leases and so on? If membership included all countries and votes were in proportion to population—which would seem appropriate since we are dealing with a gift to mankind which must mean to people, not animals or anything else—then perhaps the balance would be no different. Perhaps the key question is—can you get population as the basis of ownership and influence accepted in one case more easily than the other?

c) It can be argued that an international agency is desirable per se, in that it may help international understanding and the avoidance of conflict and may lead on to other international experiments which take the world further in this direction.

d) If nations own, rather than lease, parts of the ocean floor, they are more likely to put military installations down there.

e) The total administrative cost of many national offices disposing of parts of the ocean is likely to be greater than the cost of an international agency doing the job.

Alternative Charges

The next question is, suppose we have an international agency disposing of leases, what is the best way of charging for those leases? Many of the considerations that must be weighed here would be applicable under the alternative system whereby there was a once-for-all division of the ocean

192

bed after which nations had to decide how to dispose of and charge for their lots.

The best way to charge for the rights granted in a lease are either a tax on the rents themselves (i.e. on the profits accruing from operations as they arise year by year) or else an initial charge, levied by auction or other means such that it is proportionate to the rents that operators expect to earn. In the latter case one is making a single capital charge for the right to earn the rents, or looking at it another way, one is taking in a sum which represents the discounted value of rents that will be earned in the future.

In theory, an initial charge for the lease made, say, by auction, is best, since it should tend to induce a full surrender of the abnormal rent and yet will not entail any disincentive to production. Once the operating enterprise has paid its initial charge, there will be nothing to deter it from pursuing that output which will maximise its operating profits. Of the ways of making an initial charge, an auction is probably the best. If the price is administered, the administrator will try to fix it at that price which an auction would yield. Moreover there will then be the question how to allocate lots where there is more than one applicant.

A tax on profits, even if it is progressive, may have little, if any, effect in reducing the output of this kind below the ideal level, provided it is not set at such a high level that it deters entry into the whole business. But it is difficult to devise a profits tax which will achieve a full surrender of the abnormal rents. Added to this, there is the practical point that it may not be at all easy for an international agency to levy a tax on profits, since that would require an international standardization of accounting procedures, the right to inspect books and so on. It should probably not therefore lean on a profits tax too heavily, at least to begin with.

A big problem with the ocean floor is that the uncertainties will be extremely great, especially to begin with: it is still not clear whether operations are likely to be profitable at all. In these conditions one wants a system which does not deter people from entering the game. This means it should allow rather high rewards for the brave people who first take the plunge. In other words, it can be argued that in order to get enterprises to enter the business to start with, they should be given the prospect of retaining a large part—or all—of the abnormal rents that they would earn if they came upon a rich find. This argument, however, depends a good deal on the social system that one is considering. It applies to a competitive system in which people pursue profits. And it probably has considerable validity when applied, as here, to nations, since nations of all kinds often appear to pursue national profit rather than a higher communal objective.

The risks to the individual enterprise or nation also depend upon how far research is undertaken centrally by the international agency.

Even if high rewards have to be offered to get enterprises to embark on exploration and exploitation, there is no reason why those high rewards should continue indefinitely. As knowledge increases and the risks diminish, so the aim should be increasingly to move over to a system where the abnormal rents are taxed away as far as possible. What matters in order to get the first enterprises going is that the period for which they are assured of a high reward is sufficiently long to persuade them to start. The appropriate period will be related to the expected pattern of possible gains and to the expected time required to undertake a full investment cycle (i.e. the time required to undertake an exploration of the area and to install equipment and the expected life of the equipment before it wears out or becomes obsolete).

In the light of these considerations, there are various possible solutions:

a) an initial charge fixed by administrative means combined with an annual charge of the same kind, both to be renegotiated after some finite period.

b) an auction in which nations bid in terms of the proportion of their profits that they are ready to surrender each year to the central fund.

c) an auction in which the bidding is in terms of an initial purchase price of the lease, but the lease includes some annual charge in order to deter people from sitting on leases and doing nothing and the lease also is for a finite period.

d) an auction of a lease on the same terms as under c), except that the lease comes up for a new auction quite frequently, say every five years, but that at the new auction the present lease-holder is given an advantage by being permitted to renew the lease for only a proportion of the price reached at the auction, this proportional discount depending upon how far through one productive cycle he has gone: as the cycle proceeded the discount would diminish. The object of this scheme is that the high rents of the rich find should be surrendered more quickly to the international agency in the form of a new auction price, yet the rewards to the initial exploiter should not be reduced to the point of deterring people from embarking on new ventures.

Other Functions

This analysis suggests that the organization of research on an international basis, or at very least the sharing of the results of research, should be objectives pursued by an international agency for the sake of economy and efficiency. One way of ensuring that information is shared would be to write into the leases a clause that results of research should be sent to the international agency and made public. This would mean that an enterprise which explored one part of the ocean would make public its findings so that others would have an idea as to what might be found in an adjoining lot. This would tend to prevent wastage and duplication of research and help to ensure that the bidding at auctions for future lots took place on the basis of a common framework of knowledge and hence on a basis of fairness.

There is a variety of other problems which an international agency might handle: the technology of exploration and extraction and the right size for lots and enterprises; the right pricing and stabilization arrangements; the right distribution arrangements. There are no doubt others. The solution of many of the sea problems will, as noted earlier, influence the gains and losses of different countries and so must be brought into consideration when the equity of the total solution of the problem is weighed up.

Distribution of Proceeds

The income which the international agency derived from its operations—and there must be a fair chance that in the end there will be some—might be used in any of the following ways:

a) for the agency's own operations, for example, any research or exploitation undertaken by it;

b) to finance the United Nations or other international agencies which provide a common service to all nations. The United Nations suffers financial difficulties and does not have as strong a secretariat and research staff as those agencies which are in a stronger financial position, for example the IMF and International Bank, which have an independent income derived from interest on the funds in their hands. It can thus be argued that an independent source of income would "strengthen the United Nations", meaning that it would strengthen the secretariat. Some countries, e.g. the Soviet Union, have tended to oppose a strengthening of the secretariat. They might therefore tend to oppose this use of the funds.

c) The funds could be used to help the poorer nations of the world by being distributed to them as aid, either directly, or indirectly through international agencies which provide technical assistance and other help.

d) The income could be distributed to all member countries in proportion to their population as a kind of dividend. It is politically the most neutral and unimaginative solution.

Conclusion

The object of this paper has been not to recommend any particular solution but rather to open up the subject by exploring what alternatives might be possible and what kind of considerations need to be taken into account in choosing between them. The paper is intended to start discussion not to finish it. Below is a list of questions that have been considered in the course of the paper. The reader is invited to consider what answers he would give to them and to consider what questions he considers relevant.

Assuming that we want an international regime:

a) Should an international agency own the ocean bed, at least initially? (page 189)

b) How far out from the shore should its territory begin? (page 190)

c) Should it be an operating agency, exploiting the ocean floor alone (as a monopoly) to some extent (in competition with enterprises from different countries and groups of countries) or not at all? (page 191)

d) Should beneficial interest in the agency and control of it be distributed between nations according to population (on the grounds that the wealth of the ocean bed is a gift to the people of the world)? If not, what other basis should be used? (page 192)

e) Should the agency arrange a once-for-all distribution of titles to parts of the ocean bed to nations, say in a lottery where each nation was given tickets in proportion to its population, or should the agency offer only leases of finite period? (page 191)

f) If the agency offers leases what system of charging for the leases and distributing them—essentially what combination of an initial charge and a running charge and what method of allocation—would be best? (page 192)

g) How far should the agency undertake:

1. research and exploration;

2. price stabilization;

3. general supervision of the pace of development, and of economic and technical problems that arise? (page 194)

h) Specifically, should leases include the condition that the results of exploration by one nation or enterprise in a part of the ocean bed allocated to it should be sent to the agency and made public? (page 195)

i) Should any funds accruing to the agency from the leases be used:

1. to finance its own operations, such as research and exploration?

2. to finance the U.N.?

3. to help poor countries?

4. to be distributed to all countries in proportion to population? (page 195)

196

Shigeru Oda

Professor of International Law, Tôhoku University, Sendai, Japan

Since I participate, as a member of the Japanese delegation, in the work of the U.N. *Ad Hoc* Committee on the peaceful use of the ocean floor established pursuant to the U.N. resolution, G.A. Res. 2340 (XXII), it may be not appropriate at this present stage to express my views on Mr. Burke's paper. In this respect, I would like to introduce herewith only my views, which have been already presented elsewhere.[1] Furthermore, I wish to emphasize that these views are entirely my own and not necessarily those of the Japanese Government.

I. Outer Limit of the Continental Shelf

I submit that any proposal for internationalization would be a departure from existing rules adopted under the Continental Shelf Convention, a document which leaves no room for a new regime on deep sea mining. In other words, the Convention, as it stands, has committed itself with respect to deep sea areas. I submit that in fact deep sea resources have already been placed by the Convention under the control of certain specified States.

The coastal State itself need not necessarily engage in the exploitation of its continental shelf: each coastal State is free to grant to any foreign country or foreign nationals the right to explore its continental shelf or to exploit the natural resources therein contained. This point has often been overlooked. It is likely that the coastal States without sufficiently advanced technologies and industries will encourage foreign investment or technical assistance with a view towards the exploitation of the resources contained within the submerged areas which they claim. Thus, the concept of exploitability must be constantly reinterpreted in terms of the most advanced standards of technology and economy in the world. Hence, the exploitation of submarine resources at any point must always be reserved to the coastal State, which is empowered to claim the area when the depth of the super-

---

[1] See *International Control of Sea Resources,* Leyden, 1963, 215 pp.; The Hydrogen Bomb Tests and International Law, *Die Friedenswarte,* Bd. 53, Nr. 2 (1956); Distribution of Fish Resources of the High Seas: Free Competition or Artificial Quota? *The Future of the Sea's Resources,* (Proceedings of the Second Annual Conference on the Law of the Sea Institute, Rhode Island, 1967), pp. 29–31; Proposals for Revising the Convention on the Continental Shelf, *Columbia Journal of Transnational Law,* vol. 7, no. 1 (1968), pp. 1–31.

jacent waters admits of exploitation. It can be inferred that, under this Convention, all the submarine areas of the world have been theoretically divided among the coastal States at the deepest trenches. This is the logical conclusion to be drawn from the provision approved at the Geneva Conference.

Such an interpretation was perhaps not what the delegates at the Geneva Conference had actually thought they were affirming. Many delegates at Geneva simply and mistakenly considered the provision on "exploitability" as meaning that the coastal State would be allowed to exploit submarine resources even where the depth of the superjacent waters exceeded 200 metres. It should be noted, however, that at no point does this Convention prohibit exploitation of the submarine areas beyond the continental shelf. The concept of exploitability embodied by the Convention stems from an incorrect belief that exploitation of submarine resources, though not heretofore allowed, became permissible only in terms of the concept of the continental shelf.

By taking this stand, I do not suggest that as *lex ferenda,* the deep sea should be divided among the various coastal States. On the contrary, I am inclined to support the view that, as *lex ferenda,* the regime of the ocean floor of the deep sea should be distinct from that of the continental shelf, thus releasing deep sea areas from the exclusive control of the coastal States which they adjoin. In other words, coastal submarine areas should remain under the control of the coastal State as elements of the continental shelf, but the deep sea areas beneath the ocean should be treated differently. In order to realize this policy for deep sea areas, it is essential that the Continental Shelf Convention be revised, thus leaving the way open to free the deep sea areas from the exclusive control of the coastal State. Careful thought must still be given to whether the 200-metres depth is an appropriate criterion for determining the line between the continental shelf under the control of the coastal State and other deep sea areas free from such control. It should be recalled that a 550-metres depth line was proposed by the Netherlands delegation to the Geneva Conference.

At any rate, this move to release deep sea areas from coastal State control should be made as early as possible, before claims under the Continental Shelf Convention are asserted over deep sea areas in terms of exploitability, as provided for in the Convention.

II. Scientific Investigation of the Continental Shelf

The provision of the Continental Shelf Convention relating to the scientific investigation of the continental shelf presents many ambiguities. Paragraph

1 of article 5 based on the Danish proposal as adopted, 25: 20: 10, appears strange even at first glance, since oceanographic or other scientific research may be inevitably affected by the very existence of the installations or equipment used for the exploitation of the continental shelf. If the provision means that the coastal State is prevented from interfering with scientific research in the superjacent waters, it merely states a truism. The coastal State, entitled to the rights granted under article 2, is obliged to see to it, that the injunctions of paragraphs 5 and 6 of article 5 are observed by any enterprise connected with the exploitation of the continental shelf. There remain the questions of how the research provided for in paragraph 8 differs from the research noted in paragraph 1; whether such research may not be the same as the exploration of the continental shelf reserved exclusively to the coastal state.

III. Twelve Mile Fishery Zone

The following is a résumé of my article on Twelve Mile Fishery Zone, published in Japanese in *Kokusaihogaiko Zasshi (The Journal of International Law and Diplomacy)*, Vol. 66, Nos. 5 and 6 (1968). The table relating to the extent of fishery jurisdiction (table 1) is prepared for this paper.

La Zone de Pêche de Douze Milles

1. *Introduction*

Les Etats-Unis, qui ont proposé à la conférence de 1958 sur le droit de la mer que la zone de pêche de 12 milles serait adoptée à condition que les eaux territoriales s'étendraient seulement à 6 milles au maximum, l'ont établi eux-mêmes en 1966. Il semble que la zone de pêche de 12 milles, qui a été proposée avec des eaux territoriales étroites a été récemment considérée comme une institution indépendante des eaux territoriales.

2. *La Zone de Pêche Discutée aux Conférences de 1958 et 1960*

La zone de pêche, dont la notion a été discutée pour la première fois à Genève en 1958, y était considérée comme une zone où l'état côtier serait autorisé à exercer sa compétence concernant la pêche. En certain cas, les états étrangers, qui avaient continué la pêche pendant un certain nombre d'années, pouvaient continuer à la faire sous le règlement de l'état côtier. A la deuxième conférence de 1960, il était entendu que la continuation de la pêche traditionelle des états étrangers dans la zone de pêche cesserait d'exister après un certain nombre d'années.

3. L'Etablissement Unilatéral de la Zone de Pêche

Depuis 1960, un certain nombre d'états ont établi leur zone de pêche dans laquelle ils demandent à surveiller toutes les pêches, ou, en certain cas, à interdire toutes les pêches des états étrangers. Même dans le cas où les états étrangers ont la permission de continuer leur pêche tradition- nelle, cette concession cesse d'exister après un certain nombre d'années fixées, ou bien l'état côtier est en droit de la suspendre à n'importe quel moment.

4. Acquisecement par les Autres Etats de l'Etablissement Unilatéral de la Zone de Pêche de 12 Milles

Il y a eu certains traités internationaux, selon lesquels les nations intéres- sées approuvent l'établissement de la zone de pêche par les autres, en réservant leur droit d'y continuer la pêche sous le règlement de l'état côtier pendant un certain nombre d'années.

5. Reconnaissance Mutuelle du Droit d'Etablir la Zone de Pêche à 12 Milles

Selon un certain nombre de traités, spécialement, la convention européenne de la pêche de 1964, toutes les nations participantes reconnaissent mutuel- lement le droit de régler ou de monopoliser toutes les pêches en établissant la zone de pêche à 12 milles. On peut admettre que cet établissement est applicable seulement aux autres nations participantes. Cependant, le droit territorial est dénué de sens, s'il n'est pas appliqué à tous les états. En effet, ces traités signifient que les nations participantes reconnaissent la zone de pêche de 12 milles comme une institution générale applicable non seulement aux autres nations participantes des traités mais encore à tous les états du monde.

6. Evaluation de la Zone de Pêche de 12 Milles

La zone de pêche de 12 milles est évidemment contraire au concept tradi- tionnel de la liberté de la haute mer. Cependant, il s'agit de faire recon- naître cette institution universellement sous le droit international. Cela dépend de la situation pratique depuis ces dix dernières années. En premier lieu, le fait que les propositions pour la zone de pêche de 12 milles ont été soutenues par un grand nombre des délégations en 1958 et 1960, bien qu'elles n'aient pas été adoptée, est probablement considéré comme un facteur qui transforme la pratique simple dans le droit coutumier. En ce qui concerne la pratique de l'établissement unilatéral de la zone de pêche de 12 milles, 54 des 95 états ont revendiqué leur compétence pour régler la

Table 1. Extent of Fishery Jurisdiction   As of November 1967

	Total		Asia	Ocn.	Afr.	W.E.	E.E.	N.A.	L.A.
3 miles	16	T. 16	4	1	4	4	1	0	2
		F. 0	0	0	0	0	0	0	0
4 miles	2	T. 2	0	0	0	2	0	0	0
		F. 0	0	0	0	0	0	0	0
6 miles	9	T. 7	2	0	2	2	0	0	1
		F. 2	2	0	0	0	0	0	0
10 miles	1	T. 1	0	0	0	0	1	0	0
		F. 0	0	0	0	0	0	0	0
12 miles	54	T. 31	10	0	14	0	4	0	3
		F. 23	2	1	5	8	1	2	4
15 miles	2	T. 0	0	0	0	0	0	0	0
		F. 2	0	0	0	0	0	0	2
100 miles	1	T. 0	0	0	0	0	0	0	0
		F. 1	1	0	0	0	0	0	0
130 miles	1	T. 1	0	0	1	0	0	0	0
		F. 0	0	0	0	0	0	0	0
200 miles	8	T. 6	0	0	0	0	0	0	6
		F. 2	0	0	0	0	0	0	2
Archipelago	1	T. 1	1	0	0	0	0	0	0
		F. 0	0	0	0	0	0	0	0
Total	95	T. 65	17	1	21	8	6	0	12
		F. 30	5	1	5	8	1	2	8

Abr.: T. = territorial sea; F. = fishery zone. Ocn. = Oceania; Afr. = Africa; W.E. = Western Europe; E.E. = Eastern Europe; N.A. = North America; L.A. = Latin America.

pêche dans la zone de 12 milles dans les limites de la zone de pêche ou des eaux territoriales. 28 états seulement maintiennent leur zone de compétence pour la pêche au-dessous de 12 milles. De plus, un certain nombre d'états ont approuvé mutuellement le droit d'établir la zone de la pêche. Ces états y compris, on peut dire que 60 des 95 états soutiennent les 12 milles et seuelement 22 états maintiennent la zone au dessous de 12 milles. Le droit de continuer la pêche, qui a été souvent donné aux états étrangers, n'est qu'une concession donnée sous le système général de la zone de pêche de 12 milles. Il ne faut pas fermer les yeux sur le développement récent de la pratique tendant à institutionaliser la zone de pêche de 12 milles.

IV. Special or Preferential Right of the Coastal State
relating to the Fisheries

Article 6, paragraph 1, of the Geneva Convention on the High Seas Fisheries, is subject to different interpretations, but should not be understood in such a way as to entitle certain States to preferential fishing rights on the basis of their special situation as coastal States; nor does the Convention entrust the coastal State with any power to regulate nationals of other fishing States. The width of the coastal areas in which the coastal State is entitled to claim special interests is not provided for at all in the Convention. It is submitted that the geographical configuration of the coasts, the development of fishing methods of the coastal State, and the past practices of fishing either by the coastal State or other fishing States may be taken into consideration in order to determine the width of the area wherein the coastal State is entitled to claim special interests. Differences of opinion on this issue can be submitted to a special commission, according to the commentary on the I.L.C. draft, although there is no explicit relevant provision in the Convention. I submit, however, that this preliminary question, which is not neccessarily concerned with the conservation of resources, may be almost insusceptible of settlement by a special commission.

The coastal State is also empowered to adopt unilateral measures under the circumstances specified in article 7, paragraphs 1 and 2. The expression of "adopt unilateral measures" should not be construed as enabling the coastal State to extend its measures directly over nationals of other States. No reason is found in the Convention to upset the established rule of the freedom of the high seas, under which any person is assured of being subject only to his own flag. The fishing States are obliged to apply to their own nationals the measures unilaterally adopted by the coastal State. Even if the fishing States consider that the measures do not satisfy the necessary conditions specified in article 7, paragraph 2, they are not exempted from applying those measures in accordance with article 7, paragraphs 3 and 4.

Article 6, paragraph 4, and article 7, paragraph 3, which were based upon a proposal submitted by Burma, Chile, Costa Rica, Ecuador, Indonesia, Korea, Mexico, Nicaragua, the Philippines, Vietnam and Yugoslavia, are the most difficult to understand. The original provision of article 6, as contained in the I.L.C. draft, stipulated only that the coastal State would be entitled to participate in conservation measures, even though its nationals were not engaged in fishing. Article 6, paragraph 4, which was newly inserted as a result of a vote of 30: 28: 7 on the first reading of the third committee, is essentially incompatible with the concept of the original draft. It is hard to imagine the situation envisioned in this provision, that a State must *not* enforce conservation measures. Furthermore, conservation measures which are *opposed to* those adopted by the coastal State are also difficult to conceive of. In effect, this provision does not impose any obligation of conservation upon the fishing State but rather exempts the fishing State from the obligation to take conservation measures. Article 7, paragraph

3, based upon the concept of the eleven-power proposal, was adopted 39: 22: 4 on the first reading of the committee. This paragraph makes no sense whatsoever, since paragraph 4, which is based upon the I.L.C. draft, was also adopted.

It is submitted that some delegates to the 1958 Conference confused the concept of conservation with fishing rights themselves, and that the provisions concerning the interests of the coastal State, inserted into the Convention at their suggestion, are naturally inconsistent. In spite of diverse interpretations and expectations advanced by the delegates present at the Conference, I am of the opinion that all the provisions concerning unilateral measures were drafted to require fishing States to apply to their own nationals, in certain exceptional cases, conservation measures unilaterally prescribed by the coastal State. Nevertheless, these provisions are undoubtedly beneficial to the coastal State and place the traditional high-seas fishing State at a considerable disadvantage.

V. Treatment of Sedentary Fisheries

I find no logical reason for reviewing the exploitation of resources attached to the seabed in terms of the legal status of submerged lands in general. Nor is there any need to talk about the occupation of the seabed, when the activities involved in acquiring the resources occur in the waters above it. The only time "occupation" comes into play is when the waters above the resources being exploited are occupied for harvesting. The question should not be whether the resources swim in the ocean or are attached to the seabed but, rather, what human activities are required for their exploitation. Since both types of fishing are carried out in the high seas, the exploitation of resources attached to the seabed is no different from regular fishing, and there is no reason why the same legal rules should not apply to both. It is submitted that the so-called sedentary fisheries pertain rather to the high seas than to the seabed. A rationale similar to that used for excluding historic bays from the regime of the high seas may be invoked to create an exception for certain coastal States. It is interesting to note that, although the views on occupation of the seabed are perhaps somewhat off the mark, the ultimate goal of Hurst and other scholars was to protect historic rights; and it is submitted that their primary argument was based on prescription, with only secondary importance attached to occupation. Except for particular banks, where fishing has been carried on since time immemorial, it has not been found necessary to treat the exploitation of resources attached to the seabed any differently from ordinary fishing.

Before the 1958 Geneva Conference, I stated:

There is no logical or practical reason for separating exploitation of live re-sources attached to the seabed from the customary type of fishing. The only reason for treating the exploitation of live resources attached to the seabed differently from regular fishing should be the existence of historical rights. The consolidated treatment by the International Law Commission of sedentary fisheries and the continental shelf seems to be ill-advised. (Oda, A Reconsidera-tion of the Continental Shelf Doctrine, *Tulane Law Review,* Vol. 21 (1957/8), p. 35.)

I could not see, from a policy standpoint, any reason for dividing author-ity over the activity of fishing into different categories on the basis of *what* is caught and *how* it is caught.

VI. Fishery Management on the High Seas

We are now faced not only with the problem of how to conserve fish re-sources of the high seas from extinction, but also with the problem of how to distribute them among the nations, each of which naturally wants to maximize its own share even in sacrifice of the interest of other nations. The latter question does not fall at all into the scope of the Geneva Con-vention, and we should not exaggerate the significance of the Convention for solving this important problem relating to the high seas fisheries.

In principle, two quite opposite policies are conceivable for the alloca-tion of fish resources of the high seas. (See table 2, *infra*.) The one, which seems *still* to have a sufficient ground, is to leave all the States to compete in fishing freely among themselves, within the limit, of course, fixed by the conservation consideration.

The other is undoubtedly artificial allocation, as preferential shares for some privileged States such as coastal States or the States entitled to histor-ical titles. The latter policy is materialized in the North Pacific Fisheries Convention of 1952 between Canada, Japan and the United States, the Northwest Pacific Fisheries Convention of 1956 between Japan und the Soviet Union, some recent arrangements on Antarctic whaling, as well as the Interim Convention on Fur Seals in the North Pacific, in one way or the other. In these arrangements, some contracting parties have been successful in securing preferential shares (sometimes 100 per cent) of the admissible total catch in some high seas areas, or they have agreed upon dividing resources on the basis of a rule which itself is not necessarily based upon the principle of conservation.

In spite of these recent trends, however, I hesitate to support any gener-alization of artificial allocation of fish resources among the nations. I am quite aware that free competition is not the most ideal solution under the present circumstances, when the demands of each nation do not necessarily

Table 2

Conservation	Allocation	
Maximum Sustainable Yield	Free Competition (Whaling Convention in its original form)	
	Artificial Quota	Privileges of states entitled to historic title. Refusal of newcomer states (North Pacific Fisheries Convention of 1952).
		Special status of the coastal state with respect to anadromous fish (Northwest Pacific Fisheries Convention of 1956).
		Special quota for the coastal state. (Proposal by Iceland at the Geneva Conference of 1958.)
		Equal share for states concerned.
		Others (Antarctic whaling in its present state).

coincide with its ability. However, it is also true, on the other hand, that the international society does not provide for any supernational authority to assure the States of a fixed and guaranteed portion of the benefit on the reasonable basis in terms of the general interest of the world community. Thus, the concept of artificial allocation itself will not provide for each State concerned a satisfactory middle ground during negotiation on the amount of each share, unless each nation is guaranteed to be entitled to an equitable share of fish resources in the light of the distribution of all other resources which it enjoys. Fully admitting that free competition is not the ideal solution, we should not be in haste, on the other hand, to replace the principle of free competition—a fundamental and well-grounded rationale in modern society—by giving lip-service to the so-called "equitable" quota of fish resources of the high seas. We do not live in an age where there is a common consensus among nations on the general interest of the world community, or where each State is ready to sacrifice its own interest for the benefit of the world community.

I once wrote several years ago, as follows: "Let it suffice for the author to state that the problem of international fisheries cannot be solved solely by legal techniques. This vesting problem will require more comprehensive study by international lawyers as well as by national statesmen than it has received, if it is to be brought to a satisfactory solution."

VII. Pollution of Sea Water by Radioactive Waste

As to this subject, I would like to draw the attention of the participants to the report prepared by the "Panel on the Legal Implications of Disposal of Radioactive Waste into the Sea" convened four times by the International Atomic Energy Agency between 1961 and 1963. See IAEA, DG/WDS/L

19. Together with Dr. Manner and several other colleagues, I participated in the work of this Panel under the chairmanship of Professor Rousseau of Paris.

VIII. Military Use of the High Seas

The testing of nuclear weapons on the high seas is not prohibited, in so far as it does not infringe upon other legitimate interests, such as fishing, navigation, etc., which other States are entitled to enjoy under the established principle of the freedom of the high seas. By establishing a danger zone in the area of the test, the State is also exempted from the liability of *damnum emergens,* which it should have otherwise incurred, provided that *lucrum cessans* is paid for other legitimate interests, such as fishing, navigation, etc., in the specified area.

Annex

United Nations General Assembly
A/6695, 18 August 1967
Twenty-second session

Request for the inclusion of a supplementary item in the agenda of the twenty-second session

Declaration and treaty concerning the reservation for peaceful purposes of the sea-bed and of the ocean floor, underlying the seas beyond the limits of present national jurisdiction, and the use of their resources in the interests of mankind

Note verbale dated 17 August 1967 from the Permanent Mission of Malta to the United Nations addressed to the Secretary-General

The Permanent Mission of Malta to the United Nations presents its compliments to the Secretary-General of the United Nations and has the honour to propose under rule 14 of the rules of procedure of the General Assembly the inclusion of the following item in the agenda of the twenty-second session of the General Assembly: "Declaration and treaty concerning the reservation exclusively for peaceful purposes of the sea-bed and of the ocean floor, underlying the seas beyond the limits of present national jurisdiction, and the use of their resources in the interests of mankind".

An explanatory memorandum is attached in accordance with rule 20 of the rules of procedure.

Memorandum

1. The sea-bed and the ocean floor are estimated to constitute approximately five-sevenths of the world's area. The sea-bed and ocean floor, underlying the seas outside present territorial waters and/or the continental shelves, are the only areas of our planet which have not yet been appropriated for national use, because they have been relatively inaccessible and their use for defence purposes or the economic exploitation of their resources was not technologically feasible.

2. In view of rapid progress in the development of new techniques by technologically advanced countries, it is feared that the situation will change and that the sea-bed and the ocean floor, underlying the seas beyond present national jurisdiction, will become progressively and competitively subject to national appropriation and use. This is likely to result in the militarization of the accessible ocean floor through the establishment of fixed military

installations and in the exploitation and depletion of resources of immense potential benefit to the world, for the national advantage of technologically developed countries.

3. It is, therefore, considered that the time has come to declare the sea-bed and the ocean floor a common heritage of mankind and that immediate steps should be taken to draft a treaty embodying, *inter alia*, the following principles:

(a) The sea-bed and the ocean floor, underlying the seas beyond the limits of present national jurisdiction, are not subject to national appropriation in any manner whatsoever;

(b) The exploration of the sea-bed and of the ocean floor, underlying the seas beyond the limits of present national jurisdiction, shall be undertaken in a manner consistent with the Principles and Purposes of the Charter of the United Nations;

(c) The use of the sea-bed and of the ocean floor, underlying the seas beyond the limits of present national jurisdiction, and their economic exploitation shall be undertaken with the aim of safeguarding the interests of mankind. The net financial benefits derived from the use and exploitation of the sea-bed and of the ocean floor shall be used primarily to promote the development of poor countries;

(d) The sea-bed and the ocean floor, underlying the seas beyond the limits of present national jurisdiction, shall be reserved exclusively for peaceful purposes in perpetuity.

4. It is believed that the proposed treaty should envisage the creation of an international agency (a) to assume jurisdiction, as a trustee for all countries, over the sea-bed and the ocean floor, underlying the seas beyond the limits of present national jurisdiction; (b) to regulate, supervise and control all activities thereon; and (c) to ensure that the activities undertaken conform to the principles and provisions of the proposed treaty.

United Nations General Assembly
A/RES/2340 (XXII), 28 December 1967
Twenty-second session
Agenda item 92

Resolution adopted by the General Assembly

[on the report of the First Committee (A/6964)]

2340 (XXII). *Examination of the question of the reservation exclusively for peaceful purposes of the sea-bed and the ocean floor, and the subsoil thereof, underlying the high seas beyond the limits of present national jurisdiction, and the use of their resources in the interests of mankind*

The General Assembly,

Having considered the item entitled "Examination of the question of the reservation exclusively for peaceful purposes of the sea-bed and the ocean floor, and the subsoil thereof, underlying the high seas beyond the limits of present national jurisdiction, and the use of their resources in the interests of mankind",

Noting that developing technology is making the sea-bed and the ocean floor, and the subsoil thereof, accessible and exploitable for scientific, economic, military and other purposes,

Recognizing the common interest of mankind in the sea-bed and the ocean floor, which constitute the major portion of the area of this planet,

Recognizing further that the exploration and use of the sea-bed and the ocean floor, and the subsoil thereof, as contemplated in the title of the item, should be conducted in accordance with the principles and purposes of the Charter of the United Nations, in the interest of maintaining international peace and security and for the benefit of all mankind,

Mindful of the provisions and practice of the law of the sea relating to this question,

Mindful also of the importance of preserving the sea-bed and the ocean floor, and the subsoil thereof, as contemplated in the title of the item, from actions and uses which might be detrimental to the common interests of mankind,

Desiring to foster greater international co-operation and co-ordination in the further peaceful exploration and use of the sea-bed and the ocean floor, and the subsoil thereof, as contemplated in the title of the item,

Recalling the past and continuing valuable work on questions relating to this matter carried out by the competent organs of the United Nations, the specialized agencies, the International Atomic Energy Agency and other intergovernmental organizations,

Recalling further that surveys are being prepared by the Secretary-General in response to General Assembly resolution 2172 (XXI) of 6 December 1966 and Economic and Social Council resolution 1112 (XL) of 7 March 1966,

1. *Decides* to establish an *Ad Hoc* Committee to study the peaceful uses of the sea-bed and the ocean floor beyond the limits of national jurisdiction, composed of Argentina, Australia, Austria, Belgium, Brazil, Bulgaria, Canada, Ceylon, Chile, Czechoslovakia, Ecuador, El Salvador, France, Iceland, India, Italy, Japan, Kenya, Liberia, Libya, Malta, Norway, Pakistan, Peru, Poland, Romania, Senegal, Somalia, Thailand, the Union of Soviet Socialist Republics, the United Arab Republic, the United Kingdom of Great Britain and Northern Ireland, the United Republic of Tanzania, the United States of America and Yugoslavia, to study the scope and various aspects of this item;

2. *Requests* the *Ad Hoc* Committee, in co-operation with the Secretary-General, to prepare, for consideration by the General Assembly at its twenty-third session, a study which would include:

(a) A survey of the past and present activities of the United Nations, the specialized agencies, the International Atomic Energy Agency and other intergovernmental bodies with regard to the sea-bed and the ocean floor, and of existing international agreements concerning these areas;

(b) An account of the scientific, technical, economic, legal and other aspects of this item;

(c) An indication regarding practical means to promote international co-operation in the exploration, conservation and use of the sea-bed and the ocean floor, and the subsoil thereof, as contemplated in the title of the item, and of their resources, having regard to the views expressed and the suggestions put forward by Member States during the consideration of this item at the twenty-second session of the General Assembly;

3. *Requests* the Secretary-General:

(a) To transmit the text of the present resolution to the Governments of all Member States in order to seek their views on the subject;

(b) To transmit to the *Ad Hoc* Committee the records of the First Committee relating to the discussion of this item;

(c) To render all appropriate assistance to the *Ad Hoc* Committee, including the submission thereto of the results of the studies being undertaken in pursuance of General Assembly resolution 2172 (XXI) and Economic and Social Council resolution 1112 (XL), and such documentation pertinent to this item as may be provided by the United Nations Educational, Scientific and Cultural Organization and its Inter-governmental Oceanographic Commission, the Inter-Governmental Maritime Consultative Organization, the Foor and Agriculture Organization of the United Nations, the World Meteorological Organization, the World Health Organization, the International Atomic Energy Agency and other inter-governmental bodies;

4. *Invites* the specialized agencies, the International Atomic Energy Agency and other intergovernmental bodies to co-operate fully with the *Ad Hoc* Committee in the implementation of the present resolution.

1639th plenary meeting,
18 December 1967.

United Nations Economic and Social Council
E/4487, 24 April 1968
Forty-fifth session, Agenda item 12
E/4487/Corr. 4 and 5, 6 September 1968
Forty-fifth session, Agenda item 13(b)

Marine Science and Technology: Survey and Proposals

Report of the Secretary-General

III. The need to maximize international co-operation efforts and related proposals

246. The reasons and needs for international co-operation in the domain of marine science and technology have been stated appropriately as follows:

"The world ocean covers 71 per cent of the earth's surface. Most countries have sea coasts and make some use of the sea, although national jurisdiction extends over only a small fraction of the ocean's area; the remainder is common property. The waters of the world ocean and their contents intermingle without serious restraint. Many oceanic processes are of large scale and are driven by forces of planetary dimension. The organisms inhabiting the sea are influenced by these processes and forces, and their distribution, abundance and behaviour are often influenced by events occurring far beyond the territorial limits recognized by man."[1]

247. Rapid expansion of marine research and oceanic service activities throughout the world during the past decades has caused the creation of a variety of international organizations dealing with international co-operation within this context. Some of these attend to specific problems of only a few countries; others are regional; a number carry responsibilities that are world-wide but not comprehensive as to subject matter. Co-ordination among these organizations is considerable and continues to develop in relation to many problems, but it is neither complete nor easy and needs to be improved. A certain consolidation in the programming of intergovernmental co-operation in marine affairs is needed to facilitate proper assignment or division of responsibilities among the various organizations and bodies involved, and prevent duplication or dissipation of effort and expenditure. While planning of ocean activities is largely initiated on a national basis, and some is carried out at a regional level, an increasing amount of such planning requires a global approach because of the nature of the ocean, of its interrelation with the atmosphere and of the exploiting in-

[1] *International Ocean Affairs,* a special report prepared by a joint working group appointed by ACMRR of FAO, SCOR of ICSU and AC of WMO, preface. See also annex XIII to the present report.

dustries. Aside from such planning there is need for broadly based co-ordination of the activities in this field through national and international efforts, and collaboration in the interpretation and analyses of the results.

248. A better understanding of the marine environment and an increase on the exploitation and development of marine resources require that international co-operation be given more support at all levels. Particularly with scientific and applied research one or more of the following reasons apply: the scale of research is often greater than can be serviced by any one country alone; the research required involves a greater diversity of scientific competence or facilities than any one country possesses; solution of a problem by one country requires access to data and experience possessed by other countries; the cost effectiveness of research for each country can be increased substantially by joining forces in an international operation; the subject of research is affected by the activities or laws of another country; there is a special need to reach agreement on the employment of comparable methods of research; there is need to establish mutual confidence in observations, experiments or analyses bearing on particular problems requiring international action.

249. It is in this context that the Secretary-General presents to the General Assembly a series of considerations and specific proposals relative to a better understanding of the marine environment through science, development and exploitation of marine resources (living and mineral), prevention of pollution and education and training in marine science.

250. The questions of international concern which arise in the development and exploitation of marine resources (including questions of conservation) and in the use of the ocean generally for economic purposes are specialized and largely technical in nature, as are the related problems, such as control of marine pollution, safety of human life and property at sea and provision of technical ocean services. All are therefore best considered within the framework of the appropriate specialized organizations concerned, wherein lies the necessary technical competence and where Governments can most easily contribute effectively to international co-ordination through their appropriate national bodies. Such established international organizations are also used successfully by Governments to reach international agreements, which, of course, also have legal and even political aspects. The co-ordinating arrangements in this field appear generally to be satisfactory and the Secretary-General accordingly proposes that the General Assembly recognize and encourage the role of the specialized agencies and other organizations concerned.

251. Problems of a general legal nature relating to the development and exploitation of marine resources and to other uses of the ocean are the subject of special United Nations conferences based on extensive preparatory work by the International Law Commission. Special problems of a predominantly political nature have been taken up in the General Assembly which, for instance, in the case of the sea bed beyond the continental shelf, has appointed an *ad hoc* committee to study the subject. The Secretary-General therefore has no proposal to offer in those domains for the time being. He is glad to note, however, that provisions have been made enabling the bodies dealing with these questions to receive technical information as appropriate from the specialized organizations concerned.

252. In the field of science and the related field of education and training the Secretary-General sees the need for greatly strengthened arrangements and for an expanded programme of international collaboration. While responsibility for ensuring adequate co-ordination and collaboration in specialized scientific work is best entrusted to the specialized organizations concerned, an expanded programme of international co-operation to assist in a better understanding of the marine environment through science would involve several specialized agencies[2] and other international organizations and the Secretary-General therefore makes positive proposals in this regard.

A. *An expanded programme of international co-operation*
to assist in a better understanding of the marine
environment through science

253. The expanded programme should synthesize national and international plans in this field and might serve a dual purpose. It would enable Governments and international bodies to take cognizance of each other's plans, to adapt them as necessary, to avoid unnecessary duplication, to ensure that gaps are filled and, co-operatively or jointly, to undertake large-scale activities in research and related services which are not feasible for a single country or for a single organization. Co-operative scientific investigations of the ocean, such as those organized by the IOC, contribute greatly to the scientific foundation necessary for the development and exploitation of marine resources, both living and non-living. The expanded programme would also provide a basis for making timely and adequate provisions for finance and facilities to support the activities included in it.

[2] As an example, one could mention that the study of meteorology (especially air-sea interaction), of environmental ocean research, and of fisheries science are growing closer to each other in needs and interests. This indicates a need to strengthen the marine meteorology component of WMO as well as the ability of the various ocean organizations to interact with WMO and to deal with meteorological aspects of ocean science.

254. The expanded programme would need to be formulated by a suitable, preferably an existing, inter-governmental body occupying a focal position and related to the international organizations concerned. It should include in its membership all or most of the countries interested in a better understanding of the marine environment through science and should be so constituted as to ensure that its work is also responsive to needs with regard to the exploitation and development of marine resources, and in keeping with the over-all plans of Governments.

255. The terms of reference of the IOC established by UNESCO in 1960 already come close to those required for such an inter-governmental body. The Commission plays the most important role at present in co-ordinating national and international oceanographic programmes.

256. *The Secretary-General therefore proposes* that the General Assembly recommend to Member Goverments, UNESCO, FAO, WMO and such other organizations of the United Nations family as may be concerned that they agree as a matter of urgency to broaden the base of IOC so as to enable it to formulate and co-ordinate the expanded programme. This agreement should provide, through appropriate modification of the IOC statutes among other things, for adequate joint financial support by the agencies concerned for such a broadened IOC, for a secretariat organized jointly and for an equitable participation of the agencies concerned in organizing the Commission's work. Another necessary step will be that Member Governments concerned provide appropriate direct financial support to the Commission. The modified statutes should permit the use of directly contributed funds for all aspects of the Commission's work.

257. Support of the expanded programme and the activities of a broadened IOC by the organizations of the United Nations family can be co-ordinated adequately through the ACC and its Sub-Committee on Marine Science and its Applications; no other special co-ordinating machinery is required. To avoid unnecessary duplication of effort and proliferation of machinery, the ACC should ensure advance consultations between the secretariats of the organizations concerned regarding proposals which fall within the terms of reference of more than one of them, and ensure that any temporary arrangements made for the implementation of such proposals by one or several organizations are discontinued after completion of the tasks involved.

258. The expanded programme will, of course, require additional expenditure at various levels. Governments will have to provide directly for concerted national activities under the programme. It must be recognized that

developing countries will need assistance from developed countries and from international bodies if they are to play their part in making the programme truly global and derive full benefit from it. A substantially larger budget for marine expenditures by the organizations sponsoring the broadened IOC will be essential for the joint conduct of certain projects, organization of meetings, provision of secretariat services, arrangements for data exchange, documentation etc. In addition, the fullest collaboration of other international organizations and bodies must be sought.

259. The increased international expenditures required by the expanded programme may be financed through increased regular governmental contributions to the international organizations and bodies concerned (including non-United Nations bodies), and may have to be supplemented by direct financing and by funds from other appropriate sources.

260. *The Secretary-General therefore proposes* that the General Assembly call upon States Members of the United Nations family of organizations to provide direct financing to the broadened IOC, to give urgent consideration to increasing their national allocations for marine research activities, and to strengthen their support of international co-operation in these activities through their contributions to the organizations concerned and through their direct participation in the expanded programme.

261. The co-ordinated implementation of the expanded programme by international organizations requires improved co-ordination at the national level, in order that each Member State's position should be consistent as regards the expanded programme through all the international organizations concerned.

262. *The Secretary-General proposes* that the General Assembly call upon States Members of the United Nations family of organizations to make suitable arrangements to co-ordinate their relevant national activities in such a way as to enable their national co-ordinating mechanisms to provide adequate support for the proposed expanded programme of inter-governmental co-operation.

263. For the success of the expanded programme it is essential to ensure such a division of responsibilities and functions among the existing international organizations so as to achieve maximum efficiency in the implementation of the programme throughout the whole system.

264. *The Secretary-General proposes* that the General Assembly recommend that the expanded programme be so developed as to provide for the proper interrelation between the work of the broadened IOC and that of other inter-governmental bodies, in particular, regional organizations, as well

as international non-governmental bodies whose participation in the activities of the broadened IOC should be ensured by all appropriate means.

265. The IOC and the United Nations organizations and bodies concerned have received valuable and necessary scientific advice through committees and other bodies of scientists acting with a maximum of independence in their private capacities as individual experts.

266. *The Secretary-General proposes* that the General Assembly recommend to the IOC and the United Nations organizations concerned the preservation and strengthening of this principle of seeking independent expert advice and to arrange, in particular, for a continuation of the work started by the Joint ACMRR/SCOR/WMO (AC) Working Group in the identification of specific scientific problems which require expanded international co-operation.[3] The IOC, as well as the United Nations organizations concerned, would then be better able, in developing the expanded programme, to assign priorities and propose means of attacking the problems so identified.

267. *The Secretary-General further proposes* that the General Assembly recommend to the IOC and the United Nations organizations concerned that, in keeping with the recommended evolution of the IOC, they hold under review the mechanisms for obtaining independent scientific advice, paying due regard to trends in organization of non-governmental bodies such as, for example, the suggested merger of several ocean-related bodies of the ICSU family into an international union of marine science.

B. *International co-operation regarding development and exploitation of living marine resources*

268. The need for international co-operation in the development and exploitation of living marine resources, including the rational exploitation and conservation of fish stocks, is very great as most of the resources are not confined within national boundaries and a large part of the fishing operations takes place on the high seas with participation of nationals of different countries. Research relating to fishery resources also assumes in many respects an international character. Its progress, however, depends substantially on the availability of basic knowledge of the marine environment for the provision of which proposals are made in section A above.

269. As a consequence of the wide recognition of this need, a great deal of international machinery has been established which is providing for such co-operation in various ways. With the growth of international fishery problems and of the machinery designed to help in their solution (including

[3] See annex XIII.

more than fifteen international fishery bodies), the need for co-ordination and avoidance of duplication has also grown. This further need was recognized at the twelfth session of the Conference of FAO when Governments resolved to give that organization the status of the leading inter-governmental body in encouraging rational harvesting of food from the oceans and inland waters. The Conference of FAO therefore established an inter-governmental Committee on Fisheries *inter alia* to conduct periodic general reviews of fishery problems of an international character and to appraise such problems and their possible solutions with a view to concerted action by nations and FAO in co-operation with UNESCO, IMCO, WMO, the ILO and other inter-governmental bodies. The Committee was instructed to conduct its work so as to supplement rather than to supplant other organizations working effectively in the field of fisheries and specifically to take into account the role of commissions.

270. As the survey has shown, the FAO Committee on Fisheries has already stimulated closer co-operation between existing bodies, has identified areas where international action is needed and has been instrumental in obtaining international agreement and in creating international machinery to this end. The effectiveness of its work has been enhanced by some strengthening of the fisheries sector of FAO but has been limited by still inadequate financial support for international fishery activities (such as research, exploration, conservation and technical assistance) including particularly those of regional and specialized bodies in which developing countries should play an important role. There is still considerable scope for further improvement of international collaboration in relation to fisheries development and conservation, which can be achieved within the existing organizational framework.

271. The Secretary-General, recognizing the importance of international co-operation in fisheries, the important role played by various international organizations in this field, and specifically the leading part of FAO and its COFI, proposes that the General Assembly call upon Member States to increase their support for international co-operation, including particularly the work of regional and other specialized fishery bodies, and draw the attention of international funding organizations to the need for assisting developing countries to participate more fully in such work.

C. *International co-operation in the development and exploitation of marine mineral resources*

272. The need for international co-operation in the development and exploitation of mineral resources of the ocean in the interest of mankind is

rapidly growing as a result of the recent progress in scientific knowledge of the ocean and advances in marine technology. This need is further emphasized by the international character of the high seas. Pre-eminent in consideration of this issue is the necessity for more information about the topography, geology and sedimentary characteristics of the ocean floor, for elucidation of the pertinent ocean processes, for further development of technology and instrumentation and for resolution of associated economic, administrative and legal issues.

273. When dealing with development and exploitation of marine mineral resources, one has to consider operations relating to their exploration, evaluation or assessment and production proper. By exploration is meant the geographically broad surveys leading, by progressively narrowing the search, to the location of mineral occurrences of possible economic importance. Evaluation comprises a detailed investigation of mineral occurrences or deposits, in order to discover their nature, to establish the quantity and tenor of the contained economic minerals, to determine how best they may be exploited, and generally to take into account all other factors affecting their economic development. Production includes all the operations relating to extraction, beneficiation and transport of the minerals discovered. Most of these operations are normally carried out by public or private enterprise.

274. For international co-operation in this domain, it is appropriate to distinguish between resources on the continental shelf where exploitation is taking place today and where the question of jurisdiction is subject to the 1958 Convention on the Continental Shelf, and those of the remainder of the sea bed and ocean floor for which proper technology for recovery has not yet been developed and for which the question of the jurisdiction that could apply still remains unsettled.

275. The role of inter-governmental organizations is normally limited to the gathering and diffusion of information relating to the knowledge of mineral deposits, and technological progress affecting the instrumentation needed for their exploration, evaluation and exploitation; to providing services contributing to the programming and safety of the operations at all stages as well as to fostering the legal and administrative conditions for practical utilization of the resources. To these may be added the technical assistance given in these fields to developing countries which is still rather limited but of great potential importance.

276. As far as international arrangements are concerned, the proposals for dealing with scientific aspects are given in section A above. The technological, economic and some of the related administrative and legal aspects,

including technical assistance, are presently dealt with by the United Nations Secretariat (Resources and Transport Division of the Department of Economic and Social Affairs and ECAFE) but only for the resources of the continental shelf. Apart from scientific research and preliminary studies, very little is. being done as regards resources beyond the continental shelf.

277. *The Secretary-General therefore proposes* to the General Assembly that it takes steps to expand further the existing activities of technical assistance in the continental shelf area; and to ensure that, as far as the whole ocean beyond the limits of present national jurisdiction is concerned, the United Nations is given adequate responsibility for systematic collection and diffusion of information regarding economic marine mineral deposits, techniques appropriate for their development, as well as for assisting in resolving related juridical, organizational and political issues.

D. *International action relating to the prevention of the pollution of the sea*

278. The investigation and control of marine pollution, which is related to many of the activities discussed in the preceding section, is a matter on which international action on both regional and global scales is now becoming urgent. It involves examination of a wide variety of difficult and highly technical problems to provide a firm basis for enactment of appropriate legislation, establishment of institutional arrangements for continuing studies, and the development of necessary technical services.

279. With respect to these urgent problems of broad concern, a high degree of concerted action is being attained through existing machinery which appears satisfactory for this purpose. In this context, the ACC through its Sub-Committee on Marine Science and its Applications has, within the past two years, played a key role in making arrangements for gathering during 1967, from Governments and other sources, information and suggestions on which a realistic expanded and co-ordinated programme can be based. The bodies that have been mainly concerned, in addition to the United Nations itself, are IMCO, WHO, FAO, UNESCO and IAEA. The material thus far received has been analysed and is generally available, and a more intensified programme is being based largely upon it. The action now actively under consideration covers the joint provision of scientific and technical advice, exchange and dissemination of information and future international legislation for the control of pollution.[4]

280. The programme evolving covers all aspects of marine pollution: health, fisheries, amenity; oily and radioactive substances as well as other pollu-

[4] See annex XIV.

tants; pertinent marine research as well as control and monitoring. In several instances, a particular service function is already the responsibility of one or only a few of the organizations of the United Nations family; in other cases, many organizations may be involved. The provision of such services would therefore require active and co-ordinated contributions from all the organizations concerned. FAO, UNESCO (IOC) and IMCO have agreed to establish a joint group of experts to advise on scientific aspects related to the pollution of the sea within the competence of the sponsoring organizations. The group will remain open to other agencies should they wish to join it.

281. *The Secretary-General accordingly proposes* that the General Assembly request the organizations of the United Nations family concerned to continue, with urgency, to elaborate and implement their planned joint action with respect to marine pollution.

282. *The Secretary-General also proposes* that the General Assembly call upon States Members of the United Nations system of organizations to participate actively in the joint undertaking of the organizations concerned and that, in keeping with the progress of scientific research related to marine pollution, they take steps towards adopting, in addition to the international Convention for the Prevention of Pollution of the Sea by Oil, 1954, such effective international agreements on prevention and control of marine pollution as may appear necessary.

E. *An expanded programme of co-operation in the fields of*
education and training in marine science

283. As shown in the survey above, marine education and training programmes are part of the normal activities of a number of organizations of the United Nations family, which use widely for this purpose existing national training and education facilities. However, the scarcity of competent personnel still remains a limiting factor to the development of national efforts and of international co-operation as regards the study of the ocean and the full and rational use of its resources. This scarcity demonstrates the inadequacy of the existing national and international marine education and training programmes, which therefore need to be strengthened as a prerequisite for the implementation of the expanded programme of co-operation.

284. The necessary strengthening of marine educational and training programmes, particularly of those undertaken by the organizations of the United Nations family, may be achieved through the following means:

(a) Increased allocations for study grants, fellowships and training courses and enlarged assistance to Member States for the development of national and regional marine education and training programmes and facilities, including endowment of teaching posts through both the regular programmes of the United Nations organizations concerned and UNDP funds, as well as through the proposed international oceanographic fund;

(b) Additional contributions by Member States to the international marine education and training programmes by offers of study grants and fellowships through the organizations of the United Nations family and through extended bilateral and multilateral assistance schemes;

(c) Improvement of facilities for marine education and training at the national and regional level, with associated arrangements made for stable professional careers for scientists and technicians in their home countries or regions;

(d) Expanding the coverage, scale and continuity of scientific documentation and related services for marine scientists;

(e) Improved national arrangements to facilitate the participation of their competent personnel in international programmes of training and research.

285. *Therefore the Secretary-General proposes* that the General Assembly call upon States Members of the United Nations family of organizations and upon the organizations of the United Nations family concerned to make the necessary arrangements for the application of the above-mentioned means to strengthen the existing marine education and training programmes and to initiate new programmes wherever necessary.

United Nations General Assembly
A/RES/2467 (XXIII), 14 January 1969
Twenty-third session
Agenda item 26

Resolutions adopted by the General Assembly

[on the report of the First Committee (A/7477)]

2467 (XXIII). *Examination of the question of the reservation exclusively for peaceful purposes of the sea-bed and the ocean floor, and the subsoil thereof, underlying the high seas beyond the limits of present national jurisdiction, and the use of their resources in the interests of mankind*

A

The General Assembly,

Recalling the item entitled "Examination of the question of the reservation exclusively for peaceful purposes of the sea-bed and the ocean floor, and the subsoil thereof, underlying the high seas beyond the limits of present national jurisdiction, and the use of their resources in the interests of mankind",

Having in mind its resolution 2340 (XXII) of 18 December 1967 concerned with the problems arising in the area to which the title of the item refers,

Reaffirming the objectives set forth in that resolution,

Taking note with appreciation of the report prepared by the *Ad Hoc* Committee to Study the Peaceful Uses of the Sea-Bed and the Ocean Floor beyond the Limits of National Jurisdiction,[1] keeping in mind the views expressed in the course of its work and drawing upon its experience,

Recognizing that it is in the interest of mankind as a whole to favour the exploration and use of the sea-bed and the ocean floor and the subsoil thereof, beyond the limits of national jurisdiction, for peaceful purposes,

Considering that it is important to promote international co-operation for the exploration and exploitation of the resources of this area,

Convinced that such exploitation should be carried out for the benefit of mankind as a whole, irrespective of the geographical location of States, taking into account the special interests and needs of the developing countries,

[1] *Official Records of the General Assembly, Twenty-third Session*, agenda item 26, document A/7230.

Considering that it is essential to provide, within the United Nations system, a focal point for the elaboration of desirable measures of international co-operation, taking into account alternative actual and potential uses of this area, and for the co-ordination of the activities of international organizations in this regard,

1. *Establishes* a Committee on the Peaceful Uses of the Sea-Bed and the Ocean Floor beyond the Limits of National Jurisdiction, composed of forty-two States;

2. *Instructs* the Committee:

(a) To study the elaboration of the legal principles and norms which would promote international co-operation in the exploration and use of the sea-bed and the ocean floor, and the subsoil thereof, beyond the limits of national jurisdiction and to ensure the exploitation of their resources for the benefit of mankind, and the economic and other requirements which such a régime should satisfy in order to meet the interests of humanity as a whole;

(b) To study the ways and means of promoting the exploitation and use of the resources of this area, and of international co-operation to that end, taking into account the foreseeable development of technology and the economic implications of such exploitation and bearing in mind the fact that such exploitation should benefit mankind as a whole;

(c) To review the studies carried out in the field of exploration and research in this area and aimed at intensifying international co-operation and stimulating the exchange and the widest possible dissemination of scientific knowledge on the subject;

(d) To examine proposed measures of co-operation to be adopetd by the international community in order to prevent the marine pollution which may result from the exploration and exploitation of the resources of this area;

3. *Also calls upon* the Committee to study further, within the context of the title of the item, and taking into account the studies and international negotiations being undertaken in the field of disarmament, the reservation exclusively for peaceful purposes of the sea-bed and the ocean floor without prejudice to the limits which may be agreed upon in this respect;

4. *Requests* the Committee:

(a) To work in close co-operation with the specialized agencies, the International Atomic Energy Agency and the intergovernmental bodies dealing with the problems referred to in the present resolution, so as to avoid any duplication or overlapping of activities;

(b) To make recommendations to the General Assembly on the questions mentioned in paragraphs 2 and 3 above;

(c) In co-operation with the Secretary-General, to submit to the General Assembly reports on its activities at each subsequent session;

5. *Invites* the specialized agencies, the International Atomic Energy Agency and other intergovernmental bodies including the Intergovernmental Oceanographic Commission of the United Nations Educational, Scientific and Cultural Organization to co-operate fully with the Committee in the implementation of the present resolution.

B

The General Assembly,

Recognizing that it is in the common interest of all nations that the exploration and exploitation of the resources of the sea-bed and the ocean floor, and the subsoil thereof, should be conducted in such a manner as to avoid infringement of the other interests and established rights of nations with respect ot the uses of the sea,

Mindful of the threat to the marine environment presented by pollution and other hazardous and harmful effects which might result from exploration and exploitation of the areas under consideration,

Desiring to promote effective measures of prevention and control of such pollution and to allay the serious damage which might be caused to the marine environment and, in particular, to the living marine resources which constitute one of mankind's most valuable food resources,

Recognizing the complex problem of ensuring effective co-ordination in the wide field of environmental pollution and in the more specific area of prevention and control of marine pollution,

Noting with satisfaction the measures being undertaken by the Inter-Governmental Maritime Consultative Organization to prevent and control pollution of the sea by preparing new draft conventions and other instruments for that purpose,

Recalling, in this regard, the progress achieved towards such concerted action by intergovernmental bodies and the establishment, by the Food and Agriculture Organization of the United Nations, the United Nations Educational, Scientific and Cultural Organization and its Intergovernmental Oceanographic Commission, the Inter-Governmental Maritime Consultative Organization and the World Meteorological Organization, of a Joint Group of Experts on the Scientific Aspects of Marine Pollution,

Recalling further the competence and continuing valuable contributions of the other intergovernmental organizations concerned,

1. *Welcomes* the adoption by States of appropriate safeguards against the dangers of pollution and other hazardous and harmful effects that might arise from the exploration and exploitation of the resources of the sea-bed and the ocean floor, and the subsoil thereof, beyond the limits of national jurisdiction, notably in the form of concrete measures of international co-operation for the purpose of realizing this aim;

2. *Considers* that in connexion with the elaboration of principles underlying possible future international agreements for the area concerned, a study should be made with a view to clarifying all aspects of protection of the living and other resources of the sea-bed and ocean floor, the superjacent waters and the adjacent coasts against the consequences of pollution and other hazardous and harmful effects arising from various modalities of such exploration and exploitation;

3. *Considers further* that such a study should take into consideration the importance of minimizing interference between the many means by which the wealth of the ocean space may be harvested, and that it should extend to the examination of the circumstances in which measures may be undertaken by States for the protection of the living and other resources of those areas in which pollution detrimental to those resources has occurred or is imminent;

4. *Requests* the Secretary-General, in co-operation with the appropriate and competent body or bodies presently undertaking co-ordinated work in the field of marine pollution control, to undertake the study referred to in paragraphs 2 and 3 above and to submit a report thereon to the General Assembly and the Committee on the Peaceful Uses of the Sea-Bed and the Ocean Floor beyond the Limits of National Jurisdiction.

C

The General Assembly,

Having considered the item entitled "Examination of the question of the reservation exclusively for peaceful purposes of the sea-bed and the ocean floor, and the subsoil thereof, underlying the high seas beyond the limits of present national jurisdiction, and the use of their resources in the interests of mankind",

Reaffirming that exploration and exploitation of the resources of the sea-bed and the ocean floor, and the subsoil thereof, should be carried out for the benefit of mankind as a whole, taking into special consideration the interests and needs of the developing countries,

Recalling that international co-operation in this field is of paramount importance,

Bearing in mind its resolution 2467A above establishing the Committee on the Peaceful Uses of the Sea-Bed and the Ocean Floor beyond the Limits of National Jurisdiction, and the mandate entrusted to it,

1. *Requests* the Secretary-General to undertake a study on the question of establishing in due time appropriate international machinery for the promotion of the exploration and exploitation of the resources of this area, and the use of these resources in the interests of mankind, irrespective of the geographical location of States, and taking into special consideration the interests and needs of the developing countries, and to submit a report thereon to the Committee on the Peaceful Uses of the Sea-Bed and the Ocean Floor beyond the Limits of National Jurisdiction for consideration during one of its sessions in 1969;

2. *Calls upon* the Committee to submit a report on this question to the General Assembly at its twenty-fourth session.

D

The General Assembly,

Convinced that the nations of the world should join together, with due respect for national jurisdiction, in a common long-term programme of exploration of the ocean as a potential source of resources, which should eventually be used for meeting the needs of all mankind with due recognition of those of developing countries and irrespective of the geographical location of States,

Recalling also that in its resolution 2172 (XXI) of 6 December 1966 it requested the Secretary-General to prepare proposals for ensuring the most effective arrangements for an expanded programme of international co-operation to assist in a better understanding of the marine environment through science, and for initiating and strengthening marine education and training programmes,

Recalling further the proposals made by the Secretary-General in his report,[2] pursuant to resolution 2172 (XXI), as well as the various views expressed during the consideration of this subject by the General Assembly at its twenty-third session,

Noting that the Bureau and Consultative Council of the Intergovernmental Oceanographic Commission of the United Nations Educational, Scientific and Cultural Organization considered the proposed International

[2] E/4487 and Corr. 1–6, and Add. 1.

Decade of Ocean Exploration a useful initiative for broadening and accelerating investigations of the oceans and for strengthening international co-operation,

Endorsing the objectives expressed in Economic and Social Council resolutions 1380 (XLV), 1381 (XLV) and 1382 (XLV) of 2 August 1968 and recalling particularly the invitation to the General Assembly to endorse the concept of a co-ordinated long-term programme of oceanographic research, taking into account such initiatives as the proposal for an International Decade of Ocean Exploration and international programmes already considered, approved and adopted by the Intergovernmental Oceanographic Commission for implementation in co-operation with other specialized agencies,

Aware of the consideration given to the proposal in the *Ad Hoc* Committee to Study the Peaceful Uses of the Sea-Bed and the Ocean Floor beyond the Limits of National Jurisdiction, arising from the contribution which the Decade[a] would make to scientific research and exploration of the sea-bed and ocean floor, as an important part of a co-ordinated long-term international programme of oceanographic research,

Seeking to enrich the knowledge of all mankind by encouraging a free flow of scientific information on the oceans to all States,

1. *Welcomes* the concept of an International Decade of Ocean Exploration to be undertaken within the framework of a long-term programme of research and exploration, including scientific research and exploration of the sea-bed and the ocean floor, under the aegis of the United Nations on the understanding that all such activities falling under the national jurisdiction of a State shall be subject to the previous consent of such State, in accordance with international law;

2. *Invites* Member States to formulate proposals for national and international scientific programmes and agreed activities to be undertaken during the Decade[a] with due regard to the interests of developing countries, to transmit these proposals to the United Nations Educational, Scientific and Cultural Organization for the Intergovernmental Oceanographic Commission in time to begin the Decade in 1970, and to embark on such activities as soon as practicable;

3. *Urges* Member States to publish as soon as practicable the results of all activities which they will have undertaken within the framework of the Decade[a] as part of a long-term co-ordinated programme of scientific research and exploration, and at the same time to communicate these results to the Intergovernmental Oceanographic Commission;

[a] *For* Decade *read* International Decade of Ocean Exploration

4. *Requests* the United Nations Educational, Scientific and Cultural Organization that its Intergovernmental Oceanographic Commission:

(a) Intensify its activities in the scientific field, within its terms of reference and in co-operation with other interested agencies, in particular with regard to co-ordinating the scientific aspects of a long-term and expanded programme of world-wide exploration of the oceans and their resources of which the Decade[a] will be an important element, including international agency programmes, an expanded international exchange of data from national programmes, and international efforts to strengthen the research capabilities of all interested nations with particular regard to the needs of the developing countries;

(b) Co-operate with the Secretary-General in accordance with paragraph 4 of General Assembly resolution 2414 (XXIII) of 17 December 1968 on the resources of the sea in the preparation of the comprehensive outline of the scope of the long-term programme of oceanographic research of which the Decade[a] will be an important element, making available its views as to the appropriate relationship between the several international programmes already considered, approved and adopted by the Intergovernmental Oceanographic Commission for implementation, the Decade, and the long-term programme;

(c) Keep the Secretary-General informed of all proposals, programmes and activities of which it is informed in accordance with paragraphs 2 and 3 above together with any comments it may consider appropriate;

(d) Report through appropriate channels to the General Assembly at its twenty-fourth session on progress made in the implementation of the present resolution.

1752nd plenary meeting,
21 December 1968.

In accordance with the decision taken by the First Committee at its 1648th meeting, on 19 December 1968, the Committee on the Peaceful Uses of the Sea-Bed and the Ocean Floor beyond the Limits of National Jurisdiction, established under paragraph 1 of resolution A above, will consist of the following Member States: Argentina, Australia, Austria, Belgium, Brazil, Bulgaria, Cameroon, Canada, Ceylon, Chile, Czechoslovakia, El Salvador, France, Iceland, India, Italy, Japan, Kenya, Kuwait, Liberia, Libya, Madagascar, Malaysia, Malta, Mauritania, Mexico, Nigeria, Norway, Pakistan, Peru, Poland, Romania, Sierra Leone, Sudan, Thailand, Trinidad and Tobago, Union of Soviet Socialist Republics, United Arab Republic, United Kingdom of Great Britain and Northern Ireland, United Republic of Tanzania, United States of America and Yugoslavia.